JN494987

Early-Life Determinants of Health and Human Capital Formation: Evidence from Natural Experiments in Korea

Early-Life Determinants of
Health and Human Capital Formation:
Evidence from Natural Experiments in Korea

Copyright © Chulhee Lee 2022
First edition published by Seoul National University Press in 2022

All rights reserved. No part of this publication may be reproduced in any form without written permission from Seoul National University Press.

Seoul National University Press
1 Gwanak-ro, Gwanak-gu, Seoul 08826, Republic of Korea
Tel: +82-2-880-5252
Fax: +82-2-889-0785
Homepage: http://www.snupress.com
Facebook: @snupress1947
Instagram: @snupress
E-mail: snubook@snu.ac.kr

ISBN 978-89-521-3158-4 (93320)

Early-Life Determinants of

Health and Human Capital Formation

Evidence from Natural Experiments in Korea

Chulhee Lee

SNUPRESS
Seoul National University Press

Contents

Tables

Figures

CHAPTER 1

Introduction

Research across a range of disciplines have established that early-life health and circumstances play an important role in determining health and economic conditions at older ages. A series of studies by physicians and epidemiologists links many of the degenerative conditions of old age to exposure to infectious disease, malnutrition, and other types of biomedical and socioeconomic stress in-utero and during the early years of life. Recent research by economists suggests that early-life circumstances have strong and persistent influences on human capital accumulation and labor market performance. These effects are also possibly mediated by the deterioration in health and cognitive ability.

Debates remain regarding whether a certain age is particularly critical for determining health and human capital development over life course. As individuals age, the effects of investments in health during early childhood persist or even increase in magnitude. This finding suggests that the early years in human life comprise a distinct stage of development. Such effects on health occurring in these years are significant and cannot be fully rectified by compensatory health investments made at older ages.

A group of researchers paid particular attention to the long-term consequences of in-utero influences. In the 1990s, David J. Barker and his colleagues developed and popularized the argument widely known as the fetal origins hypothesis. The hypothesis argues that disruptions to the prenatal environment are related to various chronic health outcomes at older ages, including coronary heart disease and diabetes (Barker 1992, 1994). The hypothesis further emphasizes initial health endowment (formed in-utero), rather than postnatal conditions, as a health determinant in early ages.

A wide variety of evidence pertaining to the fetal origins hypothesis has been presented over the last three decades. Experimental studies using animals provide evidence that maternal malnutrition has a causal effect on the subsequent health of the offspring. A voluminous body of literature evaluates the health and socioeconomic consequences of low birth weight (LBW), a proxy of exposure to malnutrition, infection, or toxic substances while in-utero. Most of these studies reveal significant negative effects of LBW on human capital accumulation, socioeconomic status, and health outcomes (Currie and Hyson 1999; Behrman and Rosenzweig 2004; Black, Devereux, and Salvanes 2007; Currie and Moretti 2007). For example, Black, Devereux, and Salvanes (2007) analyzed Norwegian twins and found that LBW has long-run adverse effects on adult height, IQ, earnings, and education. Currie and Moretti (2007) stated that LBW among individuals born in California has modest but statistically significant negative effects on educational attainment and the probability of living in a wealthy neighborhood. A growing number of biomedical studies suggest that maternal stress during pregnancy may increase the likelihood of preterm birth, developmental delays, and behavioral abnormalities (Weinstock 2001; Aizer et al. 2009).

A possible concern that confronts studies on size at birth and subsequent outcomes is that the positive correlation between measures of early life and adult health can be biased by omitted variables such as genetic factors or post-birth investments.[1] A new line of research addresses this potential problem by exploiting unique opportunities offered by natural experiments, in which individuals of a particular background or cohort are randomly exposed to a type of disruption

1 Almond, Chay, and Lee (2005) compared the hospital costs, health at birth, and infant mortality rates between heavier and lighter infants of twins born in the United States to reduce potential bias arising from omitted variables such as genetic factors. They observed a minimal effect of LBW on infant mortality and other health measures from a sample of twins.

in-utero. If the probability of experiencing negative health shocks in-utero is uncorrelated with unobservable determinants of health, then the estimated effects of the shock are not subject to omitted variable bias.

Almond (2006) used the 1918 influenza pandemic as a natural experiment to test the fetal origins hypothesis. He found that the cohorts in-utero during the pandemic displayed reduced educational attainment, increased rates of physical disability, lower income, lower socioeconomic status, and higher transfer payments compared with other birth cohorts. Almond and Mazumder (2005) discovered that cohorts in-utero during the pandemic exhibited impaired health outcomes relative to those born a few months earlier or later 65 to 80 years after the event. Kelly (2009) found that people who experienced prenatal exposure to the 1957 Asian flu in Britain exhibited diminished test scores. Shih and Lin (2018) investigated the long-term effects of in-utero and postnatal exposure to malaria by using the malaria eradication campaign in Taiwan in the 1950s as a quasi-experiment. Their difference-in-difference estimation shows that malaria eradication positively affected men's education level and family income.

Historical famines were studied as natural experiments as well. At middle age, a cohort in-utero during the 1944–1945 Dutch Famine exhibited a broad spectrum of health problems such as poor self-reported health (Roseboom, Meulen, Ravelli et al. 2001), coronary heart disease morbidity (Roseboom, Meulen, Ravelli et al. 2001; Bleker et al. 2005), and adult antisocial personality (Neugebauer, Hoek, and Susser 1999). Research on the Chinese Famine (1959–1961) reported negative health and socioeconomic consequences, including heightened risk of schizophrenia (St. Clair et al. 2005), obesity among women (Luo, Mu, and Zhang 2006), height reductions (Chen and Zhou 2007), and reduction in working hours of employees (Meng and Qian 2009). Almond et al. (2010) reported that higher famine intensity is associated with a greater risk of illiteracy, dropping out of the labor force, marrying late (for men), and marrying partners with less education (for women). Neelson and Stratman (2011) claimed that exposure to the famine in Greece (1941–1942) in infancy lowered educational attainment. A recent study by Guven, Hoang, Rahman and Ulubaşoğlu (2021) investigated the impacts of the 1944–1945 Great Vietnam Famine on the early-life survivors and their offspring. They found that the cohort in-utero during the famine experienced decline in literacy, BMI, height, and weight. They also found that the second generation had lower school attendance rate, which shows the intergenerational effects of famine.

The effects of prenatal exposure to pollution were examined via natural experiments. Chay and Greenstone (2003) used variations in air pollution across counties. These variations were exogenously triggered by the implementation of the Clean Air Act of 1970 and the recession of the early 1980s. The decline in particulates significantly reduced infant death rates. Almond, Edlund, and Palme (2009) analyzed the effect of pollution stemming from the Chernobyl disaster on the subjects of a Swedish cohort who were in-utero at the time of the disaster. The subjects exposed to radiation showed significantly reduced academic performance.

The influences of maternal stress during pregnancy on offspring outcomes were investigated. Eccleston (2011) found that cohorts exposed to the stress of the September 11, 2001 terrorist attacks in-utero have lesser weight, shorter gestation length, and lower initial education attainments. Lauderdale (2006) reported that Arabic-named women in California, who experienced a period of increased harassment, violence, and workplace discrimination immediately following September 11, 2001, had increased risks of preterm birth and LBW. Currie and Rossin-Slater (2012) found that exposure to a hurricane during pregnancy increased the probability of labor and delivery complications as well as abnormal conditions of the newborn. Camacho (2008) reported that the intensity of random landmine explosion during a woman's pregnancy had a significant negative impact on child birth weight in Columbia.

More recently, Karbownik and Wray (2019) investigated the long-term consequences of fetal and postnatal exposure to tropical cyclones that hit the US south during the late 19th century. Using World War I draft records linked to census data, they found that those who experienced hurricanes in-utero or as infants had lower income 40 to 50 years later. Menclova and Stillman (2020) examined the effect of maternal stress due to the 2010 Canterbury earthquake and its aftershocks on birth outcomes. Using fixed effect regression model, they found that the exposure reduced gestational age and Apgar score. They also reported that the exposure increased the likelihood of low birth weight and preterm birth for teenage mothers. Aparicio Fenoll and González (2021) explored the effects of maternal stress due to in-utero exposure to political instability on birth outcomes by studying the case of 1981 military coup in Spain. Using difference-in-difference method, they discovered that those in-utero during the coup were born with significantly low birth weight, especially those who were exposed to the event in the first or the second trimester of pregnancy.

Unresolved issues continue to exist in spite of the growing body of evidence on the link between early-life circumstances and later economic and health outcomes. In particular, how the effects of early-life conditions differ across periods and nations remain unclear. The strength of the effect of an adverse shock to health in-utero depends on the patterns of postnatal investments in health and human capital accumulation. If postnatal interventions on the nutrition, medical care, and education of a child are effectively implemented, the prenatal damages can be rectified to a particular extent. Thus, the relationship between early-life circumstances and later socioeconomic outcomes is likely to differ across periods and countries. The differences also depend on income, quality of medical care, and educational system, as well as political and social structures.

In addition, cultural and social norms matter in determining the patterns of investments in health and human capital during childhood. In some societies, for example, parents tend to invest more in children with poorer health to achieve more equal outcomes among children (a case of compensatory investment). By comparison, parents in other societies invest in their healthiest children to increase the expected return of investment (a case of reinforcing investment). Except for studies on China, evidence for this issue is drawn largely from the US and from Europe.

This book intends to widen the scope of the literature by focusing on Korean cases that have not been thoroughly studied. Over the last eight decades, Korea has experienced a few highly experimental episodes that produced dramatic changes in early-life circumstances across birth cohorts. As widely known, Korea has achieved unusually rapid economic growth since its liberation from the Japanese occupation in 1945. Within a mere four decades after the Korean War (1950–1953), South Korea had emerged as one of the richest newly industrialized countries. Previous estimates of incomes suggest that the real GDP per capita stagnated in the early 1960s and began to increase rapidly in the following years (Pyo 2001; Kim 2012; Cha 2014). World Bank Statistics indicated that the annual growth rate for per capita GNP in South Korea was 6.6 percent in 1965–1999, the highest among all countries (Song 2003).

As a consequence of the rapid economic development and dramatic social changes associated with it, early-life experiences of the cohorts

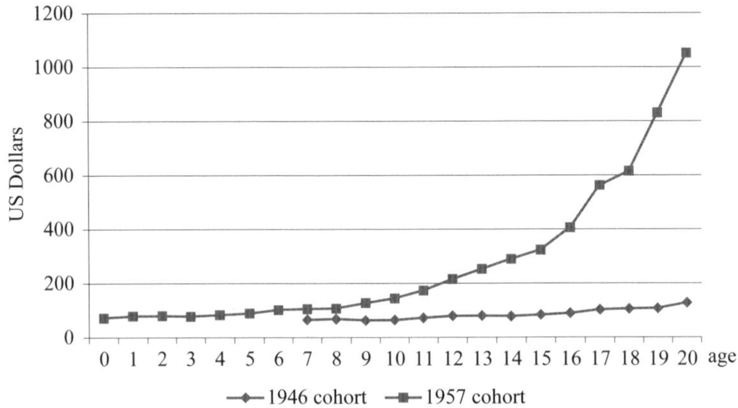

Source: Economic Statistics System (ECOS) of the Bank of Korea.

Figure 1.1 | GDP per Capita by Age of the 1946 and 1957 Birth Cohorts (US Dollars in 2010 Constant Price)

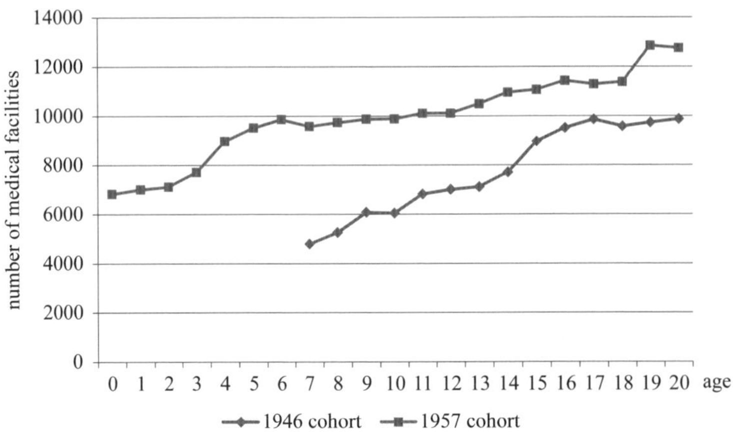

Source: Korea Statistical Office, Korea Statistical Yearbooks.

Figure 1.2 | Number of Medical Facilities by Age of the 1946 and 1957 Birth Cohorts

born shortly after 1945 substantially differed according to the year of birth. For instance, the subjects of the cohorts born just after the end of the Second World War went through the chaotic years following the liberation from Japan, severe disruptions caused by the Korean War, and the period of slow recovery from the aftermath of the devastating war.

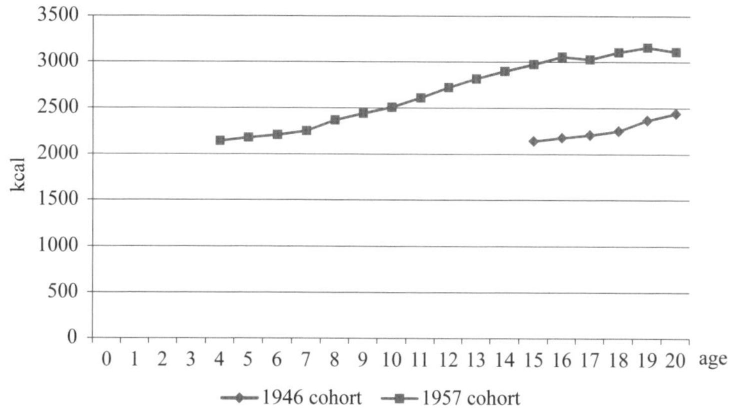

Source: Korea Statistical Office, Korea Statistical Yearbooks.

Figure 1.3 | Daily Calorie Supply per Capita by Age of the 1946 and 1957 Birth Cohorts

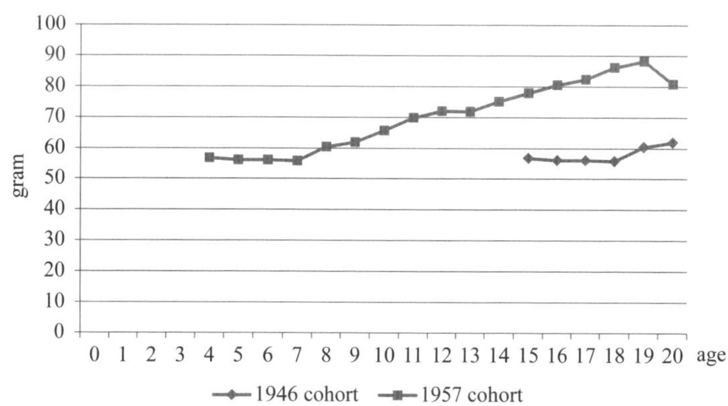

Source: Korea Statistical Office, Korea Statistical Yearbooks.

Figure 1.4 | Daily Protein Supply per Capita by Age of the 1946 and 1957 Birth Cohorts

By contrast, the cohorts born towards the end of the 1950s spent their childhood and adolescence in a prolonged peacetime when South Korea began to achieve an economic miracle.

Figures 1.1 to 1.6 compare the early-life experiences of the 1946 and 1957 birth cohorts based on several indicators of standards of living. It is apparent from the results that the two birth cohorts spent their growing ages in very different conditions, although they were born just 11 years

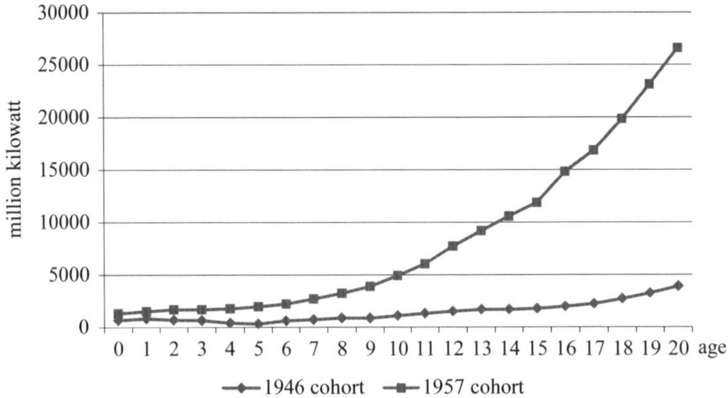

Source: Korea Statistical Office, Korea Statistical Yearbooks.

Figure 1.5 | Electric Power Supply by Age of the 1946 and 1957 Birth Cohorts

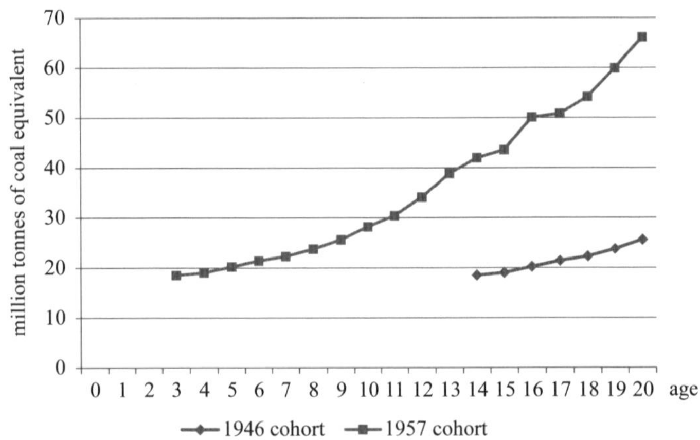

Source: Korea Statistical Office, Korea Statistical Yearbooks.

Figure 1.6 | Energy Consumption by Age of the 1946 and 1957 Birth Cohorts

apart. For instance, per capita income of South Korea (in fixed US dollars) stagnated under 130 dollars until the 1946 birth cohort reached age 20, whereas it rapidly increased from 106 dollars to 1,051 dollars during the years when the subjects of the 1957 birth cohort were aged 7 to 20 (Figure 1.1). Average Koreans were four times wealthier when the individuals born in 1957 were aged 16 than they were when those born in 1946 were at the same age.

Figure 1.2 shows that the 1957 birth cohort had much improved access to medical service in early childhood and in adolescence compared to the 1946 birth cohort. For instance, around age 7, the late birth cohort had twice the number of medical facilities that the early birth cohort had at the same age. As presented in Figures 2.3 and 2.4, it is likely that birth cohorts born in the late 1950s were better nourished in late childhood than were those born in the late 1940s. At age 15, average daily provisions of total calories and of protein were considerably larger for the late birth cohorts than for those born earlier. Likewise, the 1957 birth cohort spent their late childhood when electricity and energy in general were more abundantly supplied compared to the 1946 birth cohort (Figures 2.5 and 2.6).

As explained in the subsequent chapters of this book, early-life conditions that the subjects of each birth cohort were exposed to also depended on where they were born and lived in childhood as well. The pace of economic development and increase in food production substantially varied across different regions. Natives of particular places were hit harder by the physical and psychological damages caused by traumatic events, such as military conflict, violence, and natural disasters. The huge and exogenously-driven variations in living conditions across times and places of birth provide unique opportunity to investigate the long-term consequences of early-life circumstances.

In the present book, I look into the following three historical episodes in modern-era Korea, namely, the Korean War, the rapid and geographically uneven increase in food production, and the 1980 Gwangju uprising. Each event is expected to influence fetal and childhood health of individuals differently according to the timing and place of birth. Since these episodes took place not so long ago, many of the individuals who experienced the events in early life survived until recent years when various micro data containing the information on their late-life outcomes and even birth outcomes of their children are available. These settings and data allow me to study how early-life exposure to health shocks affect later health and human capital development in the Korean context.

The Korean War (1950–1953) offers a unique opportunity to examine the long-term effects of war-related disruptions such as arduous refugee experiences, suffering under the North Korean occupation, hunger, and direct exposure to combat. Although the war lasted for more than three years, the major war damage sustained by civilians was concentrated in the first nine months following the sudden invasion of North Korea (late June 1950 to late March 1951). At that time, the frontline rapidly and unexpectedly moved back and forth across South Korea (Halberstam 2007; Chung 2010; Yang 2010). Furthermore, the severity of wartime experience considerably differed depending on the place of residence. For example, Central Region residents were hit particularly hard because they lived closer to North Korea and their area was invaded twice by enemy forces. These specific circumstances help identify the effects of the war on maternal and fetal health through a comparison of the adult outcomes across birth cohorts and places of birth. Drawing from these features of the Korean War, Chapters 2 to 5 explore how in-utero exposure to war-related disruptions affects adult health and economic outcomes.

As South Korea achieved rapid economic growth since its liberation from the Japanese occupation in 1945, the nutritional status of the population has improved over time. The adult height, a widely-used index of cumulative net nutritional status during the growth period, shows a long-term increasing trend. The mean height of the male subject of the 1950 birth cohort at age 20 was 165.5 cm. The average height of the 1984 birth cohort at age 19 was 173.4 cm. Of the increase in height by 8 cm during the 25 years, more than 40% (3.4 cm) was gained by 1960. The growth of adult heights should be affected by secular increase in agricultural productions in Korea and institutional progress in agriculture. However, the manner by which the increased food supply and other determinants of nutritional status affected the growth and human capital development remain unexplored. Rigorous research on these issues is often considerably hampered by shortage of the appropriate data, particularly for the periods prior to the 1970s. Based on newly-collected data on military conscript records and county-level agricultural production from archival sources, Chapters 6 and 7 investigate how nutritional availability in two crucial periods of human growth, namely, early childhood (from conception to age 3) and adolescence (from age 12–16), affected the growth and human capital development of South Korean conscripts born from 1946 to 1957. The chapters also explore whether increased nutrition in adolescence mitigated the negative effects of early-life exposure to the Korean War.

The Gwangju uprising, arguably the bloodiest incident that occurred in South Korea since the end of the Korean War, took place on May 18, 1980 in the southwestern city of Gwangju in the course of political crisis that followed the assassination of President Park in October 1979.

Student demonstrations demanding democratic reform turned to mass protests by citizens who were angered by the brutal acts of violence conducted by paratroopers (special unit trained for guerrilla warfare), and the incident soon escalated into a bloody warfare between armed civilian militias (called the Citizen Army) and martial law troops. An estimated 500 civilians were killed and over 3,000 were wounded in the violence that engulfed the city (Shin and Hwang 2003, p. xvii). Even for the citizens who avoided any direct damage, the incident was extremely stressful. In Chapters 8 and 9, I investigate the hypothesis that the maternal stress in pregnancy from the Gwangju uprising negatively affected the fetal health of the children, and that the impact of the adverse early-life shock even transmitted to the health of the next generation. The chapters provide very rate evidence as to intergenerational transmission of maternal stress in pregnancy.

CHAPTER 2

The Korean War as a Natural Experiment

2.1. The Korean War

The Korean War began with the surprise invasion of South Korea by North Korea on 25 June 1950. The war lasted three years and ended when an armistice agreement was signed on 27 July 1953. Vastly unprepared in terms of equipment and training, the South Korean troops were repeatedly defeated and forced to retreat southward. The South Korean capital, Seoul, was captured by North Korean forces in only three days. The United Nations (UN) troops arrived in the south only after the resolution of the UN Security Council recommendation of military assistance to South Korea. By this time, the North Korean Army advancing into the country could not be held off. By late August 1950 (only two months after the war broke out), North Korea had occupied about 90% of the entire Korean Peninsula (see Figure 2.1). The remaining uninvaded region was a small area around Busan City, located in Southeast Korea.

In the resulting battle at the Busan perimeter from August to mid-September 1950, the South Korean and US forces managed to stave off fierce North Korean attacks meant to capture the entire peninsula. On 15 September, the UN troops countered with a successful landing at Incheon and forced the North Korean Army in the south to retreat northward to avoid a siege. The UN troops liberated Seoul on 27 September. They

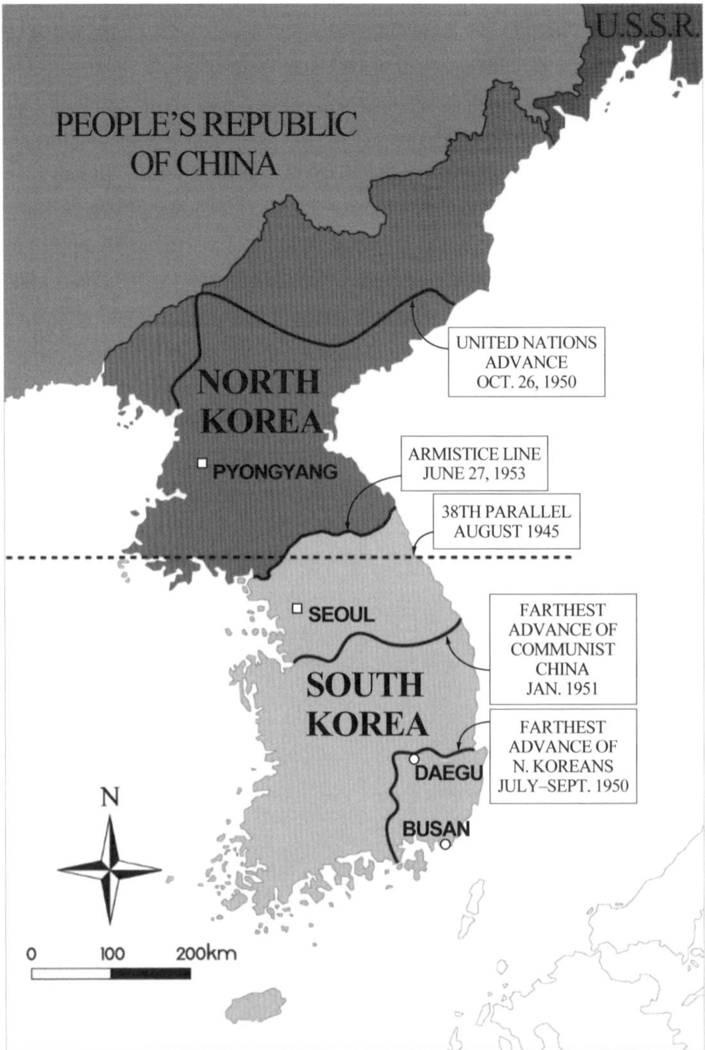

Figure 2.1 | Movements of the Frontline during the Korean War: 1950–1953

continued northward to capture Pyongyang City, the North Korean capital (19 October), and eventually reached the Amnok (Yalu) River, which divides North Korea and China.

By late November 1950, the unification of the peninsula seemed to be only a matter of time. However, Chinese communist forces secretly moved into North Korean territory and ambushed the UN troops, forcing the troops to fall back. Seoul was again lost to the enemy on 4 January 1951. Refugees from both the south and the north left their hometowns, following the retreating soldiers. Regrouped and reinforced, the UN forces stabilized the battlefront and fought back. On 14 March 1951, the UN troops drove the North Korean and Chinese armies out of Seoul. This event was the fourth conquest of the city in only nine months. After exchanging offensive actions around the 38th parallel between March and June, the war reached a stalemate that lasted until the armistice of July 1953.

The Korean War is the most brutal event that Korea has ever experienced in the modern era and one of the major international wars fought after World War II. Statistical data on human losses caused by the war are unreliable and substantially vary based on sources. According to the official statistics of South Korea published in 1955, the number of civilian casualties during the three years of hostilities totaled 990,968, including 373,599 persons killed, 229,625 injured, 84,532 abducted, and 303,212 missing in South Korea alone (Chung 2010). These estimates are likely understated. Military casualties were also heavy. An estimated 36,940 US servicemen and 245,000 to 415,000 South Korean soldiers were killed while in service during the war.

Despite its historical significance, the Korean War draws considerably less attention from people outside the country compared with World War II or the Vietnam War. Even the main participants (such as the US) who were directly involved in the campaign did not pay as much attention to the war. The "Forgotten War" is one of the best books written on the Korean War, which presents an account of the conflict that befits its current status. Relatively rich literature on political circumstances is devoted to the origin, progress, and aftermath of the war (Cumings 1981, 1990, 2010). Military actions are also reasonably well documented (Halberstam 2007). However, the social and economic aspects of the conflict remain poorly understood. In particular, documents are inadequate on how the war affected the everyday lives of civilians, and how wartime experiences influenced the subsequent health and socioeconomic performance of survivors over their life course. Studying the social history of the Korean War based on the narratives of survivors is a promising approach to fill this gap (Kim 2009; Pyo et al. 2003). However, the primary focus of such studies is the civil disputes and massacres caused by ideological conflicts.

Although quantitative evidence and systematic documentation are rare, visualizing the terrible ordeal suffered by the majority of the Koreans during the war is not difficult. With frontline troops dramatically moving back and forth across the region, practically the entire Korean Peninsula experienced the ravages of war. The chaotic situation in the early stages of the war directly exposed civilians to combat activities, which took a tremendous toll on human life. In addition to physical wounds and illnesses, a few survivors suffered from the mental damages that afflicted the soldiers, such as post-traumatic stress disorder.

During the first several months of the war, numerous South Koreans remained in the areas that were occupied by North Korean forces. The exact number of civilians who failed to escape from North Korean control remains unknown. An estimated 1 million (or 50%) residents in Seoul are believed to have remained in the city during the first three months of captivity (Yang 2010, p. 576). Many of the people under communist control suffered from atrocities such as massacres, tortures, imprisonment, and abduction. Civilians who remained under North Korean control were also victimized by heavy bombings by the UN air forces that attempted to destroy North Korean military facilities and supply lines (Kim 2008). The lessons learned from the terrible experience under the first occupation and the organized evacuation efforts by the government drove virtually all residents of the Central Region to flee southward when the Chinese Army pushed the UN forces back for a second time from late 1950 to early 1951.

Refugee experience was no less arduous. Many refugees travelled on foot for days, carrying as many of their belongings as possible. People who were fortunate to get a train ride endured overly crowded cabins. Passengers who rode on the roof bore the suffocating smoke blowing out of the steam locomotive, especially when the train passed through tunnels. Away from home, the refugees endured chronic hunger and slept without proper shelter. The refugees joined the retreating troops pushed by the Chinese attack and suffered through the harsh winter cold.[1]

The small areas in the southeast that managed to avoid occupation, especially the two large cities of Busan and Daegu, were the main refugee destinations. Busan City, with a population of about 400,000, became home to more than 1 million people in only several months.

1 See memoirs by Korean writers including Kim (2006) and Chun (2006).

Most refugees lived in shabby shelters made out of cardboard boxes, wooden planks, and makeshift tarp covering. Some people who had close relatives or friends living in Busan and Daegu fared slightly better, but they needed to cram themselves into small rooms. Emergency aid provided by the UN forces and ration distributions by the government prevented mass starvation, but these measure were still insufficient to solve the severe food shortage.

Prenatal exposure to war-related disruptions such as those described may negatively affect maternal and fetal health in different ways. First, food shortage during a war forces pregnant women to suffer from hunger. Malnutrition suffered while in-utero can increase the risk of developing various degenerative diseases at older age (Barker 1992, 1994). Second, maternal stress from exposure to combat activities and from physical or emotional hardship can adversely affect fetal health (Aizer et al. 2016; Os and Selten 1998; Selten et al. 2003; Meijer 2007). Excessive noise causes stillbirth, birth defects, and decreased birth weight as a result of changes in the uterine and placental blood flow (Geber 1970; Jones and Tauscher 1978; Knipschild et al. 1981). Among the Finnish population, Huttunen and Niskanen (1978) found that the prenatal loss of fathers increases the risks of suffering from schizophrenia and committing crimes. Rofe and Goldberg (2011) reported increases in the blood pressure of pregnant women who lived in an area in Israel that was a target of terrorist activities for a long period and suffered the effects of war.

Well-documented studies report that measures of wartime stress such as exposure to combat and imprisonment in POW camp have persistent negative effects on the health and socioeconomic outcomes of veterans (Nefzger 1970; Beebe 1975; Sutker 1991; Lee 2005; Costa and Kahn 2008; Robson et al. 2009). A long-term impact of war was found for civilians, too. Individuals who resided in war-torn countries in childhood during World War II experience greater educational and earning losses at older age compared to those from countries not involved in the war (Ichino and Winter-Ebmer 2004). Kesternich et al. (2011) reported that exposure to World War II, as measured by the number of years an individual was directly affected by the war, and to individual-level shocks caused by the war, such as hunger periods, significantly predict old-age health and socioeconomic outcomes.

Recent studies offer more clear evidence that in-utero exposure to military conflicts have persistent negative effect on later outcomes. It is well established that exposure to violence while in-utero or in early childhood negatively affect indices of physical growth, such as height and weight (Akbulut-Yuksel and Yuksel 2017; Akresh et al. 2012a, 2012b; Duque 2017; Grossman et al. 2019; Islam et al. 2017b; Minoiu and Shemyakina 2014; Oskorouchi 2019; Phadera 2019). Likewise, growing evidence suggests that early-life experiences of violent events adversely influence health outcomes (Islam et al. 2017a, 2017b; Persson and Rossin-Slater 2018; Schiman et al. 2019; Singhal 2019), and educational attainment (Akresh et al. 2017; Bundervoet and Fransen 2018; Duque 2017; Ouili 2017; Saing and Kazianga 2019).

2.2. Exploring Long-Term Consequences: Methods and Data

From the theoretical basis and empirical evidence suggested above, we may hypothesize that the various disruptions caused by the Korean War adversely affected maternal and fetal health. Measuring the magnitude of war-related negative health shocks is central to evaluating this hypothesis. Unfortunately, data that can be used to link adult health and socioeconomic outcomes to detailed wartime experiences are generally unavailable. The key strategy for measuring the effect of the war that are widely employed in the related literature is to investigate how individual socioeconomic and health outcomes at old age (available from various micro data) differ using the timing and the place of birth.

A comparison of two birth cohorts while keeping all other factors constant is infeasible. Given the linear dependence among period, age, and cohort, implementing changes in cohort necessarily imposes alterations on either age or period. Given that most socioeconomic outcomes only tend to change gradually across cohorts, identifying a cohort effect from other smooth effects is difficult. An example is the effect of changes in secular income over time.

However, one feature of the Korean War helps disentangle the cohort effect, that is, civilians were directly exposed to major war disruptions for only a relatively brief period. Although the war lasted more than three years, the major damage sustained by civilians happened in the first nine months following the sudden invasion of North Korea (late June 1950 to late March 1951). During these months, the frontline troops rapidly and unexpectedly moved back and forth across the region, and civilians suffered through occupation or refugee experience (see Figure 2.1). The war reached a stalemate around the 38th parallel after the spring of 1951, and the civilian life in the south of the battlefield more or less stabilized. Thus, a more reasonable assumption is that the fetal health of individuals born in 1951 or late 1950 is more seriously damaged by war-related disruptions than other birth cohorts.

Two more assumptions are required to add credence to the hypothesis of this study. First, following the fetal origins hypothesis, a particular wartime event is assumed to cause a stronger negative health shock while an individual is in-utero than in the postnatal period. Nearly all Koreans born either prior to or shortly after the Korean War should be negatively influenced by the war in one way or another. With all other factors being equal, if in-utero circumstances are more critical than, say, early childhood circumstances, then the adult outcomes of the cohorts who were in-utero from the summer of 1950 to the spring of 1951 should be worse than those of neighboring cohorts.

Second, all other experiences, except the war effect, is assumed to continuously or gradually change across the birth cohorts considered in the analysis (those born in 1945 through 1959). In other words, no other major events (epidemics, short-term economic shocks, institutional changes, and so on) differentially affect the 1950 to 1951 birth cohorts and those adjacent to it. This premise appears to be a reasonable assumption. For example, the number of students entering a college each year in Korea, a key institutional factor that determines the educational attainment of each birth cohort, gradually increased from 1960 to 2000, with no discriminating effect on a particular birth cohort (Figure 2.2). Similarly, although several disease epidemics occurred between 1945 and 1955, no evidence suggests that a particular birth cohort underwent a considerably worse disease environment (Chun 2011).

Two types of evidence for the cohort effect are presented in the subsequent chapters. First, the raw data on adult outcomes for each birth cohort are graphically displayed. Whether the 1950 or 1951 cohort reveals discontinuous cohort effects is determined. For measures of socioeconomic outcomes drawn from the 2000 census (reporting the place of birth), the results for individuals born in the Central Region are highlighted because they experienced particularly severe hardships during the war, as explained later in the paper.

Second, the deviations of census outcomes from smooth cohort

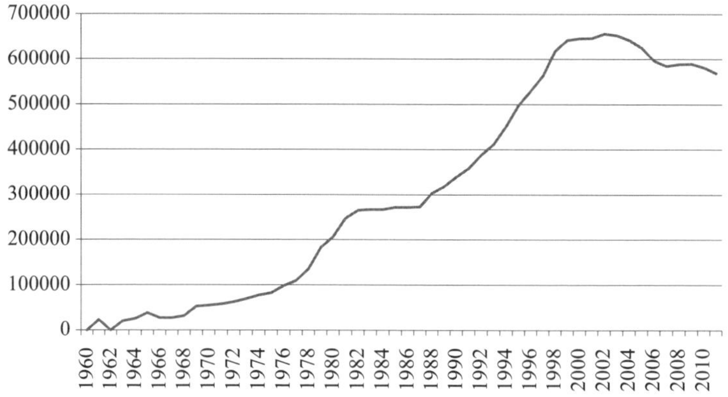

Figure 2.2 | The Number of Students Entering College: 1960–2010

trends are systematically estimated for individuals born between 1945 and 1959. The estimation is carried out using the following regression Equation 2.1:

$$\textbf{(2.1)} \quad y_i = \alpha + \sum_{t=1950}^{1951} \beta_t I_{it} + \gamma_1 YOB_i + \gamma_2 YOB_i^2 + \gamma_3 YOB_i^3 + \varepsilon_i$$

where y_i denotes adult outcome for individual i; I_t denotes the dummy variable with a value of 1 for individuals born in year t, and 0 otherwise; YOB denotes the last two digits of the birth year; and β_t measures the departure of outcomes for the birth cohorts in-utero during the Korean War from the cubic cohort trend.

The severity of wartime experiences differed by region of residence, which offers another opportunity to identify the effect of the war on maternal and fetal health. Because of the manners the frontline moved during the war, as explained in the preceding chapter, the extent of war-related disruptions experienced by a particular locality was strongly influenced by the distance to the border (the 38th parallel). That is, the closer to the 38th parallel a person was located, the more arduous his or her wartime experiences would be. For example, the residents of the Central Region, the northern provinces of South Korea, had had less time to respond to the surprise attack of the North Korean forces compared with the residents of the southern regions because of their proximity to North Korea. As a consequence, they likely suffered from the occupation of North Korean troops and the bombings by UN forces. Even if the residents of the Central Region managed to escape from the communist control, they would have had to travel a longer distance to reach the Busan perimeter. Moreover, since a large part of the Central Region was occupied by North Korea twice, many of the residents in the region were displaced twice.

The establishment of the 38th parallel as the border between North and South Korea suggests that the geographic variations in war-caused damage sustained by civilians are perhaps exogenously determined. The parallel was abruptly established as the boundary that divides Korea into two spheres, which would be split by the US and Soviet Union troops after the Second World War. The United States proposed to the Soviet Union that it would take control of the northern half of Korea, a Japanese colony at the time, in an attempt to prevent the further advance of the Red Army when the Japanese surrender in August 1945 became apparent. The 38th parallel was chosen because it roughly divides the Korean peninsula in the middle. This arbitrary decision made the temporary boundary to separate the same province, county, and even village into two. Initially, no one expected that it would become a permanent barrier separating Korea. The 38th parallel was not a formal border and people could freely cross it until the summer of 1948. The proximity to North Korea and the characteristics of a particular locality or residents are unlikely correlated, because the 38th parallel was drawn suddenly and arbitrarily, and the Korean War broke out only two years after it became a formal border.

For this study, the residence of the mother of a person who lived at the beginning of the war (summer of 1950) should be considered in constructing the location-specific measures of war-related disruptions. Unfortunately, information regarding maternal residence is unavailable. However, the place of birth of Korean War cohorts is a reasonably effective proxy for the following reasons. First, descriptive records suggest that most refugees returned home as soon as their hometowns were liberated by the UN forces. Second, even individuals who were born while in refuge regarded their permanent homes as their birthplaces. These claims are supported by the regional composition of birth-by-birth cohort (Figure 2.3). If many people were born in the unoccupied Busan perimeter [denoted as South (F) in Figure 2.3] and recorded it as their place of birth, the percentage of people born in this area should have increased during the early stages of the war. However, the figure shows that the numbers remained remarkably stable from 1949 to 1952.

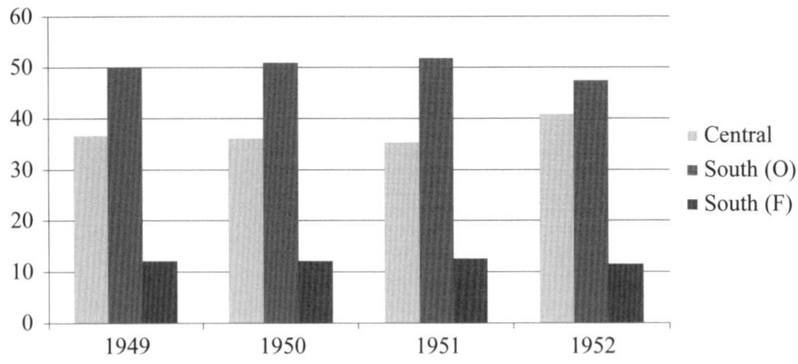

Figure 2.3 | Region of Birth by Year

To study the magnitude of wartime stress experienced while in-utero, a difference-in-difference method is employed in examining the variations across places of birth. The basic idea is that if the cohort effect captures the influences of war-related disruptions, then it should be stronger for those persons who underwent more traumatic wartime experiences. To verify this assumption, I use either OLS or logistic regression to estimate the following Equation 2.2:

$$\textbf{(2.2)} \quad y_i = \alpha + \beta_1 I_i + \beta_2 (I_i \times S_i) + \beta_3 S_i + \gamma_1 YOB_i + \gamma_2 YOB_i^2 + \delta X_i + \varepsilon_i .$$

In this equation, I denotes the dummy variable that identifies an individual as in-utero between the summer of 1950 and the spring of 1951, S is a measure of wartime stress, and X represents other location-specific factors of the given adult outcome.

The analyses provided in the next chapter use the following location-specific measures of wartime stress. First, a dummy variable indicating whether a person was born in the Central Region is used because of the higher degree of suffering that these citizens endured. Second, dummy variables show if the place of birth belongs to either of the following two categories: the localities that were occupied twice by the communist forces or the remaining areas in the Central Region captured only once. Third, the distance between the place of birth and Busan City is employed.[2] A longer distance from the major destination

2 The distance between the municipal office of each county (or district) and the

for refugees should be related to a higher probability of being occupied by the North Korean forces, a greater exposure to UN bombings, and more arduous refugee experiences. Finally, the duration of North Korean control is considered.[3] The longer the duration under occupation, the more devastating the suffering of the residents should be regardless of whether they managed to escape.

The analyses in the next chapter regarding the effect of the war on socioeconomic outcomes at older ages largely rely on the 1990 and 2000 censuses because the individuals born during the Korean War reached their prime ages (37 to 50 years old) from 1990 to 2000 in terms of socioeconomic status. Furthermore, the 1990 and 2000 censuses provides detailed geographic codes for the places of birth, which enables me to study how the effect of war differs by places of birth.[4] Conversely, the Census has two major limitations. First, it offers only a restrictive set of variables on personal characteristics, especially health outcomes. Second, it does not provide a report on the month or quarter of birth, thereby making the identification of the exact timing and duration of in-utero exposure to wartime disruptions difficult.

The following measures of socioeconomic outcomes are considered: (1) years of schooling; (2) probability of entering college; (3) probability of having primary school education or lower; (4) probability of having professional employment in 2000; (5) probability of having an unskilled

---

city hall of Busan is measured.

3 The dates of occupation of a particular place by the North Korean forces and its liberation by the UN troops are either drawn or estimated based on descriptive histories of the Korean War and maps displaying changes in the battlefield over time. If the exact timing of an event cannot be determined based on the available sources, the frontline connecting two places is assumed, for which the date of the event is known, moving with the same pace. The six-volume histories of the Korean War compiled by a government agency (The War Memorial Society 1992) and the Military Academy of the Korean Army (1998) were used as major sources.

4 The micro sample of the 1980 census also provides information on the place of birth as well as several socioeconomic outcomes. However, some individuals who belonged to the post-war birth cohorts and who were compared with the Korean War cohorts in this study were too young in 1980 to provide accurate measures of adult outcomes. For example, individuals in the 1959 birth cohort, who were included in the sample used in the analyses conducted in the balance of the study in 1980, were only 21 years old, too young to complete school, and to start a job career.

job in 2000; (6) probability of remaining never married by 2000; (7) years of the spouse's schooling in 2000; and (8) the number of children in 2000.[5] The quality of occupation is considered only for 2000 because of data problem of the 1990 census.[6] Marital status, marriage selection, and fertility are analyzed based on the 2000 census because the subjects of the youngest birth cohort considered in the study (the 1959 birth cohort) were too young to complete marriage or fertility by 1990. Analyzing the number of children was limited to the females who have ever married according to how it is reported in the censuses; for males, the number of children of the current wife is used in the analysis.

Table 2.1 presents the sample means of the socioeconomic outcomes of all male and female individuals and those who were born in the Central Region from 1945 to 1959. The mean of schooling years in the pooled censuses of 1990 and 2000 for the males and females are, respectively, 11.8 and 9.9. 22.3% of males entered college, whereas only 8.5% of females did. Individuals born in the Central Region were more educated than the entire sample. In terms of labor-market outcomes, 9.6% of males and 67.8% of females of the pooled sample were not working. Of those who worked in 2000, 25.8% of males and 9% of females held professional jobs, while 24.2% of males and 17.5% of females comprised those in unskilled occupations. Natives of the Central Region were more likely to work and to be employed in professional occupations.

Primary measures of old-age health are obtained from the 2010 census, which indicates whether a person has particular disability or limitation for all respondents. The 2010 census is the only census currently available that provides information on both the health (variables on functional limitations) and place of birth of the cohorts born during the Korean War.[7] By obtaining permission from the Korea Statistical Office,

5 The occupations include professionals, managers, officials, and technical experts (2000 census occupation codes 0 to 293). The unskilled jobs include manual labor and operatives (2000 census occupation codes 811 to 942).

6 Measures of the quality of occupation cannot be obtained from the 1990 census because of serious errors in the occupation codes given in the public-use micro sample of the 1990 census.

7 The 2000 census offers information on functional limitations only for individuals aged 65 and older; the cohorts born during the Korean War birth cohorts were 50 or younger when the census was taken. The 2005 census provides the health variables for all individuals, but does not indicate the place

Table 2.1
Sample Means of Socioeconomic Outcomes of the 1945–1959 Birth Cohorts

	All		Born in the Central Region	
	Male	Female	Male	Female
1990–2000 Censuses (pooled)				
Years of Schooling	11.8	9.9	12.3	10.5
% College or higher	22.3	8.5	26.3	10.4
% Primary or lower	11.1	24.3	8.0	18.9
% Not working	9.6	67.8	8.9	67.8
2000 Census				
% Professional job	25.8	9.0	31.7	12.0
% Unskilled job	24.2	17.5	24.8	18.3
% Never married	2.2	1.7	2.5	2.0
Spouse's schooling (married)	9.6	10.3	10.1	10.9
Fertility (married)	2.2	2.4	2.1	2.2

Source: The 2% samples of the 1990 and 2000 censuses.

Note: See text for the definition of the variables. Fertility for males refers to the total number of children born to the current wife of married men.

I analyzed the 10% sample of the census that provides a broader range of variables including the county (or district) and the exact year of birth.

The health variables available from the 2010 census include: (1) any disability or functional limitation (Disability), (2) limitations in sight, hearing or speaking (Communication), (3) limitations in walking or ascending stairs (Moving), (4) mental impairments (Mental), (5) limitations in memory, learning, or concentration (Cognitive), (6) limitations in eating, bathing, or dressing (Basic activities), (7) limitations in shopping or going to hospital (Outing), and (8) restrictions in working (Working).

Table 2.2 presents the sample means of the health outcomes of all individuals and Central Region natives born from 1945 to 1959. The fraction of the birth cohorts with any disability in the 2010 census is 12.4% for both males and females. Individuals born in the Central Region are more likely to have health problems than the entire sample. The percentage of males with a particular disability is higher than that of

of birth. The publicly available 2% micro sample of the 2010 census does not offer the variables on the place of birth.

Table 2.2
Sample Means of Health Outcomes of the 1945–1959 Birth Cohorts

	All		Born in the Central Region	
	Male	Female	Male	Female
2010 Census: functional limitation				
% Any type	12.4	12.4	13.6	13.1
% Communication (sight, hearing, speaking)	3.1	2.2	3.4	2.4
% Moving (walking, ascending stairs)	6.3	8.0	6.7	8.2
% Mental	4.5	2.9	5.4	3.5
% Cognitive (memory, learning)	4.7	3.1	5.6	3.8
% Basic activities (eating, bathing, dressing)	1.9	1.3	2.6	1.5
% Outing (shopping, going to hospital)	2.5	2.4	3.0	2.8
% Working	1.8	1.9	2.4	2.7
2005 Census				
% Disabled	5.3	5.8	N/A	N/A
% Activity limited	3.5	3.7	N/A	N/A

Source: The 10% sample of the 2010 census; 2% sample of the 2005 census.
Note: See text for the definition of the variables.

females for all but limitation in moving.

2.3. Summary

The Korean War (1950–1953) offers a unique opportunity to examine the long-term effects of war-related disruptions such as arduous refugee experiences, suffering under the North Korean occupation, hunger, and direct exposure to combat. Although the war lasted for more than three years, the major war damage sustained by civilians was concentrated in the first nine months following the sudden invasion of North Korea (late June 1950 to late March 1951). At that time, the frontline rapidly and unexpectedly moved back and forth across South Korea. Furthermore, the severity of wartime experience considerably differs depending on the place of residence. For example, Central Region residents were hit particularly hard because they lived closer to North Korea and their area was invaded twice by enemy forces. These specific circumstances help identify the effects of the war on maternal and fetal health through a comparison of the adult outcomes across birth cohorts and places of birth.

Specifically, we can investigate whether the individuals born in 1950 and 1951 (those who spent time in-utero during the first nine months of the war) show discontinuous cohort effects, and whether the cohort effects are more distinct for those born in areas hit harder by the war.

CHAPTER 3

Socioeconomic Consequences of In-Utero Exposure to the Korean War

3.1. Cohort Effects

If the disruptions caused by the Korean War adversely affected maternal and fetal health, individuals who were in-utero during the worst time of the war should reveal worse adult socioeconomic outcomes compared to the subjects of neighboring birth cohorts. As explained in Chapter 2, the first nine months from June 1950 to March 1951 were particularly harsh for civilians. Therefore, it is likely that the fetal health of the subject of the 1951 birth cohort and part of the 1950 birth cohort was impaired by war-related damages. Accordingly, I examine if socioeconomic outcomes of these birth cohorts deviate from their long-run cohort trends.

The educational attainment of individuals born in the Central Region from 1945 to 1959 were measured in terms of years of schooling (Figure 3.1), college admission (Figure 3.2), and completion of primary schooling or lower (Figure 3.3), as obtained from the pooled sample of the 1990 and 2000 Censuses. A strong upward trend in educational attainment is shown by these cohorts, with the 1950 and 1951 birth cohorts veering from this steady trend. A deviation of the 1951 cohort from the tendency for long-term increase in schooling is clearly revealed; the1951 cohort subjects received approximately two months less schooling than those born in 1949. They were less likely to enter college and more likely to

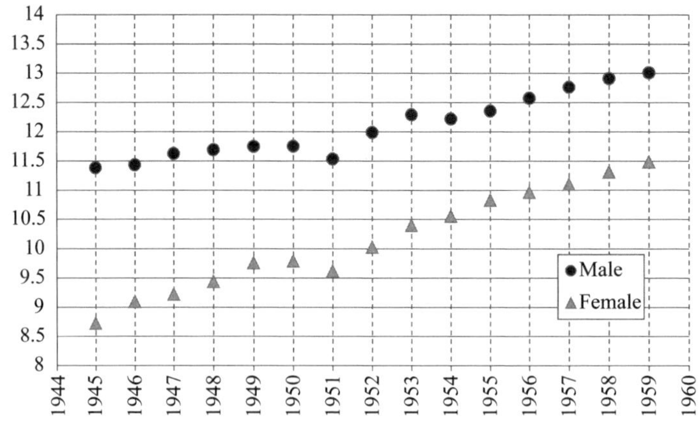

Source: Pooled data of the 2% samples of the 1990 and 2000 censuses.

Figure 3.1 | Years of Schooling by Birth Cohort: Born in the Central Region

achieve the lowest educational attainment.[1]

Figure 3.4 presents two measures of success in the labor market for male subjects born in the Central Region from 1945 to 1959. The percentages of those professionally employed and those who were manual laborers were calculated from the 2000 census.[2] The analysis is limited to males because of the low labor force participation of females belonging to the cohorts. As with schooling trends, the lower occupational achievement of the 1951 male birth cohort is evident. Male workers born in 1951 are much less likely to be employed in a professional job and more likely to hold unskilled manual occupation than predicted by long-

---

1 Although not presented here, digression of the 1951 birth cohort from the trend is also observed in the entire sample, albeit at a smaller magnitude. Educational attainment either stagnated (admission to college or higher for males and females, and primary school or lower for females) or improved at a rate slower than the predicted long-term trend (years of schooling for males and females, and primary school or lower for males) from the 1950 to the 1951 cohorts.

2 These measures of labor market outcomes are computed for the entire sample, including non-participants in the labor market and the unemployed. The unconditional percentages provide similar implications that the results are not primarily driven by decisions on labor force participation.

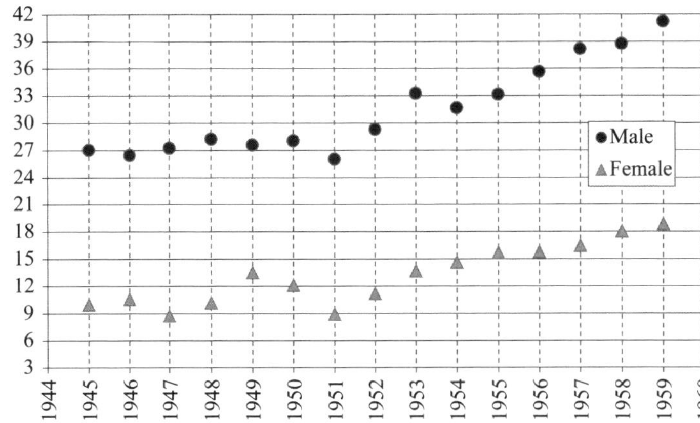

Source: The 2% micro sample of the 2000 census.

Figure 3.2 | % College or Higher in 2000 by Birth Cohort: Born in the Central Region

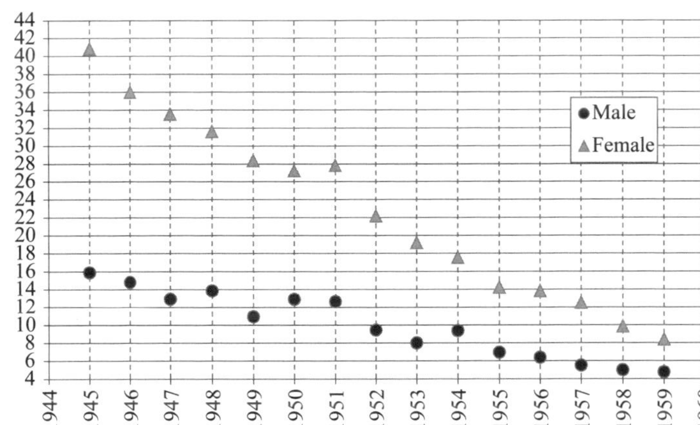

Source: The 2% micro sample of the 2000 census.

Figure 3.3 | % Primary School or Less in 2000 by Birth Cohort: Born in the Central Region

term trends.[3]

3 The same measures constructed for the entire sample (also not presented here) show similar handicaps for the 1951 birth cohort, although the magnitude of

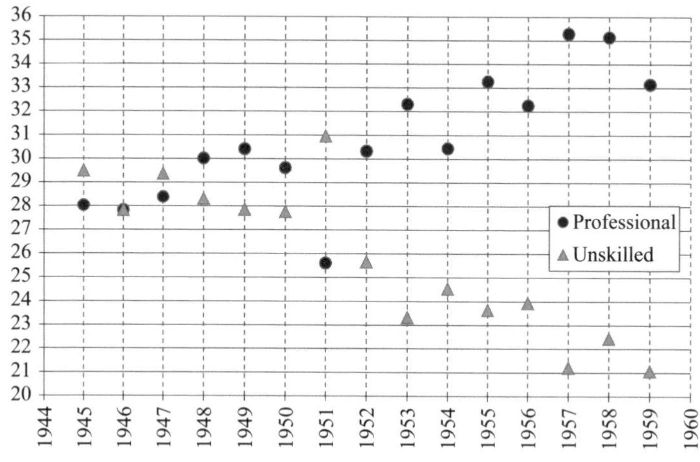

Source: The 2% sample of the 2000 census.

Figure 3.4 | % Professionals and Unskilled Workers among Employed Males in 2000: Born in the Central Region

Adult outcomes on marriage and reproduction were also compared across birth cohorts, as shown in Figures 3.5 to 3.7. Males born in 1951 are more likely to remain unmarried compared with the neighboring male birth cohorts. In contrast, the percentage of females who never married is higher for the 1952 and 1953 birth cohorts (Figure 3.5). The spouses of men and women born in 1951 are more negatively selected in terms of educational attainment compared with the adjacent birth cohorts (Figure 3.6). The lifetime fertility of females born in 1951 is higher than the predicted long-term cohort trend (Figure 3.7).

Columns 1 and 2 of Table 3.1 provide the estimates of β_t in Equation 2.1, indicating the magnitude of the outcome deviation of male subjects born in 1950 and 1951 from the cubic cohort trend. Standard errors were adjusted in testing the statistical significance for the clustering of birth year and region levels.[4] The regression results confirm that educational attainment, employment rate, quality of occupation, and education of the

---

deviation from the trend is smaller compared to that in the Central Region.

4 All the coefficients of interest are jointly significant at the 1% level for all the regressions reported in this chapter.

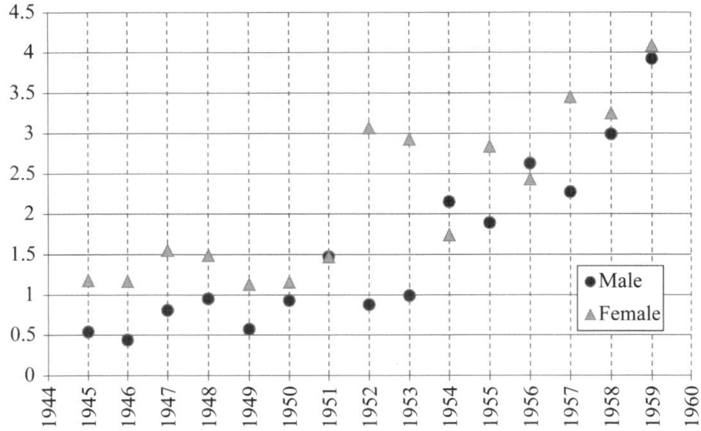

Source: The 2% sample of the 2000 census.

Figure 3.5 | % Never Married Persons in 2000: Born in the Central Region

Source: Currently married males and ever married females in the 2% sample of the 2000 census.

Figure 3.6 | Spouse's Years of Schooling in 2000 by Birth Cohort: Born in the Central Region

spouse of the 1951 birth cohort are significantly low, especially among subjects born in the Central Region.[5] If born in the Central Region, the

5 The negative effect of being born in 1951 on the quality of occupation is not

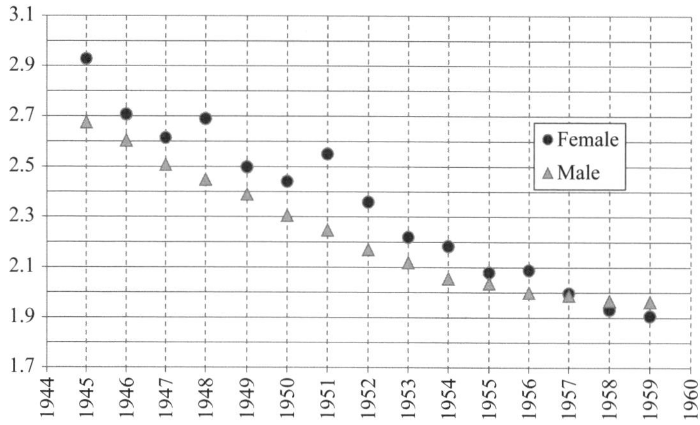

Source: The 2% sample of the 2000 census.

Note: The total number of children of famales who have ever married; and the number of children for the current wife for males.

Figure 3.7 | Number of Children in 2000: Born in the Central Region

male subjects of the 1951 birth cohort are more likely to remain bachelors, and the percentage of those who never married is low for all males born in 1951. The fertility of the female spouse is higher for the 1951 male birth cohort than that predicted by the cubic cohort trend. For all measures, the 1951 cohort effect is statistically significant in the sample limited to people born in the Central Region (Table 3.1, Column 2). This effect remains statistically significant when the entire sample is used (Column 1) but at a small magnitude. However, the sign of the coefficient changes for the probability of being never married. By contrast, the cohort effect is insignificant for individuals born in the Southern Region, including the areas occupied by North Korea (not reported in the table).

Columns 3 and 4 of Table 3.1 present the regression results for females, which correspond well with the patterns of the cohort effect. Female subjects of the 1951 birth cohort, who were born in the Central Region, exhibit clear disadvantages in all three measures of educational

---

fully explained by the disadvantage in educational attainment of the cohort. Although the education factor is controlled, the 1951 cohort effect remains statistically significant.

Table 3.1

Deviation of the 1950 and 1951 Birth Cohorts' Adult Socioeconomic Outcomes from 1945–1959 Trend

Outcome	Males				Females			
	(1) South Korea		(2) Central Region		(3) South Korea		(4) Central Region	
	$\partial y/\partial x$	P-value	$\partial y/\partial x$	P-value	$\partial y/\partial x$	P-value	$\partial y/\partial x$	P-value
A. Years of schooling								
Born in 1950	**-0.0911**	0.0228	**-0.1703**	0.0008	**-0.1023**	0.0001	0.0321	0.4613
Born in 1951	**-0.1660**	0.0003	**-0.4323**	<.0001	**-0.1681**	<.0001	**-0.2883**	<.0001
B. College or higher								
Born in 1950	**-0.0099**	0.0046	**-0.0113**	0.0049	-0.0001	0.9543	**0.0103**	0.0489
Born in 1951	**-0.0122**	0.0014	**-0.0281**	<.0001	**-0.0074**	0.0005	**-0.0173**	0.0012
C. Primary or less								
Born in 1950	**0.0052**	0.0261	**0.0187**	<.0001	**0.0109**	0.0006	-0.0026	0.3678
Born in 1951	**0.0070**	0.0036	**0.0178**	<.0001	**0.0153**	<.0001	**0.0234**	<.0001
D. Not working								
Born in 1950	**0.0079**	<.0001	**0.0056**	0.0206	**-0.0079**	<.0001	-0.0001	0.9772
Born in 1951	0.0004	0.6978	**0.0077**	0.0012	**-0.0032**	0.0203	-0.0022	0.2832
E. Professional job								
Born in 1950	-0.0034	0.3194	-0.0028	0.6054	**-0.0055**	0.0459	-0.0039	0.5231
Born in 1951	**-0.0176**	<.0001	**-0.0485**	<.0001	-0.0001	0.9502	-0.0068	0.1981
F. Unskilled job								
Born in 1950	**0.0122**	<.0001	**0.0084**	0.0306	**0.0123**	<.0001	**0.0349**	<.0001
Born in 1951	**0.0122**	<.0001	**0.0471**	<.0001	0.0026	0.2273	**0.0333**	<.0001
G. Never married								
Born in 1950	0.0007	0.2728	0.0007	0.6564	-0.0017	0.1354	**-0.0087**	0.0307
Born in 1951	**-0.0012**	0.0792	**-0.0048**	0.0058	**-0.0027**	0.0078	**-0.0067**	0.0738
H. Spouse's schooling								
Born in 1950	-0.0287	0.1803	**-0.0596**	0.0228	**-0.0867**	0.0196	**-0.0961**	0.0316
Born in 1951	**-0.1684**	<.0001	**-0.4065**	<.0001	**-0.1764**	<.0001	**-0.2632**	<.0001
I. Number of children								
Born in 1950	0.0039	0.5225	-0.0024	0.8276	**0.0525**	0.0045	-0.0123	0.6903
Born in 1951	**0.0123**	0.0332	**0.0564**	<.0001	**0.1096**	<.0001	**0.1696**	<.0001

Source: The pooled sample of the 2% micro sample of the 1990 and 2000 population censuses.

Note: (a) "South Korea" includes persons who were born in North Korea and those for whom the place of birth is not reported; (b) For Panels E through I, the 2% sample of the 2000 census is utilized, and for Panels E and F, the sample is limited to persons who were employed at the time of census enumeration; (c) Polynomials of the year of birth (YOB, YOB^2 and YOB^3) are included in the regressions; (d) The number of children for males (Columns 1 and 2 of Panel I) is the total number of children born to the wife of currently married men; (e) Standard errors are adjusted for clustering at the levels of year and region of birth; and (f) The estimated coefficient in bold number is statistically significant at 10% level.

attainment, the percentage of the unskilled among the employed, and spouse's schooling (Panels A to C, F, and H of Column 4). Females born in 1951 had more children than the neighboring birth cohorts as in the case of males. However, unlike males, this female cohort does not significantly differ from other cohorts in terms of employment status and the percentage of workers employed in professional occupation. This unremarkable effect on female labor market outcomes is unsurprising, given the low labor-force participation of women from this cohort. No negative effect on female socioeconomic outcomes (not reported here) was observed among those born in the Southern Region in 1951.

A possible concern of the baseline regressions conducted above is that a cubic function of the year of birth may not accurately capture the actual smooth cohort trend. To address this concern, a more flexible cohort trend is applied to the cohort analysis, in which a quadratic cohort trend is allowed to change across the pre-war (1945 to 1949), wartime (1950 to 1954), and post-war (1955 to 1959) cohorts. The results are similar to those based on the cubic specification, especially for males born in 1951. For females, the negative effects of birth in 1950 or 1951 on education and occupation are more strongly revealed if the new specification is applied.

3.2. Difference-in-Difference Estimations

If the deviation of Census outcomes of the 1951 birth cohort reflects the influences of war-related disruptions experienced while in-utero, then its magnitude should be larger for individuals exposed to worse in-utero circumstances during the war. This hypothesis is consistent with the fact that the disadvantages of the 1951 birth cohort are particularly pronounced among individuals born in the Central Region. Further analyses employing more direct and detailed measures of wartime stress confirm that the 1951 cohort effect is indeed stronger for individuals with more arduous in-utero wartime experiences.

Figure 3.8 compares the schooling years of males from the 1951 birth cohort against those of neighboring cohorts (either 1950 or 1952) using the distance between their place of birth and Busan, a measure of wartime stress. Individuals born near Busan (within 200 kilometers) and

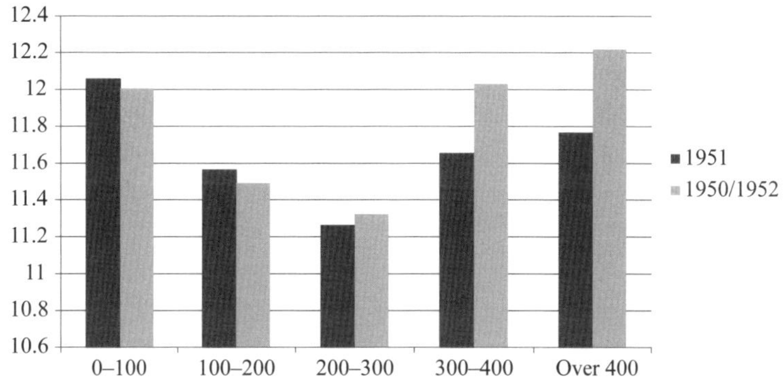

Source: The 2% sample of the 2000 census.

Figure 3.8 | Years of Male Schooling by Distance from Busan

who were from the 1951 birth cohort acquired slightly more schooling than those from adjacent cohorts. The direction of this schooling gap is reversed for areas that are 200 km to 300 km away from Busan. The disadvantages in schooling for the 1951 cohort versus other cohorts are particularly pronounced for individuals born far from Busan. The results obtained from female samples are similar to those from males, wherein the 1951 cohort effect increases with the severity of wartime stress measured by the distance from Busan. Analyses in which either an alternative measure of wartime stress (such as the duration of occupation) or a different adult outcome (such as the quality of occupation) present remarkably similar implications.

Similar comparisons across birth cohorts were conducted using different measures of socioeconomic outcomes and wartime stress. Lower schooling of the 1951 birth cohort is apparent among individuals born in areas under communist control for a prolonged period (Figure 3.9). The disadvantages experienced by the 1951 male cohort in terms of labor market performance (measured by the percentage of unskilled workers) are also larger among those exposed to more serious war-related disruptions, which are represented by the greater distance from Busan or the longer occupation by enemy forces (Figure 3.10). Similar results are obtained using percentage of males with professional employment as measure of occupational success (not reported here).

Regressions are conducted based on a difference-in-difference model, as displayed in Equation 2.2. If the 1951 cohort effect increases

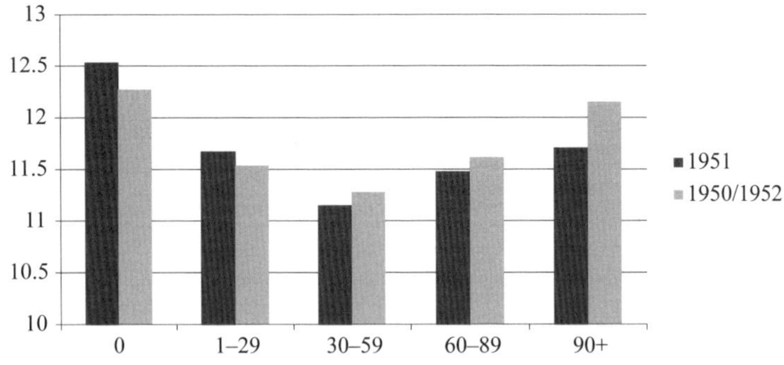

Source: The 2% micro sample of the 2000 census.

Figure 3.9 | Years of Male Schooling by Duration of Occupation (Days)

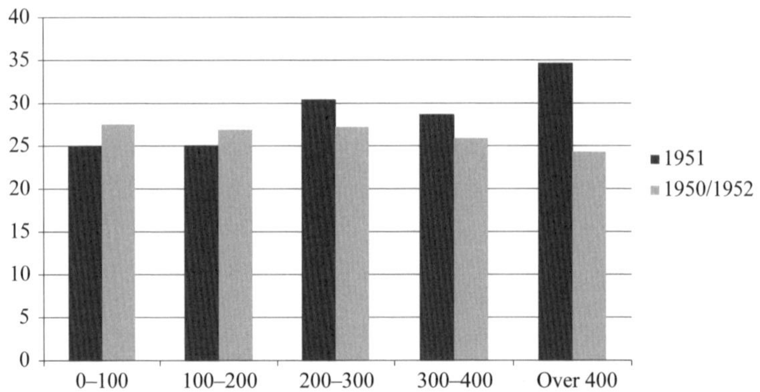

Source: The 2% micro sample of the 2000 census.

Figure 3.10 | % Manual Laborers among Employed Males by Distance from Busan (km)

with the magnitude of wartime stress, then the coefficient of interaction between the dummy variable for the 1951 birth (BORN1951) and the measure of wartime stress should be negative if the dependent variable is a desirable outcome. The cubic cohort trend (i.e., YOB, YOB^2, and YOB^3), dummy variable for the 1951 birth, and measure of negative shocks caused by the war are controlled.

Four measures of wartime stress are employed: (a) dummy variable for birth in the Central Region (CENTRAL); (b) dummy variables

Table 3.2

Summary of Regressions for Difference-in-Difference Model: Interaction between Measure of Wartime Stress and Deviation of the 1951 Birth Cohort's Adult Outcomes from 1945–1959 Trend

Outcome	Interaction between Measure of Wartime Stress and the 1951 Birth							
	(1) CENTRAL× BORN1951		(2) CENOCCUP2× BORN1951		(3) BUSAN_DIST× BORN1951		(4) DUROCCUP× BORN1951	
	∂y/∂x	P-value	∂y/∂x	P-value	∂y/∂x	P-value	∂y/∂x	P-value
1. Males								
A. Years of schooling	**-0.3212**	0.0071	**-0.5232**	0.0042	**-0.1852**	0.0012	**-0.1426**	0.0075
B. College or higher	**-0.0236**	0.0942	**-0.0552**	0.0069	**-0.0147**	0.0302	-0.0107	0.1069
C. Primary or less	0.0058	0.5388	0.0085	0.5147	**0.0100**	0.0134	**0.0099**	0.0153
D. Not working	**0.0145**	0.0748	**0.0269**	0.0279	**0.0084**	0.0333	**0.0059**	0.0852
E. Professional job	**-0.0540**	0.0092	**-0.0584**	0.0654	**-0.0155**	0.0924	-0.0064	0.5452
F. Unskilled job	**0.0539**	0.0057	**0.0783**	0.0043	**0.0282**	0.0014	**0.0289**	0.0055
G. Never married	0.0044	0.3754	0.0083	0.3478	0.0016	0.5425	-0.0003	0.9207
H. Spouse's schooling	**-0.3116**	0.0487	-0.3475	0.1827	**-0.1620**	0.0308	**-0.1730**	0.0378
I. Number of children	**0.0664**	0.0427	0.0554	0.2449	**0.0327**	0.0276	**0.0265**	0.0896
2. Females								
A. Years of schooling	**-0.2581**	0.0524	-0.2402	0.2270	**-0.1378**	0.0674	-0.0991	0.1386
B. College or higher	**-0.0283**	**0.0033**	-0.0303	0.0613	**-0.0133**	0.0331	**-0.0092**	0.0820
C. Primary or less	0.0063	0.6799	-0.0036	0.8705	0.0075	0.3120	0.0087	0.2106
D. Not working	0.0004	0.9775	0.0024	0.9013	-0.0051	0.4641	-0.0002	0.9799
E. Professional job	-0.0229	0.1641	-0.0300	0.2177	-0.0072	0.4019	-0.0142	0.1429
F. Unskilled job	0.0309	0.2070	0.0116	0.7288	**0.0260**	0.0067	**0.0294**	0.0064
G. Never married	-0.0050	0.1801	-0.0076	0.1488	**-0.0040**	0.0413	-0.0026	0.2625
H. Spouse's schooling	-0.1694	0.3402	-0.3092	0.2153	-0.0812	0.3484	-0.0795	0.4076
I. Number of children	0.0987	0.1116	0.1324	0.1811	0.0349	0.2388	0.0375	0.2353

Source: The pooled data of the 2% micro sample of the 1990 and 2000 population censuses.

Note: (a) Summary of 72 regressions; (b) The sample is limited to those for whom the place of birth is reported; (c) For Panels E through I, the 2% sample of the 2000 census is utilized, and for Panels E and F, the sample is limited to persons who were employed at the time of census enumeration; (d) A cubic cohort trend is included in each regression but omitted from the table; (e) The number of children for males (Panel 1-I) is the total number of children born to the current wife of married men; (f) Standard errors are adjusted for clustering at the levels of year and county of birth; and (g) The estimated coefficient in bold number is statistically significant at 10% level.

for birth in the localities occupied twice (CENOCCUP2) and birth in other places in the Central Region that were captured only once (CENOCCUP1); (c) the distance between the place of birth and Busan, measured in 100 kilometers (BUSAN_DIST); and (d) the number of months under occupation by North Korean forces (DUROCCUP).

Table 3.2 reports the summary results of 72 difference-in-difference regressions conducted on the 9 measures of socioeconomic outcomes cited in this study. The results suggest that for a wide range of socioeconomic outcomes, the 1951 cohort effect is stronger for individuals who suffered more serious wartime stress while in-utero. For males, the coefficient of the interaction between birth in 1951 and wartime stress is statistically significant in 26 out of 36 regressions. In all adult outcomes, except the probability of being never married (Panel 1-G), the coefficient for interaction is statistically significant in at least 2 specifications; in 7 out of 9 measures, it is significant in at least 3 specifications.[6]

The results among females are similar to those among males in terms of educational attainment. However, prenatal exposure to war-related disruptions had considerably weaker effects on the labor-market, marriage, and fertility outcomes of women than men. Only the probability of employment in unskilled occupations in 2000 was significantly affected by the interaction between birth in 1951 and measure of wartime stress (Panel 2-F, Columns 3 and 4). The significantly lower and, presumably, more selective labor force participation of women born prior to 1960 is a possible explanation for the gender difference in labor-market outcomes.[7]

The measures of the intensity of the war likely capture the exogenously-determined distance between the place of birth and the 38th parallel, but they might be correlated with selections of the treated group (i.e. the 1951 birth cohort born in the Central Region) as well. Accordingly, a number of control variables pertaining to the characteristics of the place of birth were added to the difference-in-difference regressions, including (a) the extent of urbanization, (b) educational attainment, (c) province dummy, and (d) urbanization and education combined. To construct the variables for extent of urbanization, places of birth were classified as

---

6 The entire Southern Region is the omitted category in the regressions in which CENTRAL and CENOCCUP2 are used as measures of wartime stress (Columns 1 and 2 of Table 3.2). If Busan is chosen as the omitted category, the absolute magnitudes of the regression coefficients for the interaction terms generally increase. For example, the estimated coefficient of CENTRAL interacting with BORN1951 for male schooling changes from -0.3212 (1-A of Column 1) to -0.3793 (p-value=0.0271). Female schooling changes from -0.2581 to -0.4266 (0.0466).

7 The possibility of the effect of in-utero exposure to war-related disruptions on change across ages was also investigated. The pooled sample of the 1990 and 2000 censuses is used by allowing the change in regression coefficients over the decade. The results for the years of schooling, not reported here, suggest that the differences between the two census years are statistically insignificant.

follows: (a) Seoul; (b) five metro cities, namely, Busan, Incheon, Daegu, Daejeon, and Gwangju; (c) all other smaller cities; and (d) rural areas (omitted category). For variables on educational attainment of each province or birth, we computed the percentage of the adult population with each of the following education category: (a) primary school or less (omitted category), (b) middle school, (c) high school, and (d) college or higher.

Table 3.3 presents the regression results for selected adult measures on which the interaction term of the 1951 birth and measure of wartime stress has a relatively strong effect in the original regressions (Table 3.2). Only the coefficient of the interaction term is reported for 112 regressions (seven adult outcomes, four measures of wartime stress, and four models). Except female years of schooling and male college education (Panels 2 and 3), the results of difference-in-difference estimations do not change much by applying different specifications. As far as the majority of male adult outcomes and a particular type female educational outcome are concerned, it is likely that the 1951 cohort effect captures the long-term consequence of in-utero exposure to disruptions directly related with combat activities.

I also examined whether the effect of interaction between the 1951 birth and the measure of war-caused damage is sensitive to the functional form of cohort trend by including birth year dummies (1945 is the omitted category) interacting with each measure of wartime stress in the regressions, as represented by the following Equation 3.1:

$$\textbf{(3.1)} \quad y_i = \alpha + \sum_{t=1946}^{1959} \beta_{1,t} I_{i,t} + \sum_{t=1946}^{1959} \beta_{2,t} (I_{i,t} \times S_i) + \beta_3 S_i + \delta X_i + \varepsilon_i .$$

Figures 3.11 and 3.12 plot the coefficients for the interaction terms estimated from the regressions in which education is used as the dependent variable. The Central Region dummy and the distance from Busan are applied as measures of wartime stress. The coefficient for the 1951 dummy for males, which interacts with wartime stress measure, stands out as a clear downward outlier (Figure 3.11). It is the only statistically significant coefficient at the 5% level. A discontinuous drop in the magnitude of the coefficient between 1950 and 1951 is clearly observed in females, too. However, unlike males, the 1951 female birth cohort is less clearly distinguished from other wartime birth cohorts born in 1952 or 1953 (Figure 3.12).

Table 3.3

Robustness Tests for Difference-in-Difference Model: Interaction between Measure of Wartime Stress and Deviation of the 1951 Birth Cohort's Adult Outcomes from 1945–1959 Trend

	Model 1 + Urbanization:		Model 2 + Education		Model 3 + Province dummy		Model 4 + Urbanization & Education	
	∂y/∂x	P-value	∂y/∂x	P-value	∂y/∂x	P-value	∂y/∂x	P-value
1. Male schooling								
A. CENTRAL*B1951	**-0.2054**	0.0503	-0.2536	0.1411	-0.2376	0.1624	-0.2491	0.1440
B. CENOCCUP2*B1951	**-0.3987**	0.0035	**-0.3758**	0.0826	**-0.3686**	0.0789	**-0.3610**	0.0789
C. BUSAN_DIST*B1951	**-0.1144**	0.0089	**-0.1232**	0.0492	**-0.1221**	0.0466	**-0.1197**	0.0499
D. DUROCCUP*B1951	**-0.0831**	0.0561	**-0.1424**	0.0546	**-0.1565**	0.0303	**-0.1300**	0.0864
2. Female schooling								
A. CENTRAL*B1951	-0.1096	0.2854	-0.1671	0.2714	-0.1454	0.3249	-0.1598	0.2858
B. CENOCCUP2*B1951	-0.0673	0.6234	-0.1496	0.4861	-0.1335	0.5049	-0.1506	0.4663
C. BUSAN_DIST*B1951	-0.0604	0.2243	-0.0775	0.2724	-0.0707	0.3250	-0.0731	0.2758
D. DUROCCUP*B1951	-0.0309	0.5364	**-0.1422**	0.0825	-0.1383	0.1004	-0.1309	0.1106
3. Male college								
A. CENTRAL*B1951	-0.0212	0.1084	0.0260	0.2297	-0.0236	0.2704	-0.0249	0.2419
B. CENOCCUP2*B1951	**-0.0488**	0.0037	-0.0412	0.1393	-0.0393	0.1522	-0.0387	0.1480
C. BUSAN_DIST*B1951	-0.0069	0.2371	-0.0035	0.6826	-0.0037	0.6615	-0.0029	0.7335
D. DUROCCUP*B1951	-0.0027	0.6547	0.0016	0.8770	-0.0007	0.9450	0.0032	0.7666
4. Female college								
A. CENTRAL*B1951	**-0.0222**	0.0043	**-0.0353**	0.0019	**-0.0319**	0.0041	**-0.0334**	0.0023
B. CENOCCUP2*B1951	**-0.0233**	0.0524	**-0.0409**	0.0173	**-0.0378**	0.0208	**-0.0389**	0.0188
C. BUSAN_DIST*B1951	-0.0068	0.1299	**-0.0100**	0.0804	-0.0087	0.1398	**-0.0095**	0.0895
D. DUROCCUP*B1951	-0.0033	0.4451	**-0.0123**	0.0961	-0.0111	0.1400	-0.0113	0.1272
5. Male not working								
A. CENTRAL*B1951	**0.0156**	0.0494	**0.0144**	0.0773	**0.0154**	0.0569	**0.0148**	0.0643
B. CENOCCUP2*B1951	**0.0277**	0.0234	**0.0267**	0.0285	**0.0273**	0.0255	**0.0270**	0.0272
C. BUSAN_DIST*B1951	**0.0089**	0.0223	**0.0086**	0.0302	**0.0087**	0.0271	**0.0087**	0.0273
D. DUROCCUP*B1951	**0.0061**	0.0671	**0.0056**	0.0969	**0.0059**	0.0835	**0.0055**	0.0992
6. Male unskilled								
A. CENTRAL*B1951	**0.0468**	0.0148	**0.0493**	0.0097	**0.0488**	0.0098	**0.0480**	0.0114
B. CENOCCUP2*B1951	**0.0714**	0.0051	**0.0737**	0.0044	**0.0728**	0.0048	**0.0716**	0.0050
C. BUSAN_DIST*B1951	**0.0246**	0.0033	**0.0250**	0.0029	**0.0262**	0.0016	**0.0247**	0.0031
D. DUROCCUP*B1951	**0.0252**	0.0101	**0.0266**	0.0064	**0.0278**	0.0031	**0.0259**	0.0088
7. Male spouse schooling								
A. CENTRAL*B1951	-0.1906	0.1575	**-0.3269**	0.0551	**-0.3267**	0.0550	-0.2050	0.1777
B. CENOCCUP2*B1951	-0.2385	0.2271	-0.3341	0.2082	-0.3637	0.1695	-0.2249	0.3132
C. BUSAN_DIST*B1951	**-0.0948**	0.0894	**-0.1825**	0.0235	**-0.1822**	0.0230	**-0.1188**	0.0638
D. DUROCCUP*B1951	-0.0998	0.1423	**-0.1995**	0.0308	**-0.1858**	0.0422	-0.1276	0.1033

Source: The 2% micro samples of the 1990 and 2000 population censuses.

Note: (a) Summary of 112 regressions; (b) The sample is limited to those for whom the place of birth is reported; (c) For Panels 6 and 7, the 2% sample of the 2000 census is utilized, and the sample is limited to persons who were employed (Panel 6) and the currently married (Panel 7) at the time of census enumeration; (d) A cubic cohort trend is included in each regression but omitted from the table; (e) Standard errors are adjusted for clustering at the levels of year and county of birth; and (f) The estimated coefficient in bold number is statistically significant at 10% level.

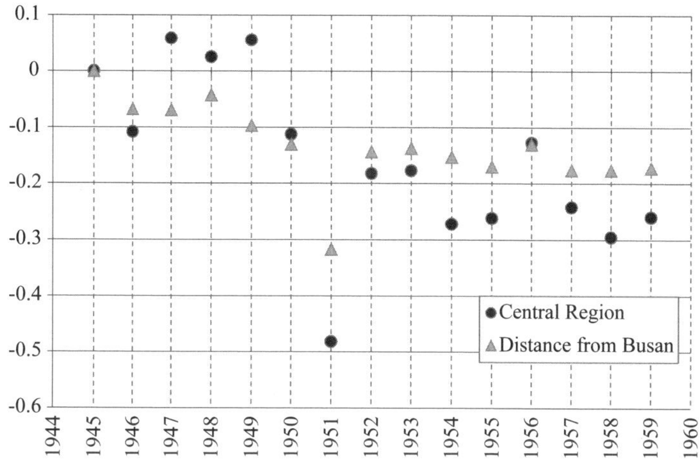

Source: Regression results from the pooled sample of the 1990 and 2000 censuses.

Figure 3.11 | Estimated Coefficients for Birth Year Dummies Interacted with Measure of Wartime Stress: Years of Schooling for Males

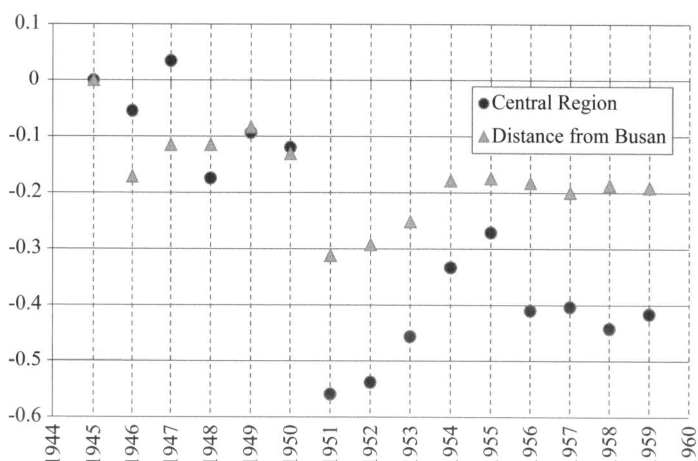

Source: Regression results from the pooled sample of the 1990 and 2000 censuses.

Figure 3.12 | Estimated Coefficients for Birth Year Dummies Interacted with Measure of Wartime Stress: Years of Schooling for Females

Table 3.4

Summary of Quantile Regressions for Difference-in-Difference Model: Interaction between Measure of Wartime Stress and Deviation of the 1951 Birth Cohort's Years of Schooling from 1945–1959 Trend

(1) Male			(2) Female		
Quantile	∂y/∂x	P-value	Quantile	∂y/∂x	P-value
A. 0.116: middle-school dropouts	**-0.7613**	<.0001	A. 0.248: middle school-dropouts	**-0.0000**	0.9720
B. 0.250	-0.0000	0.9681	B. 0.250	**-0.0000**	0.0260
C. 0.320: high school-dropouts	**-0.0000**	<.0001	C. 0.500	-0.0000	0.9932
D. 0.500	-0.0000	0.9649	D. 0.534: high school-dropouts	**-0.0183**	<.0001
E. 0.750	**-0.4908**	<.0001	E. 0.750	**-0.0000**	0.0440
F. 0.756: college-dropouts	**-0.5480**	<.0001	F. 0.903: college-dropouts	**-0.4950**	<.0001

Source: The pooled data of the 2% micro sample of the 1990 and 2000 population censuses.

Note: (a) Summary of 12 regressions; (b) The sample is limited to those for whom the place of birth is reported; (c) A cubic cohort trend is included in each regression but omitted from the table; (d) The measure of wartime stress is the distance from the City of Busan; and (e) The estimated coefficient in bold number is statistically significant at 10% level.

Quantile regressions are also conducted to determine how the effect of exposure to the war on the years of schooling differs across various quantiles of the schooling distribution. The distance from Busan is employed as the measure of wartime stress because the coefficient of the interaction of this variable and the 1951 birth dummy is significantly negative for both males and females (Table 3.2). Moreover, this measure is the most continuous among all variables on wartime stress used in the analysis. Variations in the years of schooling in Korea largely come from those among graduates of primary school (six years), middle school (nine years), high school (12 years), and college (16 years). Accordingly, the coefficient of the interaction term is estimated for the three quantiles corresponding to average middle school, high school, and college-dropouts as well as the three quantiles of schooling. The results reported in Table 3.4 suggest that the effect of in-utero exposure to the war on male schooling is particularly strong at the quantiles corresponding to middle school and college dropouts. Female schooling is most strongly influenced by wartime stress along the borderline between high school and college graduates. These results are consistent with the outcomes of the difference-in-difference regressions (Table 3.2): for males, both the probabilities of primary school education and college entrance are significantly affected by the interaction term; for females, only the effect on the probability of college entrance is significant.

3.3. Summary

This chapter investigated how in-utero exposure to the Korean War affected adult socioeconomic outcomes. A number of socioeconomic outcomes from the 1990 and 2000 census were significantly lower for the 1951 birth cohort. For instance, males and females of this cohort received significantly less schooling than predicted by the smooth cohort trends. Controlling for cubic cohort trends in these measures shows that males born in 1951 are less likely to have professional employment, as well as more likely to be a manual laborer around the age of 50 (in 2000) than other male birth cohorts.

The disadvantages in socioeconomic outcomes experienced by the 1951 birth cohort are particularly pronounced for those born in the Central Region of South Korea. This result can be attributed to the extensive collateral damage experienced by the residents of this region when the war broke out: a larger percentage of residents endured North Korean occupation; refugees from this region traveled longer distances; and the region fell under communist control twice. By exploiting these geographic variations in wartime disruptions, a difference-in-difference model was estimated using several location-specific measures of wartime stress, including the distance from Busan and the duration of occupation by North Korean forces. Regression results suggest that the magnitude of the negative cohort effect is significantly larger for individuals more seriously traumatized by the war.

CHAPTER 4

Early Exposure to the Korean War and Health Outcomes

4.1. Cohort Effects

To determine the long-term health consequences of early-life exposure to the Korean War, I examine if health outcomes of the birth cohorts who were exposed to various war-driven disruptions during pregnancy deviate from their long-run cohort trends. The primary measure of old-age health outcomes used in the analysis is the rates of all and particular type of functional limitation.

The rate of particular type of functional limitation for each birth cohort was computed from the 2010 census (see Chapter 2). The percentage of persons born in the Central Region with any disability by birth cohort is presented in Figure 4.1. A strong downward trend in the rate of disability is shown by these cohorts, with the 1950 and 1951 birth cohorts veering from this steady trend. In particular, a deviation of the 1951 cohort from the tendency for long-term decrease in the disability rate is clearly revealed.[1]

1 Although not presented here, digression of the 1951 birth cohort from the trend is also observed in the entire sample, albeit at a smaller magnitude.

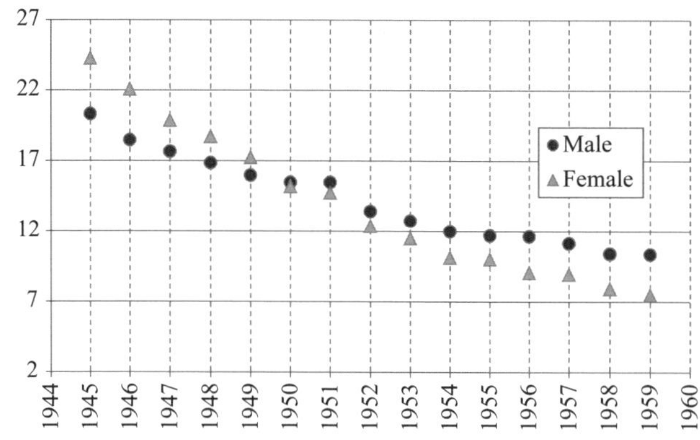

Source: The 10% sample of the 2010 census.

Figure 4.1 | % Persons with Any Disability in 2010 by Birth Cohort: Born in the Central Region

The fraction of the Central Region natives with a particular type of disability is compared across birth cohorts, as shown in Figures 4.2 to 4.8. As with the trend of disability in general, the disadvantage of the 1951 birth cohort is graphically evident for six out of seven types of functional limitations, namely, restrictions in moving (Figure 4.3), mental impairments for males (Figure 4.4), cognitive disability (Figure 4.5), limitations in basic activity for females, limitations in outing (Figures 4.6 and 4.7), and restrictions in working (Figure 4.8). In particular, the male subjects of the birth cohort born in 1951 were at much higher risks of suffering from mental condition, cognitive disability, and restriction in working.

Table 4.1 provides the estimates of β_t in Equation 2.1, indicating the magnitude of the health outcome deviation of male and female subjects born in 1950 and 1951 from the cubic cohort trend. Standard errors were adjusted in testing the statistical significance for the clustering of birth year.[2] The regression results confirm that the rates of overall disability and particular types of disability among the 1951 birth cohort are significantly high, especially among the subjects born in the Central

2 All the coefficients of interest are jointly significant at the 1% level for all the regressions reported in this chapter.

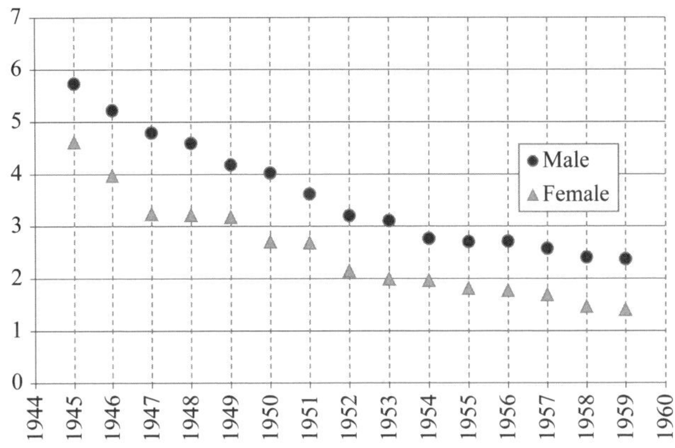

Source: The 10% sample of the 2010 census.

Figure 4.2 | % Persons with Limitations in "Communication" in 2010 Birth Cohort: Born in the Central Region

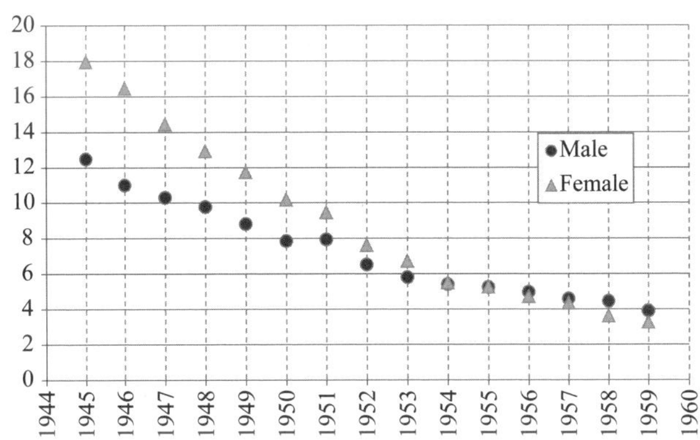

Source: The 10% sample of the 2010 census.

Figure 4.3 | % Persons with Limitations in "Moving" in 2010 Birth Cohort: Born in the Central Region

Region. Two exceptions are found in the results for "moving" and "mental" for females that show the statistically insignificant 1951 cohort effect.

The regression results for males and females, though largely similar with each other, are different in several respects. First, it appears that the

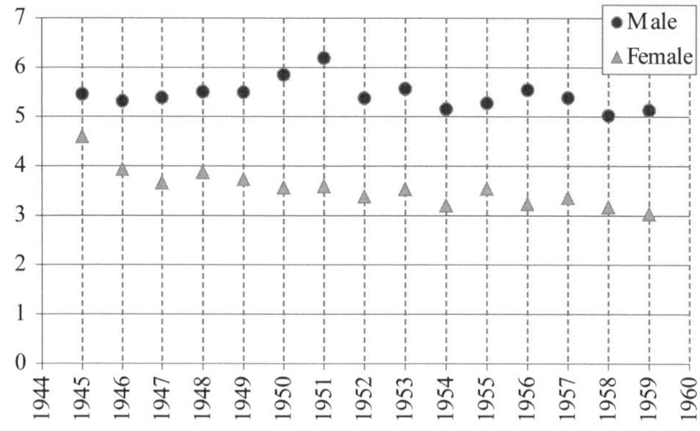

Source: The 10% sample of the 2010 census.

Figure 4.4 | % Persons with Mental Impairments in 2010 Birth Cohort: Born in the Central Region

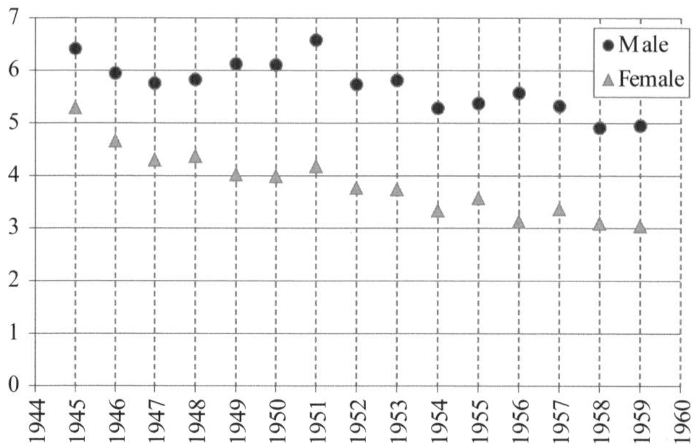

Source: The 10% sample of the 2010 census.

Figure 4.5 | % Persons with "Cognitive" Limitations in 2010 by Birth Cohort: Born in the Central Region

health of the males was more strongly influenced by in-utero exposure to the Korean War than that of females. The estimated coefficients for the 1950 and 1951 birth dummy variables are larger and statistically more significant for males in general. Second, for females, the negative health consequences of early exposure to the war are found only for the 1951 birth cohort, whereas the male subjects of the 1950 birth cohort were

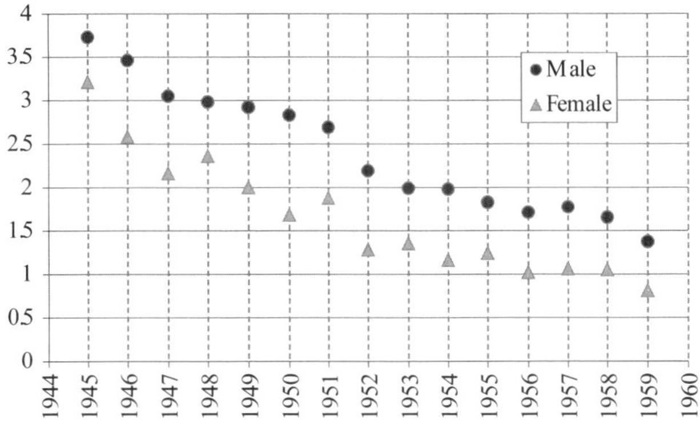

Source: The 10% sample of the 2010 census.

Figure 4.6 | % Persons with Limitations in Basic Activities in 2010 by Birth Cohort: Born in the Central Region

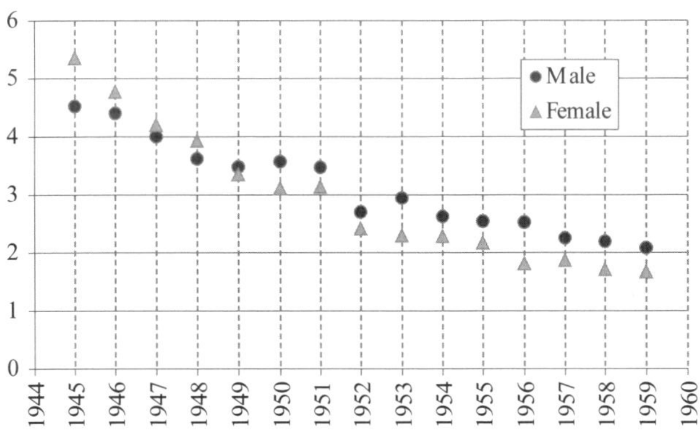

Source: The 10% sample of the 2010 census.

Figure 4.7 | % Persons with Limitations in Outing in 2010 by Birth Cohort: Born in the Central Region

significantly more likely to suffer from disability. Third, the particularly strong negative effect of the war sustained by the Central Region natives compared to the entire sample are more clearly revealed among females than among males.

The results of Chapter 3 show that in-utero exposure to the Korean War significantly affected adult socioeconomic outcomes, including

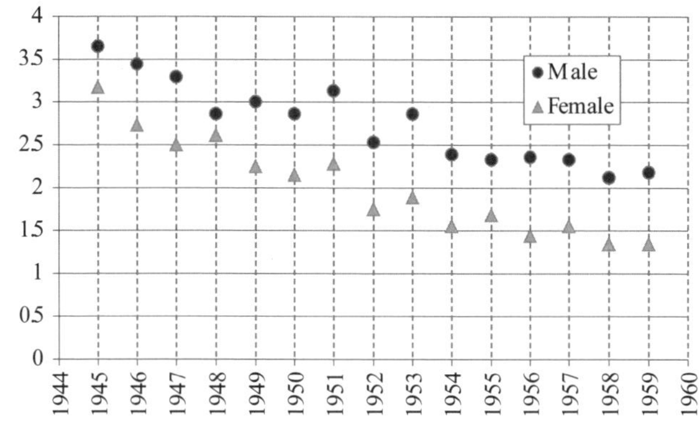

Source: The 10% sample of the 2010 census.

Figure 4.8 | % Persons with Limitations in Working in 2010 by Birth Cohort: Born in the Central Region

educational attainment, occupation, and marital status. Since old-age health can be influenced by socioeconomic status, the regression results reported in Table 4.1 may in part capture the indirect effects of early exposure to the war through different socioeconomic outcomes. To examine if this is the case, Equation 2.1 is estimated with controlling for the years of schooling and dummy variable on marital status (=1 if married and =0 otherwise).

Columns 1 and 3 of Table 4.2 present the results for males and females born in the Central Region. In the case of males (Column 1), the coefficient for the 1951 birth cohort remains significantly positive for all categories of functional limitations if socioeconomic variables are added, except "communication" (Panel B). However, the magnitude of the 1951 cohort effect modestly diminishes: as for the probability of having any disability (Panel A), for instance, the magnitude of the regression coefficient for the 1951 birth decreases by 24%. For females (Column 3), the 1951 cohort effect is statistically significant for five out of eight measures of health. Overall, the results suggests that the long-term direct impact of early exposure to the Korean War is a more likely explanation for the negative 1951 cohort effect on health than possible indirect influences of the war via socioeconomic status.

A possible concern of the baseline regressions conducted above is that a cubic function of the year of birth may not accurately capture the actual smooth cohort trend. To address this concern, a more flexible

Table 4.1
Deviation of the 1950 and 1951 Birth Cohorts' Health Outcomes from 1945–1959 Trend

Outcome	Males				Females			
	(1) South Korea		(2) Central Region		(3) South Korea		(4) Central Region	
	$\partial y/\partial x$	S.E.	$\partial y/\partial x$	S.E.	$\partial y/\partial x$	S.E.	$\partial y/\partial x$	S.E.
A. Disability								
Born in 1950	**0.0033**	0.0011	**0.0060**	0.0009	-0.0018	0.0017	-0.0005	0.0020
Born in 1951	**0.0076**	0.0010	**0.0136**	0.0009	**0.0042**	0.0016	**0.0087**	0.0018
B. Communication								
Born in 1950	**0.0016**	0.0006	**0.0021**	0.0004	-0.0003	0.0009	0.0011	0.0011
Born in 1951	**0.0017**	0.0005	**0.0009**	0.0004	**0.0017**	0.0007	**0.0030**	0.0009
C. Moving								
Born in 1950	0.0003	0.0011	-0.0004	0.0011	-0.0008	0.0013	0.0009	0.0011
Born in 1951	**0.0038**	0.0009	**0.0072**	0.0010	0.0016	0.0012	**0.0060**	0.0010
D. Mental								
Born in 1950	**0.0014**	0.0005	**0.0042**	0.0005	-0.0001	0.0005	0.0006	0.0008
Born in 1951	**0.0054**	0.0005	**0.0077**	0.0005	-0.0002	0.0005	**0.0014**	0.0008
E. Cognitive								
Born in 1950	0.0006	0.0007	**0.0032**	0.0011	-0.0002	0.0006	0.0009	0.0007
Born in 1951	**0.0063**	0.0006	**0.0085**	0.0010	**0.0026**	0.0007	**0.0040**	0.0006
F. Basic activity								
Born in 1950	**0.0019**	0.0004	**0.0029**	0.0006	-0.0008	0.0006	-0.0001	0.0010
Born in 1951	**0.0017**	0.0003	**0.0031**	0.0005	**0.0011**	0.0005	**0.0035**	0.0008
G. Outing								
Born in 1950	**0.0014**	0.0005	**0.0034**	0.0007	-0.0005	0.0004	0.0006	0.0006
Born in 1951	**0.0021**	0.0005	**0.0041**	0.0007	**0.0010**	0.0004	**0.0036**	0.0005
H. Working								
Born in 1950	0.0005	0.0005	0.0005	0.0008	0.0001	0.0004	0.0005	0.0007
Born in 1951	**0.0033**	0.0005	**0.0042**	0.0008	**0.0017**	0.0004	**0.0032**	0.0006

Source: The 10% micro sample of the 2010 population census.

Note: (a) "South Korea" includes persons who were born in North Korea and those for whom the place of birth is not reported; (b) Polynomials of the year of birth (YOB, YOB^2 and YOB^3) are included in the regressions; (c) Standard errors are adjusted for clustering at the level of year of birth; and (d) The estimated coefficient in bold number is statistically significant at 10% level.

cohort trend is applied to the cohort analysis, in which a quadratic cohort trend is allowed to change across the pre-war (1945 to 1949), wartime (1950 to 1954), and post-war (1955 to 1959) cohorts. The results reported in Columns 2 and 4 of Table 4.2 are similar to those based on the cubic specification, especially for males born in 1951. For females, the negative effects of birth in 1951 on mental and cognitive limitations are less strongly revealed if the new specification is applied.

Table 4.2
Deviation of the 1950 and 1951 Birth Cohorts' Health Outcomes from 1945–1959 Trend: Robustness Tests

Outcome	Males born in the Central Region				Females born in the Central Region			
	(1) + Schooling and marital status		(2) More flexible cohort trend		(3) + Schooling and marital status		(4) More flexible cohort trend	
	∂y/∂x	S.E.	∂y/∂x	S.E.	∂y/∂x	S.E.	∂y/∂x	S.E.
A. Disability								
Born in 1950	**0.0029**	0.0011	0.0020	0.0029	-0.0025	0.0020	-0.0024	0.0043
Born in 1951	**0.0058**	0.0010	**0.0082**	0.0012	0.0031	0.0019	**0.0088**	0.0022
B. Communication								
Born in 1950	**0.0013**	0.0004	**0.0027**	0.0012	0.0006	0.0011	-0.0012	0.0023
Born in 1951	**-0.0013**	0.0004	**0.0013**	0.0007	0.0016	0.0009	**0.0026**	0.0090
C. Moving								
Born in 1950	-0.0017	0.0010	0.0001	0.0023	-0.0003	0.0011	0.0011	0.0027
Born in 1951	**0.0039**	0.0010	**0.0080**	0.0011	**0.0027**	0.0011	**0.0061**	0.0016
D. Mental								
Born in 1950	**0.0025**	0.0005	0.0030	0.0024	-0.0001	0.0009	-0.0045	0.0027
Born in 1951	**0.0034**	0.0006	**0.0068**	0.0015	-0.0008	0.0008	-0.0010	0.0016
E. Cognitive								
Born in 1950	0.0015	0.0014	-0.0045	0.0033	0.0002	0.0008	-0.0059	0.0023
Born in 1951	**0.0042**	0.0012	**0.0042**	0.0019	**0.0018**	0.0008	0.0000	0.0013
F. Basic activity								
Born in 1950	**0.0023**	0.0007	**0.0039**	0.0016	-0.0004	0.0010	-0.0003	0.0022
Born in 1951	**0.0016**	0.0006	**0.0039**	0.0007	**0.0026**	0.0008	**0.0039**	0.0011
G. Outing								
Born in 1950	**0.0025**	0.0007	**0.0072**	0.0020	0.0000	0.0006	0.0034	0.0009
Born in 1951	**0.0020**	0.0007	**0.0065**	0.0014	**0.0021**	0.0006	**0.0058**	0.0004
H. Working								
Born in 1950	-0.0002	0.0009	0.0004	0.0029	0.0002	0.0007	-0.0002	0.0021
Born in 1951	**0.0024**	0.0008	**0.0039**	0.0020	**0.0022**	0.0007	**0.0030**	0.0014

Source: The 10% micro sample of the 2010 population census.

Note: (a) "South Korea" includes persons who were born in North Korea and those for whom the place of birth is not reported; (b) In Columns 1 and 3, years of schooling, dummy variable for marital status, and polynomials of the year of birth (YOB, YOB^2 and YOB^3) are included; (c) In Columns 2 and 4, a quadratic cohort trend is allowed to change across the pre-war (1945 to 1949), war-time (1950 to 1954), and post-war (1955 to 1959) cohorts; (d) Standard errors are adjusted for clustering at the level of year of birth; and (e) The estimated coefficient in bold number is statistically significant at 10% level.

The 2005 census is used as supplementary data for analyzing the difference in disability rate across birth cohort. A weakness of the census is that it does not contain information on the place of birth. Therefore, the analysis cannot be conducted separately according to the region of birth

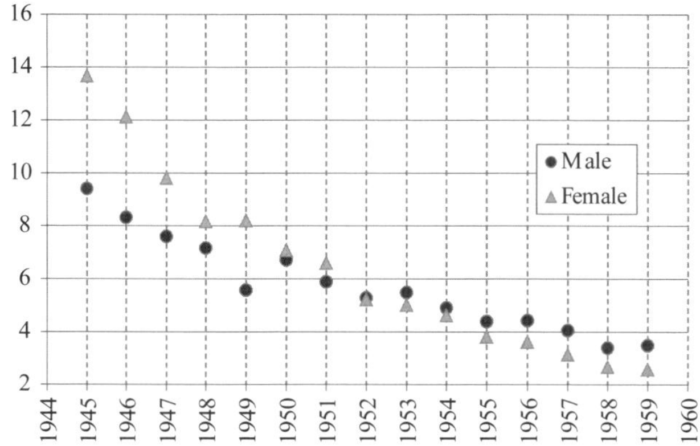

Source: The 2% sample of the 2005 census.

Figure 4.9 | % Persons with Disability in 2005 by Birth Cohort

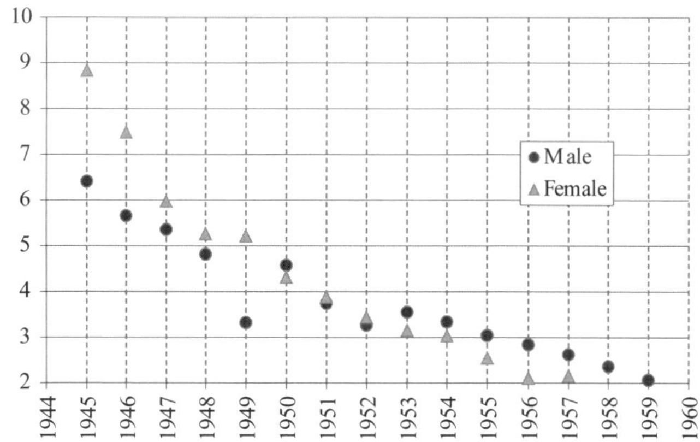

Source: The 2% sample of the 2005 census.

Figure 4.10 | % Males with Limited Activity in 2005 by Birth Cohort

with the data. However, the data provide an opportunity to observe health outcomes of wartime birth cohorts in younger ages (around mid-50s).

Figures 4.9 and 4.10 present two health outcomes drawn from the 2005 census: the percentages of individuals with disability and individuals with limited daily activity. The charts suggest that the 1950 and 1953 male subjects exhibit upward deviations from the long-term trend in terms of disability and limitations in activity. Among females,

Table 4.3
Deviation of the 1950–1951 Birth Cohorts' Health Outcomes in 2005 from 1945–1959 Trend

	Male				Female			
	(1) Disabled		(2) Activity Limited		(3) Disabled		(4) Activity Limited	
	$\partial y/\partial x$	P-value	$\partial y/\partial x$	P-value	$\partial y/\partial x$	P-value	$\partial y/\partial x$	P-value
A. Model 1								
Born in 1950	**0.0086**	0.0033	**0.0082**	0.0059	0.0036	0.1569	0.0007	0.6783
Born in 1951	0.0037	0.1059	0.0020	0.3637	0.0064	0.0071	0.0011	0.4188
B. Model 2								
Born in 1950	**0.0116**	0.0050	**0.0182**	<.0001	0.0004	0.9291	-0.0053	0.1267
Born in 1951	**0.0038**	0.0915	**0.0065**	0.0001	**0.0057**	0.0160	-0.0015	0.2895

Source: The 2% micro sample of the 2005 population census.

Note: The sample includes 83,649 males and 85,994 females who were aged 46 to 60 in 2005. In model 1, polynomials of the year of birth (YOB, YOB^2 and YOB^3) are included in the regressions, whereas quadratic cohort trend is allowed to change across the pre-war (1945 to 1949), war-time (1950 to 1954), and post-war (1955 to 1959) cohorts in model 2; (d) Standard errors are adjusted for clustering at the level of year of birth; and (e) The estimated coefficient in bold number is statistically significant at 10% level.

conversely, no clear departure of the 1950 birth cohort from long-term trends in health outcomes appears whereas the 1949 birth cohort shows particularly high rates of disability and limited activity. It also appears that females born in 1951 were somewhat more likely to be disabled than predicted by smooth cohort trend.

The regressions are conducted where cubic cohort trend (model 1) and quadratic trend allowed to change across the pre-war (1945 to 1949), wartime (1950 to 1954), and post-war (1955 to 1959) cohorts (model 2) are applied. The results in Table 4.3 confirm that the 1950 male birth cohort is more likely to possess disability or limitations in daily activities than other birth cohorts. No similar statistically significant 1950 cohort effect is observed among females. The results obtained from the 2005 census are somewhat different from those drawn from the 2010 census. Such inconsistencies could be explained by (a) different age of measuring health outcomes, (b) difference across regions that could not be considered with the 2005 census, and (c) the consequences of population selections. More detailed explanations are offered in Chapter 5.

4.2. Timing and Length of Exposure

The long-term effects of early exposure to war-related disruptions could differ by the timing and length of exposure. Previous studies suggest that the consequences of prenatal exposure depend on which trimester of pregnancy the shock is received. Since the Korea Statistical Office only provides the year of birth in the micro sample of the censuses, it is difficult to fully identify the timing and duration of exposure. However, utilizing the information on the age at the time of census enumeration (November 1) and the year of birth, it is possible to identify if a person was born prior to November 1 in a given year. Among the subjects of the 1951 birth cohort, for instance, if a person's age is reported 59 in the 2010 census, his or her birth month should be January to October; if the age is reported as 58, the person's birth month should be either November or December.

To investigate if there were differences in the old-age health outcomes by the timing of birth among the 1951 birth cohort, regressions based on Equation 2.1 are conducted where dummy variables on birth in January to October 1951 and birth in November to December 1951 are included instead of dummy variables for the 1950 and 1951 birth cohorts. Two specifications with cubic and more flexible cohort trends are employed. Standard errors are adjusted for clustering at the level of the two periods (January to October and November to December) of the birth year.

The results reported in Table 4.4 suggest that the adverse cohort effect is more strongly revealed for those born prior to November 1. Except for the case of male limitations in communication, the individuals born in January to October 1951 were more likely to suffer from functional limitations. In contrast, the estimated coefficient for the birth in November to December 1951 is either insignificant or even significantly negative for 23 out of 32 regressions. For the nine regressions in which the coefficient for the birth cohort born in November or December is significantly positive, the magnitudes of the cohort effect on disability are generally similar between the two groups of individuals born in 1951.

With the information on the month of birth for the generations born during the Korean War, the Korean Longitudinal Study of Aging (KLoSA) can supplement the results related to the differences by the timing of birth. Two health outcomes, the average score of self-reported

Table 4.4
Deviation of the 1951 Birth Cohorts' Health Outcomes from 1945–1959 Trend by the Month of Birth

Outcome	Males born in the Central Region				Females born in the Central Region			
	(1) Cubic cohort trend		(2) More flexible cohort trend		(3) Cubic cohort trend		(4) More flexible cohort trend	
	∂y/∂x	S.E.	∂y/∂x	S.E.	∂y/∂x	S.E.	∂y/∂x	S.E.
A. Disability								
Born in Jan. to Oct. 1951	**0.0134**	0.0016	**0.0115**	0.0021	**0.0114**	0.0018	**0.0126**	0.0032
Born in Nov. to Dec. 1951	**0.0086**	0.0016	**0.0068**	0.0021	**-0.0033**	0.0018	-0.0021	0.0032
B. Communication								
Born in Jan. to Oct. 1951	0.0015	0.0009	0.0009	0.0018	**0.0028**	0.0006	**0.0032**	0.0005
Born in Nov. to Dec. 1951	**-0.0040**	0.0009	**-0.0045**	0.0018	**0.0028**	0.0006	**0.0033**	0.0005
C. Moving								
Born in Jan. to Oct. 1951	**0.0070**	0.0009	**0.0077**	0.0007	**0.0073**	0.0011	**0.0071**	0.0023
Born in Nov. to Dec. 1951	**0.0087**	0.0009	**0.0094**	0.0007	-0.0016	0.0011	-0.0018	0.0023
D. Mental								
Born in Jan. to Oct. 1951	**0.0082**	0.0010	**0.0066**	0.0014	**0.0027**	0.0008	**0.0027**	0.0010
Born in Nov. to Dec. 1951	0.0011	0.0010	-0.0005	0.0014	**-0.0056**	0.0008	**-0.0056**	0.0010
E. Cognitive								
Born in Jan. to Oct. 1951	**0.0095**	0.0012	**0.0081**	0.0013	**0.0057**	0.0009	**0.0049**	0.0014
Born in Nov. to Dec. 1951	0.0007	0.0012	-0.0008	0.0013	**-0.0050**	0.0009	**-0.0058**	0.0014
F. Basic activity								
Born in Jan. to Oct. 1951	**0.0028**	0.0007	**0.0022**	0.0010	**0.0042**	0.0006	**0.0049**	0.0009
Born in Nov. to Dec. 1951	**0.0013**	0.0007	0.0008	0.0010	-0.0002	0.0006	0.0005	0.0009
G. Outing								
Born in Jan. to Oct. 1951	**0.0042**	0.0009	**0.0036**	0.0015	**0.0046**	0.0008	**0.0052**	0.0013
Born in Nov. to Dec. 1951	0.0005	0.0009	-0.0001	0.0015	**-0.0018**	0.0008	-0.0013	0.0013
H. Working								
Born in Jan. to Oct. 1951	**0.0063**	0.0008	**0.0060**	0.0013	**0.0030**	0.0007	**0.0031**	0.0012
Born in Nov. to Dec. 1951	**-0.0059**	0.0008	**-0.0062**	0.0013	**0.0032**	0.0007	**0.0033**	0.0012

Source: The 10% micro sample of the 2010 population census.

Note: (a) Polynomials of the year of birth (YOB, YOB^2 and YOB^3) are included in Columns 1 and 3; (b) A quadratic cohort trend is allowed to change across the pre-war (1945 to 1949), war-time (1950 to 1954), and post-war (1955 to 1959) cohorts; (c) Standard errors are adjusted for clustering at the level of two periods (January to October and November to December) of the year of birth; and (d) The estimated coefficient in bold number is statistically significant at 10% level.

health and the percentage of individuals having any disability, are plotted based on data from the 2006 KLoSA for each birth quarter from 1948 to 1955. Place of birth is not identified in the KLoSA, thus the results pertain to the entire sample. Figure 4.11 and Figure 4.12 present the

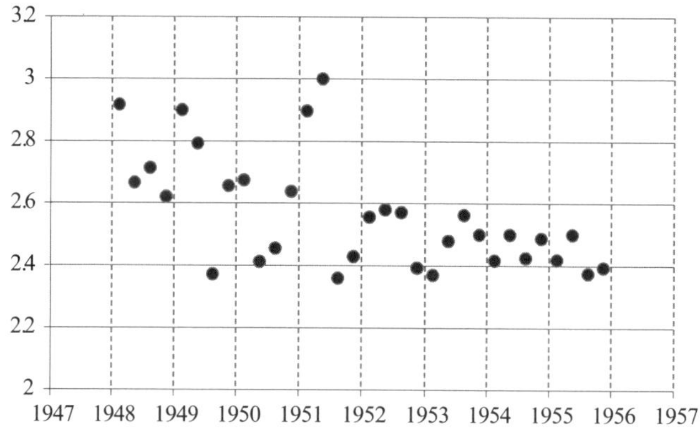

Source: 2006 Korea Longitudinal Study of Aging.

Figure 4.11A | Score of Male Self-Reported Health in 2006

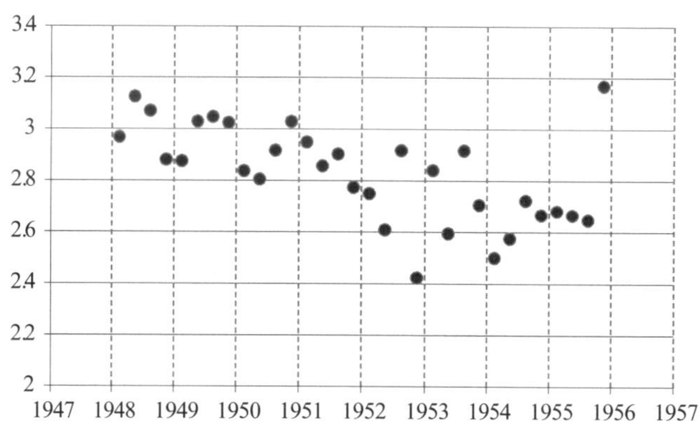

Source: 2006 Korea Longitudinal Study of Aging.

Figure 4.11B | Score of Female Self-Reported Health in 2006

results for males and females.

Although the measures of health considered in the analysis considerably fluctuate across birth quarters (perhaps because of the small sample size), the male subjects born in the second quarter of 1951 clearly deviate from long-term patterns predicted in the two health outcomes. In the case of self-reported health, the males born in the first half of 1951 were more likely to report poorer health status than the neighboring birth cohorts (Figure 4.11A). In contrast, the plotted variables for females do

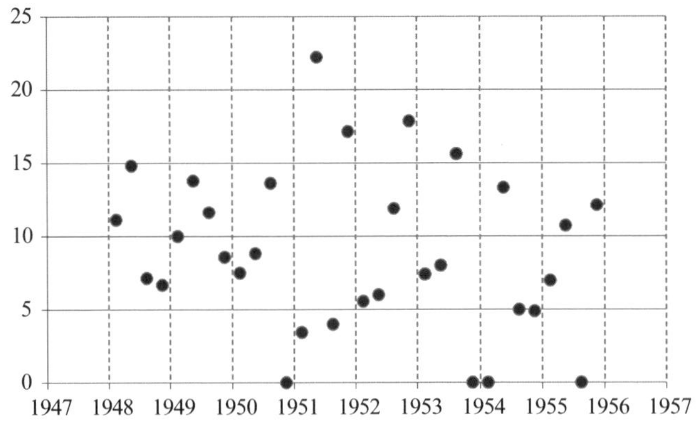

Source: 2006 Korea Longitudinal Study of Aging.

Figure 4.12A | % Males with Disability in 2006

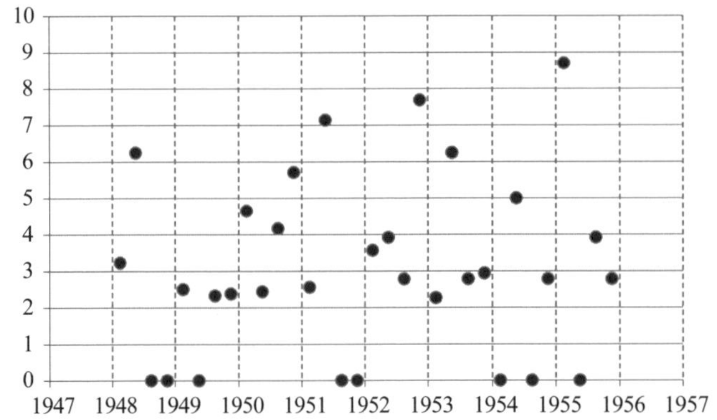

Source: 2006 Korea Longitudinal Study of Aging.

Figure 4.12B | % Females with Disability in 2006

not reveal any clear cohort effects (Figures 4.11B and 4.12B).

Regression results for self-reported health and disability are consistent with the patterns of cohort effects displayed by the figures (not reported here). The male subjects born in the first and second quarters of 1951 are significantly more likely to report poorer health; those born in the second quarter of 1951 are more likely to have disability. Females who were in-utero for any length of time during the worst nine months of the war do not exhibit any significant disadvantages in self-reported health and disability.

It cannot be determined by the available evidence whether the timing or duration of exposure produces the worse health outcomes of the persons born in the earlier months of 1951 compared to those born at the end of the year. Given that the war-related disruptions experienced by civilians were largely concentrated in the nine months from late June 1950 to late March 1951, the subjects of the 1951 cohort born in November or December were exposed to the difficulties caused by the war only during the first trimester of pregnancy. In contrast, the persons born the spring of 1951 spent the entire prenatal period during the worst nine months of the war. The persons born in the first half of 1951 spent at least the first and second trimesters of pregnancy during the worst time of the war. The males born in the second quarter of 1951, the biggest victims of the war in terms of self-reported health and disability reported in the KLoSA, passed at least the first and second trimesters of pregnancy under the highly stressful nine months of the war. Thus, the evidence given here suggests: (1) the longer the duration of prenatal exposure to the war-caused disruptions the worse the old-age health outcomes; or (2) exposure during the second trimester of pregnancy is especially harmful for old-age health outcomes.

4.3. Difference-in-Difference Estimations

If the deviation of health outcomes of the 1951 birth cohort reflects the influences of war-related disruptions experienced while in-utero, then its magnitude should be larger for individuals exposed to worse in-utero circumstances during the war. This hypothesis is consistent with the fact that the disadvantages of the 1951 birth cohort are particularly pronounced among individuals born in the Central Region. Figure 4.13 compares the percentage of each birth cohort with any disability between the natives of the Central and the South. The upward deviation of the disability rate of the 1951 birth cohort is observed only among those born in the Central Region.

Regressions are conducted based on a difference-in-difference model, as displayed in Equation 2.2. If the 1951 cohort effect increases with the magnitude of wartime stress, then the coefficient of interaction

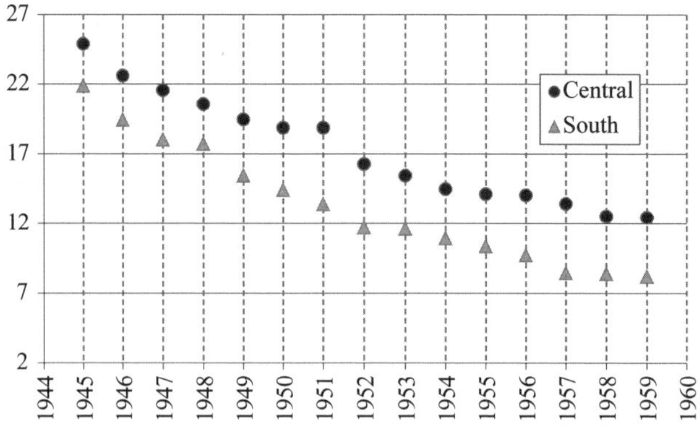

Source: The 10% sample of the 2010 census.

Figure 4.13A | % Males with Disability in 2010 by Birth Cohort: Comparison between the Central and the South

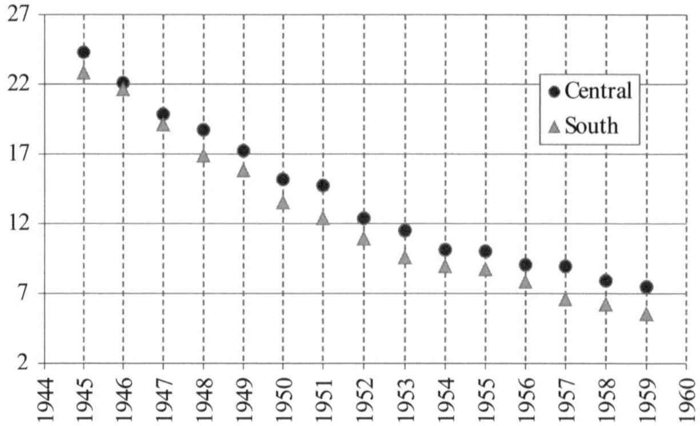

Source: The 10% sample of the 2010 census.

Figure 4.13B | % Females with Disability in 2010 by Birth Cohort: Comparison between the Central and the South

between the dummy variable for the birth in January to October 1951 and the dummy variable for the birth in the Central Region should be positive if the dependent variable is the probability of suffering from a disability. The cubic cohort trend (i.e., YOB, YOB^2, and YOB^3), dummy variable for the birth in January to October 1951, and the Central Region dummy are controlled.

The first column of Table 4.5 reports the summary results (the coef-

Table 4.5

Summary of Regressions for Difference-in-Difference Model: Interaction between the Central Region dummy and deviation of the Health Outcomes of the birth cohort born in Jan. to Oct. 1951 from 1945 to 1959 Trend

	(1) Baseline Model		(2) + Schooling and marital status		(3) + Urbanization		(4) + Schooling, marital status, urbanization	
	∂y/∂x	S.E.	∂y/∂x	S.E.	∂y/∂x	S.E.	∂y/∂x	S.E.
1. Males								
A. Disability	**0.0099**	0.0038	**0.0062**	0.0032	**0.0086**	0.0038	**0.0061**	0.0033
B. Communication	**-0.0019**	0.0019	-0.0031	0.0019	-0.0021	0.0019	-0.0029	0.0019
C. Moving	**0.0064**	0.0032	0.0046	0.0033	**0.0059**	0.0032	0.0049	0.0033
D. Mental	**0.0051**	0.0026	**0.0037**	0.0019	**0.0044**	0.0025	**0.0032**	0.0019
E. Cognitive	**0.0057**	0.0025	**0.0042**	0.0023	**0.0049**	0.0025	**0.0040**	0.0022
F. Basic activity	**0.0038**	0.0013	**0.0032**	0.0014	**0.0036**	0.0013	**0.0031**	0.0013
G. Outing	**0.0041**	0.0011	**0.0032**	0.0013	**0.0038**	0.0011	**0.0031**	0.0013
H. Working	0.0025	0.0015	0.0017	0.0015	0.0024	0.0015	0.0019	0.0015
2. Females								
A. Disability	**0.0111**	0.0060	0.0076	0.0051	0.0099	0.0057	0.0075	0.0052
B. Communication	**0.0031**	0.0016	0.0022	0.0016	**0.0029**	0.0016	0.0023	0.0017
C. Moving	**0.0108**	0.0037	**0.0084**	0.0034	**0.0101**	0.0037	**0.0085**	0.0034
D. Mental	0.0036	0.0025	0.0027	0.0023	0.0031	0.0025	0.0026	0.0024
E. Cognitive	0.0040	0.0032	0.0030	0.0029	0.0034	0.0030	0.0028	0.0030
F. Basic activity	**0.0059**	0.0014	**0.0055**	0.0015	**0.0058**	0.0014	**0.0055**	0.0015
G. Outing	**0.0057**	0.0014	**0.0048**	0.0014	**0.0054**	0.0014	**0.0048**	0.0014
H. Working	0.0029	0.0019	0.0024	0.0018	0.0028	0.0020	0.0024	0.0019

Source: The 10% micro sample of the 2010 population census.

Note: (a) Summary of 64 regressions; (b) A cubic cohort trend is included in each regression but omitted from the table; (c) Standard errors are adjusted for clustering at the levels of province of birth; and (d) The estimated coefficient in bold number is statistically significant at 10% level.

ficient of the interaction term) of 16 difference-in-difference regressions conducted on eight measures of health outcomes of males and females. The results suggest that for all health outcomes except male "communication" the 1951 cohort effect is stronger for individuals who suffered more serious wartime stress while in-utero. The coefficient of the interaction between the birth in 1951 and wartime stress is significantly positive in 11out of 16 regressions. The results among females are similar to those among males in terms of general disability and particular functional limitations such as those in moving, basic activity, and outing. However, prenatal exposure to war-related disruptions had considerably weaker effects on mental and cognitive limitations for females than for men.

As explained in the preceding chapter, the measures of the intensity of the war likely capture the exogenously-determined distance between the place of birth and the 38th parallel, but they might be correlated with selections of the treated group (i.e. the 1951 birth cohort born in the Central Region) as well. Accordingly, a number of control variables pertaining to the characteristics of the person and the place of birth were added to the difference-in-difference regressions, including (a) personal characteristics including the years of schooling and marital status (Column 2), (b) the extent of urbanization of the place of birth (Column 3), and (c) personal characteristics and urbanization combined (Column 4). To construct the variables for extent of urbanization, places of birth were classified as follows: (a) Seoul; (b) five metro cities, namely, Busan, Incheon, Daegu, Daejeon, and Gwangju; (c) all other smaller cities; and (d) rural areas (omitted category).

Columns 2 to 4 of Table 4.5 present the regression results with additional controls. For males, the results of difference-in-difference estimations do not change much by applying different specifications. The notable difference is that the magnitude of the coefficient modestly diminishes if the variables on schooling and marital status are controlled. The regression results with additional controls for females are qualitatively similar to those of the baseline regressions, too. However, only the coefficients for "moving," "basic activity," and "outing" remain statically significant. These gender differences in the difference-in-difference regressions are consistent with the results of the cohort analyses (reported in Tables 4.1 and 4.2): the long-term health effects of early exposure to the war-related disruptions are weaker and less robust for females than for males, especially in mental and cognitive limitations.

This chapter also examined whether the effect of interaction between the 1951 birth and the measure of war-caused damage (birth in the Central Region) is sensitive to the functional form of cohort trend by including birth year dummies (1945 is the omitted category) interacting with each measure of wartime stress in the regressions, as represented by the following equation:

(4.1) $$h_i = \alpha + \sum_{t=1946}^{1959} \beta_{1,t} I_{i,t} + \sum_{t=1946}^{1959} \beta_{2,t} (I_{i,t} \times S_i) + \beta_3 S_i + \delta X_i + \varepsilon_i .$$

Figure 4.14 plots the coefficients for the interaction terms estimated

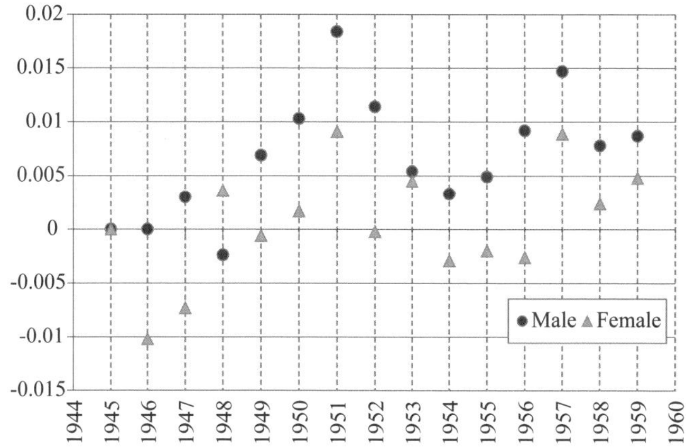

Source: Regression results from the 10% sample of the 2010 censuses.

Figure 4.14 | Estimated Coefficients for Birth Year Dummies Interacted with Measure of Wartime Stress: Probability of Disability

from the regressions in which the probability of having any disability is used as the dependent variable. The coefficient for the 1951 dummy for males interacted with the Central Region dummy stands out as a clear upward outlier. It is the only statistically significant coefficient at the 5% level for males. A discontinuous drop in the magnitude of the coefficient between 1950 and 1951 is clearly observed in females, too. However, unlike males, the 1951 female birth cohort is less clearly distinguished from the neighboring wartime birth cohorts, and the coefficient is statistically insignificant.

4.4. Summary

This chapter investigated how in-utero exposure to the Korean War affected health outcomes at old age. The results suggest that the probabilities of suffering from a particular type of functional limitation as well as any disability were significantly higher among the individuals born in 1951, who were in-utero during the worst time of the war. The results of difference-in-difference estimations suggest that the magnitude of the adverse 1951 cohort effect on health is significantly larger for individuals whose places of birth were more seriously devastated by the war.

CHAPTER 5

Long-Term Effects of the Korean War: Discussion and Implication

5.1. Potential Bias Arising from Population Selections

Several types of population selections possibly influenced the composition of war-time birth cohorts, including (a) marriage and fertility behaviors; (b) deaths of pregnant women; (c) prenatal deaths; and (d) postnatal deaths. A natural concern in interpreting the results of Chapters 3 and 4 is the pattern of selection of Korean War birth cohorts that survived five to six decades after the conflict. If individuals who were in-utero during the worst time of the war were positively selected in terms of characteristics correlated with later life health and economic outcomes, then maternal health can no longer be considered as explanation for the results given in the preceding section.

Marriage and fertility behaviors before June 1950 were not affected by the war. Thus, cohort subjects born prior to the spring of 1951 should not be selected in terms of conception. The probability of conception for cohort subjects born after March 1951 and the probability of prenatal death during conception by subjects born after June 1950 were deemed influenced by the war. No direct evidence is available as to which subjects were more likely to be pregnant or have live birth. A possible source of selection in fertility behaviors is selective enlistment in the military (Brown 2011).

Documentations of military conscription during the Korean War do not show how men were selected into the armed forces. However, the process was obviously extremely chaotic, especially in the early stage of the war. Immediately following the outbreak of the war, the South Korean military attempted to recruit more than 200,000 men on compulsory basis. However, these mobilization efforts were seriously hampered by rapid advancing of the North Korean force and by a paralyzed administrative infrastructure. A number of men were, in fact, conscripted by force on the street, bypassing formal enlistment procedures including medical examination, and being sent directly to training camps (Korean Military Manpower Administration 1985, pp. 264–286; Tucker 2002, pp. 354–359). Under these circumstances, men from particular socioeconomic backgrounds were unlikely to be recruited more than the others.

How fertility behaviors differed among socioeconomic classes during the war is likewise unclear. Brown (2011) suggested that higher-income U.S. families concerned with providing higher quality education to their children during the First World War postponed reproduction until the war was over. However, given the fact that Korea circa 1950 was a poor agrarian society in which the fertility transition had not begun, women who were under a more favorable socioeconomic circumstance can be assumed to have better chances of conceiving than those in poorer conditions.[1]

The majority of civilians who died during the Korean War were victims of either combat activities or politically motivated murders (Chung 2010). Considering the unexpected outbreak and highly chaotic progress of the war, visualizing that pregnant women from a particular background were more likely to be hit by bullets or bombs is difficult. Descriptive documents suggest that migrants from North Korea, as well as family members of South Korean policemen and soldiers, were more likely to escape to the southern region for fear of punishment by the North Korean forces (Chung 2010). However, whether the people who failed to escape considerably differ in terms of socioeconomic status from refugees in the Busan perimeter is difficult to determine. Refugees had

1 Total fertility rate in South Korea was 5.99 in 1960, and the country is believed to have undergone its first fertility transition during the 1960s (Kim et al. 2002, pp. 84–87).

their own share of hardships. Although the possibility of selection cannot be precluded, survival during the Korean War should be more randomly determined compared with events such as famines or epidemics.

5.1.1. Selections in Birth and Survival in Childhood

I investigated if there were selections in birth and survival in childhood among the birth cohorts who were exposed to the Korean War in pregnancy. A comparison of socioeconomic characteristics of the parents across different birth cohorts would be useful in determining the magnitude and direction of potential section bias. Figure 5.1 provides the average years of schooling of the parents by the children's year of birth, computed from the 2006 Korea Longitudinal Study of Aging.[2] Beginning with the 1949 birth cohort, parental education increased across cohorts. The years of schooling for both the fathers and the mothers of children born in 1951 are longer than those predicted by long-term cohort trends. This suggests that the subjects of the 1951 birth cohort are positively selected in terms of family background.

A micro sample of the 1960 census can offer more direct evidence as to the direction and magnitude of selections in conception, live birth, and childhood death. In the censuses, parental characteristics can be

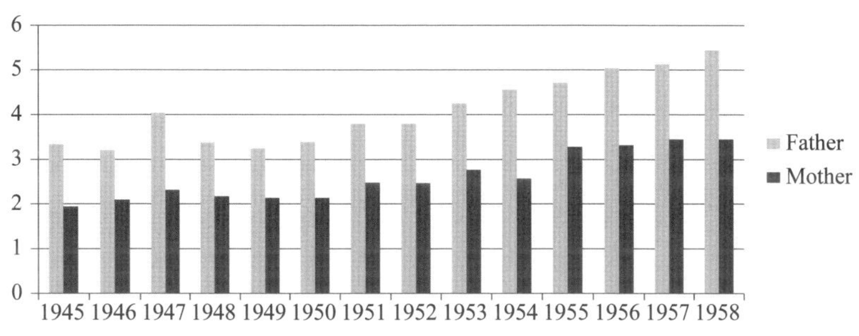

Source: The 2006 Korea Longitudinal Study of Aging.

Figure 5.1 | Parents' Years of Schooling by Children's Year of Birth

2 The sample size of each birth cohort ranges from 236 (1951) to 368 (1957).

observed only when the person co-resides with his or her parents. Any evidence from the censuses after 1960 cannot determine the direction of potential selections because parental survival and co-residence decisions are not random. But in 1960, the birth cohorts considered in this study (1945 to 1959) were under age 15, and thus the majority of them were expected to live with their parents.

The following parental characteristics are compared across the birth cohorts born from 1947 to 1957 to examine if there were any selections in the quality of family backgrounds among the individuals who were prenatally exposed to the disruptions caused by the war. Firstly, if the father or mother was absent in the household in 1960 is considered (parent absent). Five variables on parental socioeconomic status are constructed for individuals who resided with a parent: unable to read or write (illiterate), years of schooling, high school graduation (high school or higher), no formal education (no schooling), and currently working (working). The sample is further limited to the persons with a working parent for constructing variables on occupation: being employed as a wage worker (wage worker) and in a professional job (professional). Table 5.1 presents the sample means and standard deviations of these variables.

Figures 5.2 to 5.7 plot these variables on parental characteristics

Table 5.1

Parental Socioeconomic Characteristics of the 1947–1957 Birth Cohorts in 1960

Variable	(1) Father		(2) Mother	
	Mean	S.D.	Mean	S.D.
A. Parent absent	0.0645	0.2457	0.0112	0.1052
B. Illiterate	0.2121	0.4088	0.4568	0.4982
C. Years of schooling	4.1333	4.3123	2.3130	3.2927
D. High school or higher	0.0681	0.2520	0.0156	0.1237
E. No schooling	0.4480	0.4973	0.6380	0.4806
F. Working	0.9636	0.1872	0.3003	0.4584
G. Wage workers	0.2267	0.4188	0.0250	0.1562
H. Professional	0.0975	0.2966	0.0140	0.1175

Source: The 1% samples of the 1960 census.

Note: See text for the definition of the variables. The sample consists of 66,251 children aged 3 to 13 in 1960. For Panels B to F, the sample was restricted to the children whose father (Column 1) or mother (Column 2) was present in the household (the number of observations is 61,976 and 65,509, respectively). For Panels G and H, children of working father (Column 1: N = 59,613) or mother (Column 2: N = 19,641) were included in the sample.

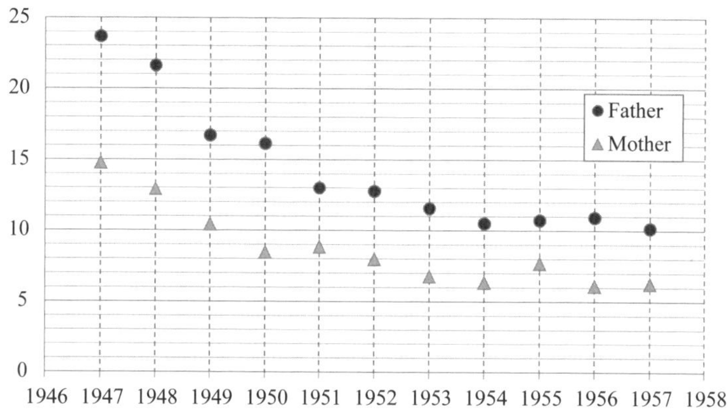

Source: The 1% sample of the 1960 census.

Figure 5.2 | % Absence a Parent in 1960 by Year of Birth of Children

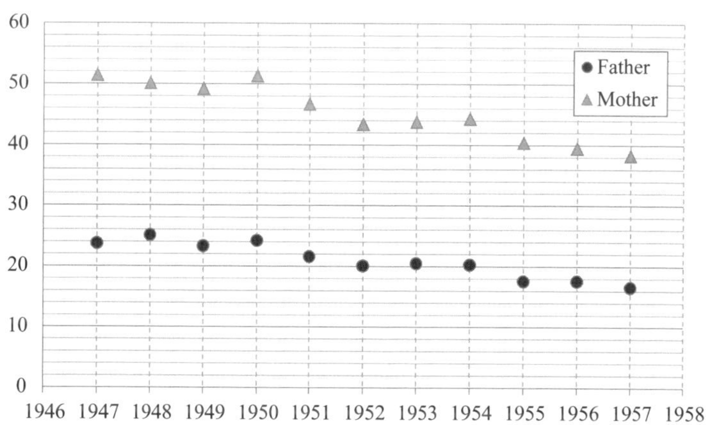

Source: The 1% sample of the 1960 census.

Figure 5.3 | % Illiterate Parents in 1960 by Year of Birth of Children

as of 1960 by the year of birth of children. Judging from graphical presentations, it appears that the subjects of the 1950 and 1954 birth cohorts were negatively selected in terms of parental characteristics, whereas the 1951 birth cohort does not deviate from smooth cohort trends. The children born in 1950 were more likely to live without their father (Figure 5.2), to have illiterate parents (Figure 5.3), and to have

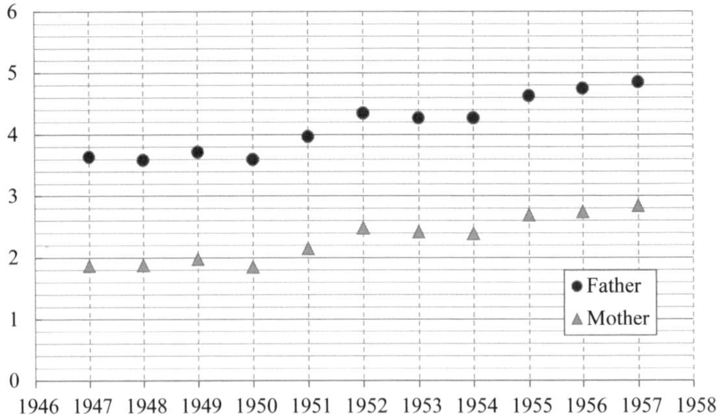

Source: The 1% sample of the 1960 census.

Figure 5.4 | Parent's Years of Schooling in 1960 by Year of Birth of Children

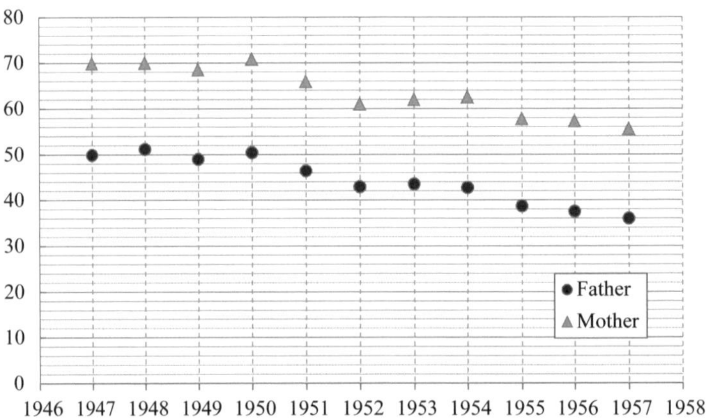

Source: The 1% sample of the 1960 census.

Figure 5.5 | % Parent with No Schooling in 1960 by Year of Birth of Children

low-educated parents (Figures 5.4 to 5.6) than the adjacent birth cohorts. The fathers of the 1950 birth cohort were less likely to be employed in a professional job (Figure 5.7). Similarly, the subjects of the 1954 birth cohort were more likely to have illiterate parents (Figure 5.3), and to have parents with lower educational attainment (Figures 5.4 to 5.6); the fathers of the cohort were less likely to be employed in a wage and salary

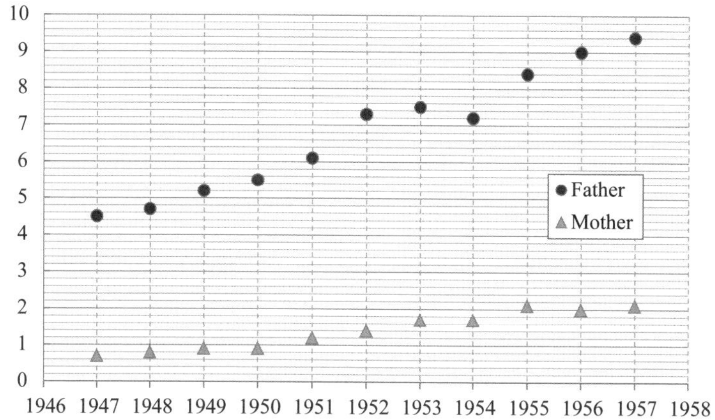

Source: The 1% sample of the 1960 census.

Figure 5.6 | % Parent with Highschool Diploma by Year of Birth of Children

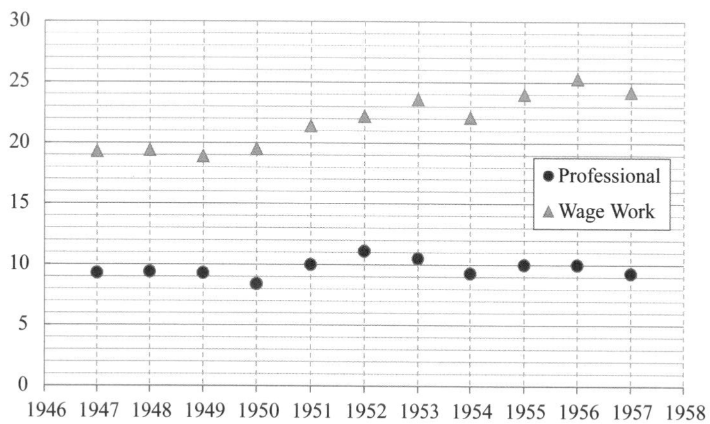

Source: The 1% sample of the 1960 census.

Figure 5.7 | % Fathers with Professional Jobs and % Fathers with Wage and Salary Jobs in 1960 by Year of Birth of Children

job or to hold a professional occupation (Figure 5.7).

The deviations of the parental characteristics from smooth cohort trends are systematically estimated for individuals born between 1947 and 1957. The estimation is carried out using the following regression equation:

Table 5.2
Deviation of the 1950–1954 Birth Cohorts' Parental Characteristics in 1960 from 1947–1957 Trend

	Father				Mother			
	(1) Quadratic Trend		(2) Cubic Trend		(3) Quadratic Trend		(4) Cubic Trend	
	∂y/∂x	P-value	∂y/∂x	P-value	∂y/∂x	P-value	∂y/∂x	P-value
A. Absence of a parent								
Born in 1950	0.0061	0.1633	0.0071	0.2600	0.0005	0.6853	-0.0003	0.8461
Born in 1951	**-0.0086**	0.0704	-0.0079	0.1899	-0.0003	0.8289	-0.0009	0.5278
Born in 1952	-0.0027	0.5326	-0.0024	0.6278	**0.0024**	0.0858	0.0021	0.1043
Born in 1953	-0.0007	0.8629	-0.0007	0.8415	0.0005	0.6743	0.0005	0.5578
Born in 1954	**0.0062**	0.0803	**0.0058**	0.0601	0.0002	0.8525	0.0005	0.4656
B. Illiterate								
Born in 1950	**0.0199**	0.0037	**0.0123**	0.0763	**0.0404**	<.0001	**0.0365**	<.0001
Born in 1951	-0.0008	0.9048	-0.0069	0.2725	0.0049	0.2934	0.0018	0.5332
Born in 1952	-0.0044	0.5338	-0.0076	0.1742	**-0.0143**	0.0102	**-0.0158**	<.0001
Born in 1953	0.0076	0.2855	**0.0079**	0.0989	0.0067	0.1472	**0.0069**	0.0047
Born in 1954	**0.0135**	0.0496	**0.0164**	0.0012	**0.0210**	0.0002	**0.0227**	<.0001
C. Years of schooling								
Born in 1950	**-0.3106**	0.0002	**-0.2065**	0.0006	**-0.2743**	<.0001	**-0.2153**	<.0001
Born in 1951	-0.0450	0.4931	0.0383	0.3538	-0.0720	0.1368	**-0.0254**	0.0112
Born in 1952	**0.1695**	0.0326	**0.2125**	<.0001	**0.1457**	0.0120	**0.1687**	<.0001
Born in 1953	-0.0151	0.8246	-0.0177	0.4256	-0.0231	0.6268	**-0.0265**	0.0359
Born in 1954	**-0.1794**	0.0105	**-0.2186**	<.0001	**-0.1381**	0.0058	**-0.1625**	<.0001
D. High school or higher								
Born in 1950	**-0.0031**	0.0555	-0.0002	0.8154	**-0.0029**	0.0225	**-0.0013**	<.0001
Born in 1951	0.0005	0.7726	**0.0018**	0.0440	-0.0011	0.4157	0.0001	0.5755
Born in 1952	**0.0056**	0.0118	**0.0068**	<.0001	-0.0013	0.3761	**-0.0007**	0.0844
Born in 1953	0.0017	0.3586	**0.0016**	0.0119	0.0006	0.6738	0.0005	0.2846
Born in 1954	**-0.0069**	0.0009	**-0.0080**	<.0001	-0.0017	0.1753	**-0.0023**	0.0005
E. No schooling								
Born in 1950	**0.0327**	0.0002	**0.0225**	0.0170	**0.0427**	<.0001	**0.0331**	<.0001
Born in 1951	0.0035	0.6166	-0.0047	0.5410	0.0096	0.2202	0.0020	0.2898
Born in 1952	-0.0112	0.1559	**-0.0154**	0.0283	**-0.0234**	0.0141	**-0.0271**	<.0001
Born in 1953	0.0055	0.4568	0.0058	0.1965	0.0027	0.7267	0.0033	0.1562
Born in 1954	**0.0181**	0.0157	**0.0220**	<.0001	**0.0202**	0.0119	**0.0242**	<.0001
F. Work								
Born in 1950	**-0.0055**	0.0111	**-0.0081**	0.0433	**0.0213**	0.0038	**0.0096**	0.0769
Born in 1951	0.0028	0.1589	0.0007	0.8312	**-0.0173**	0.0273	**-0.0265**	0.0004
Born in 1952	-0.0010	0.6243	-0.0021	0.4526	**-0.0198**	0.0197	**-0.0244**	0.0011
Born in 1953	-0.0006	0.7585	-0.0005	0.7767	-0.0039	0.5833	-0.0032	0.5806
Born in 1954	-0.0009	0.5743	0.0001	0.9343	-0.0016	0.7857	0.0032	0.5844
G. Wage worker								
Born in 1950	**-0.0127**	0.0939	-0.0017	0.5335	0.0027	0.4671	0.0022	0.6854
Born in 1951	-0.0019	0.8163	**0.0070**	0.0501	-0.0002	0.9600	-0.0006	0.9006
Born in 1952	0.0004	0.9570	0.0051	0.2184	**-0.0070**	0.0959	-0.0072	0.1132
Born in 1953	0.0085	0.2797	**0.0083**	0.0972	-0.0023	0.5323	-0.0021	0.5117
Born in 1954	**-0.0134**	0.0547	**-0.0174**	0.0047	-0.0037	0.2299	-0.0034	0.1835

Table 5.2 (continued)

	Father				Mother			
	(1) Quadratic Trend		(2) Cubic Trend		(3) Quadratic Trend		(4) Cubic Trend	
	∂y/∂x	P-value	∂y/∂x	P-value	∂y/∂x	P-value	∂y/∂x	P-value
H. Professional job								
Born in 1950	**-0.0138**	<.0001	**-0.0103**	<.0001	-0.0008	0.6654	0.0002	0.9187
Born in 1951	-0.0025	0.2796	0.0004	0.4894	**-0.0050**	0.0340	**-0.0042**	0.0627
Born in 1952	**0.0109**	0.0007	**0.0124**	<.0001	0.0013	0.5348	0.0016	0.4140
Born in 1953	0.0031	0.1713	**0.0031**	0.0056	-0.0030	0.1481	-0.0032	0.1110
Born in 1954	**-0.0075**	0.0017	**-0.0088**	<.0001	-0.0013	0.4522	-0.0019	0.3137

Source: The 1% micro sample of the 1960 census.

Note: The polynomials of the year of birth were included in the regressions, but omitted from the table. For Panels B to H, the sample was restricted to the children whose father (Columns 1 and 2) or mother (Columns 3 and 4) was present in the household. For Panels G and H, children of working father (Columns 1 and 2) or mother (Columns 3 and 4) were included in the sample. Standard errors were adjusted for clustering at the level of year of birth.

$$\textbf{(5.1)} \quad Z_i = \alpha + \sum_{i=1950}^{1954} \beta_i I_i + \gamma_1 YOB_i + \gamma_2 YOB_i^2 + \gamma_3 YOB_i^3 + \varepsilon_i$$

where Z_i denotes a given parental characteristic of the birth cohort i; I_i denotes the dummy variable with a value of 1 for the birth cohort i, and 0 otherwise; *YOB* denotes the last two digits of the birth year; and β_i measures the departure of the parental variable for the birth cohorts in-utero during the Korean War from the cubic cohort trend. Regressions are also conducted in which a quadratic cohort trend employed instead of a cubic cohort trend.

The results of the regressions reported in Table 5.2 confirm that there is no evidence that the subjects of the 1951 birth cohort were positively selected in terms of parental characteristics. Although statistically insignificant, they were less likely to live without a parent, and were more likely to have parents with higher educational attainment. In contrast, the parental socioeconomic status of the 1950 and 1954 birth cohorts is significantly lower than predicted by smooth cohort trends. It is also notable that the subjects of the 1952 birth cohort show signs of positive selections: lower mother's illiteracy rate (Cols. 3 and 4 of Panel A), higher parental years of schooling (Panel C), and higher percentage of persons with professional father (Panel H).

Table 5.3
Deviation of the 1950–1954 Birth Cohorts' Parental Characteristics in 1960 from 1947–1957 Trend: Year by Year

	(1) Absence of Father		(2) Father Illiterate		(3) Father's years of schooling		(4) Father with professional jobs	
	∂y/∂x	P-value	∂y/∂x	P-value	∂y/∂x	P-value	∂y/∂x	P-value
A. Born in 1947	**-0.0214**	0.0030	**-0.0248**	0.0213	0.2155	0.1356	0.0049	0.5232
B. Born in 1948	**0.0118**	0.0005	**0.0131**	0.0033	-0.0751	0.1647	0.0008	0.7518
C. Born in 1949	-0.0056	0.2298	-0.0058	0.3628	0.0447	0.5968	0.0002	0.9630
D. Born in 1950	**0.0111**	0.0044	**0.0166**	0.0021	**-0.2777**	0.0004	**-0.0140**	0.0009
E. Born in 1951	**-0.0098**	0.0090	**-0.0118**	0.0540	0.0684	0.4913	0.0003	0.9468
F. Born in 1952	-0.0026	0.4162	**-0.0134**	0.0145	**0.2916**	0.0005	**0.0154**	0.0002
G. Born in 1953	-0.0015	0.5671	0.0037	0.5220	0.0280	0.7495	0.0045	0.2904
H. Born in 1954	**0.0074**	0.0007	**0.0160**	0.0015	**-0.2588**	0.0001	**-0.0123**	0.0007
I. Born in 1955	**-0.0045**	0.0688	**-0.0118**	0.0143	0.0679	0.4104	-0.0000	0.9927
J. Born in 1956	**0.0035**	0.0891	0.0022	0.5902	0.0333	0.5240	0.0028	0.2365
K. Born in 1957	-0.0074	0.1502	-0.0024	0.7895	-0.0052	0.9704	-0.0002	0.9810

Source: The 1% micro sample of the 1960 census.

Note: Presented is a summary of the 52 OLS regressions that provide the estimated coefficient for the dummy variable indicating a particular birth cohort. The polynomials of the year of birth (YOB, YOB^2, and YOB^3) were included in the regressions, but omitted from the table. Standard errors were adjusted for clustering at the level of year of birth.

Year-by-year regressions are also conducted for four measures of paternal characteristics where the dummy variable for each birth cohort born from 1947 to 1957 is included one by one. The results of 44 regressions summarized in Table 5.3 confirm the baseline results reported in Table 5.2. The percentages of fatherless children and of those with illiterate fathers are significantly lower for the 1951 birth cohort, whereas the subjects of the 1950 and 1954 cohorts are negatively selected in terms of the absence, illiteracy, year of schooling, and occupation of their fathers. The fathers of the 1952 birth cohorts were more educated (Col. 3), less likely to be illiterate (Col. 2), and more likely to have a professional job (Col. 4).

5.1.2. Selections in Death after Childhood

Direct evidence regarding the selections in survival after childhood is difficult to obtain, yet the pattern of change in the population size of each birth cohort over time provides circumstantial evidence. Figure 5.8 shows the size of each cohort born from 1948 to 1955, as enumerated

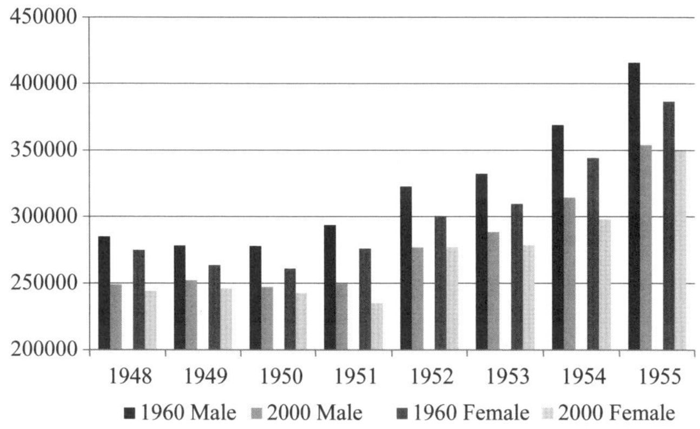

Source: Korean Statistics Information System (KOSIS).

Figure 5.8 | Population by Sex and Year of Birth: 1960 and 2000

by the censuses of 1960 and 2000. More 1951 birth cohort subjects died between 1960 and 2000 than other birth cohorts. The size of the 1951 cohort was reduced by 15%, while the 1950 and 1952 cohorts decreased by 9% and 11%, respectively, during these four decades. The cause of the rapid decline in population of the 1951 birth cohort compared with other cohorts is unclear. While this may be attributed to the in-utero circumstances faced by this cohort, further research is required to verify this claim. Regardless of the cause, cohort subjects with frailer health tended to die by 2000. Consequently, the 1951 birth cohort subjects who were still alive in 2000 are positively selected in terms of health or robustness compared with other cohorts with lower mortality rates since 1960.

I then compare mortality rates across different birth cohorts from 1991 to 2010 when the socioeconomic and health outcomes used in Chapters 3 and 4 were observed. This is to examine the potential consequences of population selections in younger and middle ages. The micro data of the universe of digitalized death registration records in Korea (Vital Statistics for death) were used for this analysis. The average number of deaths per 100,000 persons during a given period is computed for the subject of each birth cohort.

Figure 5.9 presents how the 20-year mortality rates of males and females changed across birth cohorts. The graph shows a long-term downward trend across cohorts, with the 1952 and 1955 birth cohorts

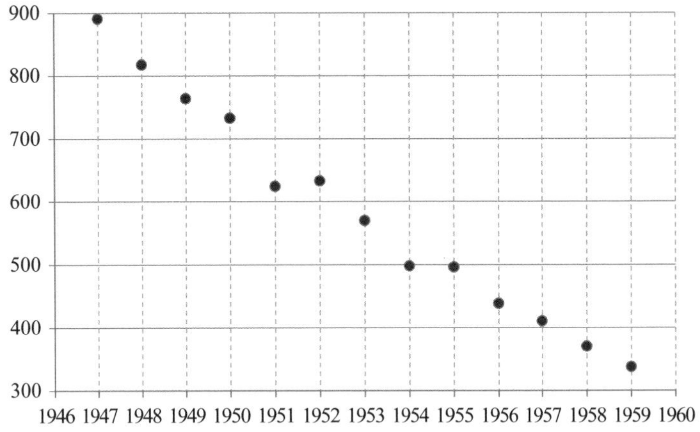

Source: The Vital Statistucs for 1991–2010.

Figure 5.9A | Average Number of Deaths per 100,000 by Year of Birth: Males for 1991–2010

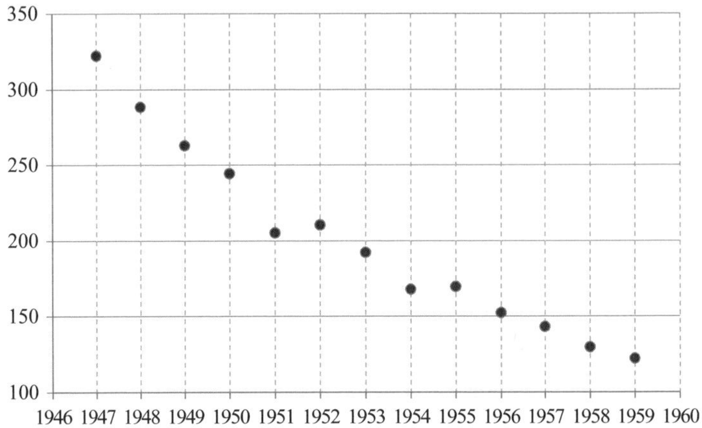

Source: The Vital Statistics for 1991–2010.

Figure 5.9B | Average Number of Deaths per 100,000 by Year of Birth: Females for 1991–2010

veering from the steady trend. It is also apparent that the 1951 and 1954 birth cohorts deviate downward from the smooth cohort trend. Though less clearly revealed, the subjects of the 1950 birth cohort were more likely to die than predicted by the long-term smooth trend.

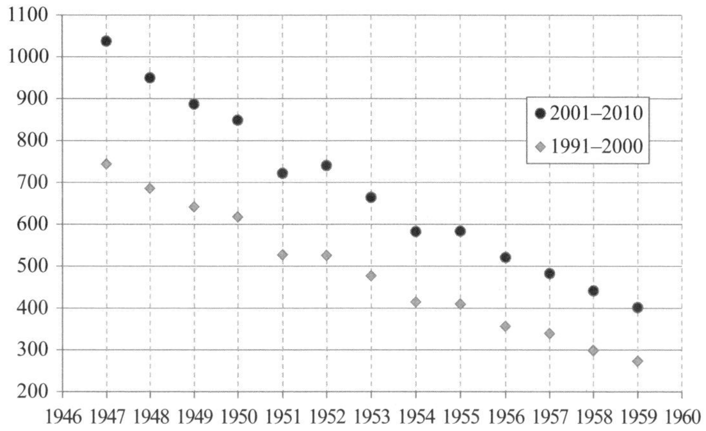

Source: The Vital Statistics for 1991–2010.

Figure 5.10A | Average Number of Deaths per 100,000 by Year of Birth: Males for 1991–2000 and 2001–2010

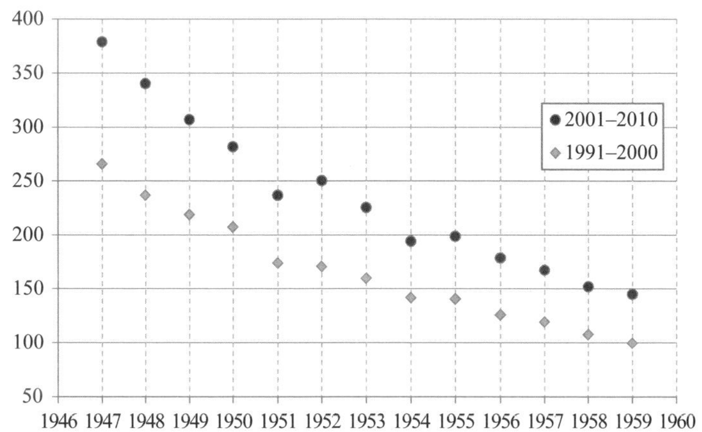

Source: The Vital Statistics for 1991–2010.

Figure 5.10B | Average Number of Deaths per 100,000 by Year of Birth: Females for 1991–2000 and 2001–2010

Figure 5.10 provides the mortality rates of males and females for each of the two decades (1991 to 2000 and 2001 to 2010) under investigation. The result shows that the deviations of the Korean War birth cohorts from the long-term smooth downward trend emerge more

Table 5.4
Deviation of the 1950–1954 Birth Cohorts' Death Rate from 1947–1959 Trend

	Male				Female			
	(1) Deaths per 100,000 A. 583.231 B. 485.017 C. 681.444		(2) Log (Deaths per 100,000) A. 6.303 B. 6.130 C. 6.476		(1) Deaths per 100,000 A. 200.783 B. 166.599 C. 234.967		(2) Log (Deaths per 100,000) A. 5.237 B. 5.066 C. 5.408	
	$\partial y/\partial x$	P-value	$\partial y/\partial x$	P-value	$\partial y/\partial x$	P-value	$\partial y/\partial x$	P-value
A. 1991–2010								
Born in 1950	**23.8711**	0.0356	**0.0305**	0.0014	3.8205	0.4597	0.0118	0.4160
Born in 1951	**-33.6143**	0.0040	**-0.0563**	<.0001	**-15.8099**	0.0031	**-0.0829**	<.0001
Born in 1952	**21.7801**	0.0528	**0.0280**	0.0003	6.0754	0.2358	0.0131	0.3596
Born in 1953	2.4781	0.8138	0.0002	0.9810	2.4566	0.6093	-0.0009	0.9476
Born in 1954	**-27.6812**	0.0054	**-0.0563**	<.0001	**-9.3712**	0.0386	**-0.0623**	<.0001
B. 1991–2000								
Born in 1950	**21.7253**	0.0205	**0.0331**	0.0101	**7.7517**	0.0520	0.0292	0.1598
Born in 1951	**-24.9746**	0.0095	**-0.0519**	0.0001	**-9.6610**	0.0185	**-0.0670**	0.0020
Born in 1952	14.4472	0.1175	**0.0237**	0.0605	0.6893	0.8604	-0.0075	0.7140
Born in 1953	3.5738	0.6786	0.0044	0.7110	1.3077	0.7225	-0.0053	0.7849
Born in 1954	**-21.5877**	0.0086	**-0.0523**	<.0001	**-5.8995**	0.0897	**-0.0516**	0.0050
C. 2001–2010								
Born in 1950	**26.0170**	0.0440	**0.0281**	0.0218	-0.1107	0.9861	-0.0057	0.7755
Born in 1951	**-42.2540**	0.0016	**-0.0607**	<.0001	**-21.9589**	0.0010	**-0.0988**	<.0001
Born in 1952	**29.1132**	0.0233	**0.0323**	0.0080	**11.4616**	0.0710	**0.0338**	0.0882
Born in 1953	1.3824	0.9076	-0.0039	0.7263	3.6056	0.5427	0.0035	0.8505
Born in 1954	**-33.7747**	0.0031	**-0.0602**	<.0001	**-12.8429**	0.0223	**-0.0729**	<.0001

Source: The year-by-cohort number of deaths is computed from the micro data on the Vital Statistics from 1991 to 2010. The year-by-cohort mid-year population is drawn from the Projected Population from 1991 to 2010.

Note: The polynomials of the year of birth (YOB, YOB^2, and YOB^3) and the year dummy were included in the regressions, but omitted from the table.

strongly for the years from 2001 to 2010 than for the previous decade. In particular, the higher mortality rate experienced by the subjects of the 1952 birth cohort is much more clearly revealed for the period 2001-2010 than for the previous 10 years.

The deviations of the year-by-year mortality rates from smooth cohort trends were systematically estimated for individuals born between 1947 and 1959. The estimation was carried out using the following regression equation:

$$\textbf{(5.2)} \quad M_{it} = \alpha + \sum_{i=1950}^{1954} \beta_i I_{it} + \gamma_1 YOB_{it} + \gamma_2 YOB_{it}^{\ 2} + \gamma_3 YOB_{it}^{\ 3} + \sum_{t=1992}^{2010} \delta_t Y_{it} + \varepsilon_{it}$$

where M_{it} denotes the death rate for the birth cohort i in year t; I_{it} denotes the dummy variable with a value of 1 for the birth cohort i, and 0 otherwise; *YOB* denotes the last two digits of the birth year; Y_{it} denotes the year dummy variable; and β_i measures the departure of outcomes for the birth cohorts in-utero during the Korean War from the cubic cohort trend.

The results of regressions reported in Table 5.4 confirm the patterns of changes in mortality across birth cohorts that the death rates of the 1950 and 1952 male birth cohorts were higher than predicted by the cubic cohort trend whereas the mortality of the 1951 and 1954 male birth cohorts deviates downward from the smooth trend. For females, only the downward deviations of the 1951 and 1954 birth cohorts from the cubic trend are statistically significant. The results of regressions separately performed for each of the two decades, 1991–2000 and 2001 to 2010 (Panels B and C of Table 5.4) suggest that the cohort effects are stronger for the latter half of the 20 years under investigation, as graphically presented by Figure 5.9.

Year-by-year regressions were also conducted where the dummy variable for each birth cohort born from 1947 to 1959 was included one by one. The results of 52 regressions summarized in Table 5.5 confirm the baseline results reported in Table 5.4. The adult mortality rates of the persons born in 1951 or 1954 are lower than predicted by the smooth cohort trend whereas the subjects of the 1952 birth cohort and of 1950 male birth cohort were more likely to die than the neighboring cohorts. Deviations from the long-term smooth trend in mortality are largely observed among the Korean War cohorts (born between 1950 and 1954) who were either conceived or born during the Korean War. An exception is the subjects of the 1955 birth cohort who were significantly more likely to die than predicted by the cubic cohort trend in mortality. The mortality rates of other birth cohorts do not deviate significantly from the cubic cohort trend.

The cohort effects on cause-specific mortality were also examined. Equation 5.2 is estimated where all-cause mortality rate was replaced by the rate of death caused by each of the 16 categories of disease or accident. Several notable results emerge from the results reported in Table 5.5. First, individuals who were born or conceived during the Korean War (males born in 1950, 1952, or 1954, and females born in 1952 or 1953) were more likely to be killed by endocrine or metabolic diseases. Second, except for endocrine or metabolic diseases, the Korean

Table 5.5
Deviation of the Death Rate of Each Birth Cohort from 1947–1959 Trend

	Male				Female			
	(1) Deaths per 100,000		(2) Log (Deaths per 100,000)		(1) Deaths per 100,000		(2) Log (Deaths per 100,000)	
	$\partial y/\partial x$	P-value	$\partial y/\partial x$	P-value	$\partial y/\partial x$	P-value	$\partial y/\partial x$	P-value
A. Born in 1947	10.3938	0.5264	0.0068	0.6813	1.8390	0.8001	-0.0070	0.7543
B. Born in 1948	-9.9665	0.3209	-0.0112	0.2694	-1.6848	0.7048	-0.0050	0.7175
C. Born in 1949	-1.7324	0.8590	-0.0006	0.9481	0.8859	0.8374	0.0109	0.4138
D. Born in 1950	**30.0242**	0.0022	**0.0440**	<.0001	7.3533	0.0919	**0.0375**	0.0052
E. Born in 1951	**-44.1278**	<.0001	**-0.0670**	<.0001	**-18.0417**	<.0001	**-0.0831**	<.0001
F. Born in 1952	**28.6937**	0.0024	**0.0441**	<.0001	**10.1512**	0.0155	**0.0413**	0.0014
G. Born in 1953	6.4237	0.4952	0.0118	0.2122	5.4226	0.1926	0.0223	0.0838
H. Born in 1954	**-29.3326**	0.0019	**-0.0565**	<.0001	**-9.4150**	0.0249	**-0.0563**	<.0001
I. Born in 1955	**19.3079**	0.0475	**0.0387**	<.0001	7.1317	0.0985	**0.0436**	0.0010
J. Born in 1956	-6.2727	0.5257	-0.0153	0.1245	0.6938	0.9978	-0.0058	0.0073
K. Born in 1957	5.0820	0.6022	0.0170	0.0830	0.0120	0.9978	0.0089	0.5051
L. Born in 1958	-2.1837	0.8280	-0.0070	0.4905	-3.6201	0.4153	-0.0226	0.1005
M. Born in 1959	-0.6530	0.9683	-0.0037	0.8233	6.3228	0.3832	0.0248	0.2900

Source: The year-by-cohort number of deaths is computed from the micro data on the Vital Statistics from 1991 to 2010. The year-by-cohort mid-year population is drawn from the Projected Population from 1991 to 2010.

Note: Presented is a summary of the 52 OLS regressions that provide the estimated coefficient for the dummy variable indicating a particular birth cohort. The polynomials of the year of birth (YOB, YOB^2, and YOB^3) and the year dummy were included in the regressions, but omitted from the table.

War cohorts were generally less likely to be killed by diseases than predicted by the cubic cohort trend. In particular, the lower mortality of the 1951 male birth cohort resulted largely from their lower mortality caused by diseases (infectious/parasites, cancer, circulatory, respiratory, and unclassified symptoms). Third, it appears that the relatively higher mortality of males born in 1950 or 1952 was the outcome of their higher rates of accident-caused deaths, such as traffic accidents, drowning, toxic substance, and homicide. Males born in 1951 were more likely to be victimized by homicide than the neighboring cohorts. In contrast, male subjects of the 1954 birth cohort were generally less likely to die from non-disease causes.

5.1.3. Conclusion on Selection Bias Issues

In summary, the adverse long-term effects of in-utero exposure to the

Korean War found in the preceding chapters are unlikely driven by selection bias. Available evidence suggests that the subject of the 1951 birth, whose fetal health was most seriously damaged by the Korean War, were actually positively selected by the period between 1990 and 2010 when their adult outcomes were observed for the analyses provided in Chapters 3 and 4. They were more likely to have parents with better socioeconomic characteristics compared to the parents of neighboring birth cohorts in 1960. The 1951 birth cohort experienced lower all-cause and disease-caused mortality compared to adjacent birth cohort from 1991 to 2010. This is perhaps because relatively robust individuals among the 1951 birth cohort remained alive by older age due to higher mortality during younger ages.

Further studies are needed for a better understanding of why the direction of selections in birth and survival changed across the cohorts born from 1950 to 1954, but some conjectures can be offered. The positive selections of the 1951 and 1952 birth cohorts in terms of parental characteristics may be attributable to the severe wartime disruptions from the summer of 1950 to the spring of 1951. Under the highly unfavorable circumstance, the advantages of the individuals with higher socioeconomic status would be more strongly revealed in fertility behaviors and survival of children. By contrast, the negative selections of the 1950 and 1954 birth cohorts could result from the relatively favorable conditions of 1949 to early 1950 (following the establishment of the South Korean government in August 1948) and of late 1953 to early 1954 (following the end of the Korean War in July 1953).

5.2. Differences by Gender, Cohort, and Year

5.2.1. Differences by Gender

The results presented in Chapters 3 and 4 do not explain why the health outcomes of females were less strongly affected by the Korean War, compared to those of males. It is unclear, either, why the advantage of the 1951 birth cohort in mortality from 1991 to 2010 is more strongly revealed for females. Four possible explanations are examined, without implying that these are exhaustive or mutually exclusive.

First, the war-related shocks could have less severely impaired the fetal health of females than of males because of the biological differences between genders. In the prenatal period and early childhood, females are generally known to be more robust than males, as suggested by the lower rates of still births and infant mortality among females. However, previous studies examining other disastrous events such as famines and epidemics provide mixed results regarding gender differences in the relationship between in-utero circumstances and adult health outcomes. For example, the adverse effect of prenatal exposure to the 1918 pandemic influenza on adult disability in the United States is more strongly revealed for males than for females (Almond and Mazumder 2005), whereas female disability is more heavily affected by early-life exposure to the 1959 to 1961 Chinese famine (Mu and Zhang 2008). No clear consensus exists on gender difference in the association between birth weight and systolic blood pressure in later life (Lawlor et al. 2002). A possible explanation for the distinct results of this study is that varied types of shocks to fetal health can affect the adult health outcomes of males and females in different ways.

Second, the gender differences in the health effects of the Korean War could have been generated by the gender bias in parental investments in children. This hypothesis is based on the following assumptions. First, the effects of the Korean War on health were mediated by different parental investments in children. Second, more parental investments were made in healthier children to increase investment return. Finally, parents made minor investments in the wellbeing of their daughters during the mid-20th century because of the strong preference for sons in Korea. Under these conditions, the disparity in in-utero circumstances among girls would not produce any differences in their adult health because their parents did not spend much to improve their daughter's health in the first place. However, testing this hypothesis is difficult because neither the mechanism by which the negative influences of the Korean War affected adult health nor the patterns of parental response to health shocks on children are known.

Given the evidence that parents prefer sons over daughters even in developed countries today (Dahl and Moretti 2008; Lhila and Simon 2008), such a bias is assumed to significantly influence parental investment in children in Korea circa 1950, although its magnitude is difficult to determine. Evidence pertaining to parental response to health shocks is even harder to obtain. A study by Conti et al. (2011),

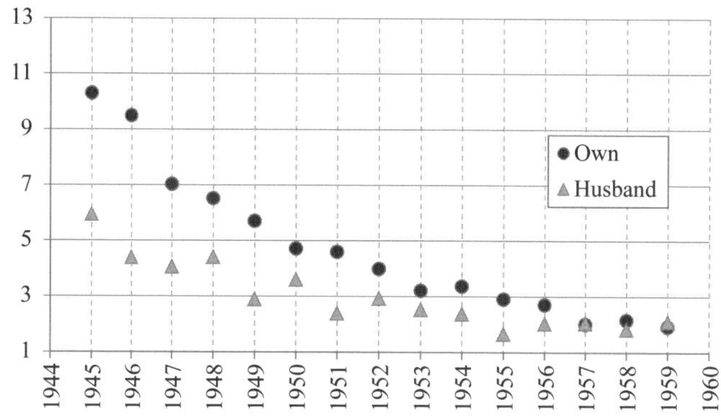

Source: The 2% micro sample of the 2005 census.

Figure 5.11 | % Married Women with Disability/Limited Activity in 2005 by Own and Husband's Birth Year

based on a sample of twins in China, suggests that parental investments in children's health are compensatory, whereas their investments in children's cognitive development are reinforcing. Although Korea and China share several common cultural features, similarities in the patterns of parental investments in children in Korea six decades ago and those of China today are unclear, considering these countries' institutional and socioeconomic differences.

Third, only a small fraction of females born during the Korean War participated in the labor market and virtually all of them eventually married. Thus, the husband's health and socioeconomic status possibly played a more important role in determining the health of older women. An underlying assumption is that the effect of war-driven negative health shocks on adult health was mediated by different economic statuses. Using a sample from the 2005 Census, this hypothesis is tested by selecting married women whose families were headed by the husband. The health outcomes (the probability of having any disability) of these women are displayed in terms of their husbands' birth years and their own birth years (Figure 5.11).

The regressions on the health outcomes of married women employed smooth cohort trends and dummy variables of birth by the couples during wartime (Table 5.6). Women married to subjects from the 1950 male birth cohorts were more likely to have disability or limitations in daily activities in 2005 than predicted by smooth cohort trends, although its

Table 5.6
Effects of Own and Husband's Birth Year on the Probability of Having Disability of Married Women in 2005

	Model 1				Model 2			
	(1) Own YOB		(2) Husband's YOB		(3) Own YOB		(4) Husband's YOB	
	$\partial y/\partial x$	P-value	$\partial y/\partial x$	P-value	$\partial y/\partial x$	P-value	$\partial y/\partial x$	P-value
A. Logistic Regression								
Born in 1950	-0.0032	0.4034	**0.0059**	0.0547	-0.0033	0.3725	0.0041	0.1599
Born in 1951	0.0004	0.9069	0.0015	0.6899	0.0012	0.7361	0.0004	0.9157
Born in 1952	-0.0025	0.4443	0.0048	0.1793	-0.0020	0.5174	0.0036	0.2916
Born in 1953	-0.0022	0.5157	0.0060	0.1103	-0.0015	0.6522	0.0045	0.2015
Born in 1954	0.0012	0.7060	0.0015	0.6990	0.0007	0.8061	0.0014	0.6901
Husband Disabled					**0.0713**	<.0001	**0.0709**	<.0001
B. OLS Regression								
Born in 1950	-0.0064	0.2711	0.0052	0.1387	-0.0062	0.2646	0.0038	0.2529
Born in 1951	-0.0009	0.8690	0.0002	0.9448	0.0002	0.9688	-0.0009	0.7742
Born in 1952	-0.0045	0.2507	0.0037	0.2432	-0.0037	0.3194	0.0032	0.2849
Born in 1953	-0.0034	0.3431	0.0050	0.1211	-0.0023	0.5172	0.0044	0.1533
Born in 1954	0.0007	0.8179	0.0016	0.5695	0.0005	0.8764	0.0020	0.4592
Husband Disabled					**0.2351**	<.0001	**0.2349**	<.0001

Source: The 2% micro sample of the 2005 population census.

Note: (a) The sample includes 42,541 married couples aged 46 to 60 in 2005; (b) The year of birth (YOB) and the year of birth squared (YOB^2) were included in the regressions, but omitted from the table; and (c) Standard errors are adjusted for clustering at the levels of year of birth for Panel B.

statistical significance is sensitive to change in specification (Column 2). In contrast, the married women's own birth years had no significant effect on their health at old age (Column 1). This finding implies that the previously cited gender differences in the effects of the Korean War on health are at least partly explained by the strong influence on female health by the husband's economic and/or health status.

The last two regressions reported in Table 5.6 (Columns 3 and 4) include a dummy variable indicating whether the husband has any disability. The results suggest that the effect of the husband's birth year on the wife's disability can be mediated by the husband's poor health. The husband's disability strongly increases the likelihood of disability in the wife (Column 3). Once the husband's disability is controlled, the effect of being married to a man born in 1950 on the probability of having disability diminishes in magnitude by a third and becomes statistically insignificant (Column 4). The wives of disabled men are likely to become handicapped themselves in the course of providing care. Alternatively, economic hardship caused by the breadwinner's incapacity can adversely affect the health of the wife.

Finally, a stronger population selection among females could have produced the gender differences in the effects of the Korean War on health outcomes. This hypothesis may partly explain the more pronounced lower mortality in females than in males from the 1951 birth cohort compared with that in the neighboring cohorts (Table 5.4). As noted above, the size of the 1951 birth cohort decreased more rapidly than that of neighboring cohorts from 1960 to 2000 (Figure 5.8). Normally, the male-to-female ratio of a cohort is about 1.05 at the time of birth, which continuously declines with age because the rate of male deaths exceeds that of females. Figure 5.8 shows that for the majority of birth cohorts, the male-to-female ratio substantially dropped between 1960 and 2000. However, the gender ratio for the 1951 cohort remained remarkably stable during the four decades. The estimated mortality rate between 1960 and 2000 for the 1951 cohort is 14.7% for females and 15.1% for males. These rates suggest that compared with the population decline in other birth cohorts, population selection in the 1951 cohort is much more pronounced among females than among males. As noted by previous studies (Stanner et al. 1997; Bozzoli, Deaton, and Quintana-Domeque 2009), this stronger population selection should leave more robust females alive within the 1951 cohort. On the contrary, the 1950 birth cohort shows that females were more likely to survive than males by 2000 if they were alive in 1960.[3]

5.2.2. Differences by Birth Cohorts

Another puzzling finding is that different aspects of human capital for the 1950 and 1951 cohorts were significantly damaged by their in-utero exposure to the Korean War. Considering the census outcomes, the 1950

---

3 The question of gender differences in mortality during childhood (prior to 1960) is also considered. Male-to-female ratios of the 1950 and 1951 birth cohorts in 1960 (1.065 and 1.064, respectively) are close to the normal gender ratio at birth (1.05). Therefore, it is unlikely that considerably more girls than boys were killed among the 1950 and 1951 cohorts, resulting in a stronger population selection among females by 1960.

cohort mostly exhibits health-related negative consequences from the war, whereas the 1951 cohort shows lower socioeconomic outcomes than neighboring cohorts.

This result can be attributed to the difference in pregnancy stages during which the two birth cohorts were exposed to negative health shocks. Individuals born at the end of 1950 had already spent four months as a fetus or in-utero by the time the war broke out in late June; thus, majority of this cohort survived the first half of pregnancy before the war. In particular, the 1950 cohort in-utero during the first three months of the Korean War spent only the final trimester of pregnancy during what is considered as the most chaotic period of the war. Conversely, the majority of the 1951 cohort subjects were exposed to the war during the early stages of pregnancy.

The effects of prenatal exposure to negative health shocks differ according to the stage of pregnancy at which the shocks were received (Barker 1994). The human brain develops between the 8th and 25th weeks of pregnancy. Thus, the 1951 birth cohort was more likely to be exposed to war-related disruptions as a fetus during these weeks than the 1950 cohort. This study considers socioeconomic outcomes, which are closely related to cognitive skills including educational attainment and quality of occupation. Therefore, with all factors considered, the education and labor market outcomes of the 1951 cohort were significantly worse than predicted by long-term trends because in-utero development of the subjects' brains was adversely affected by the war. In contrast, the subjects of the 1950 birth cohort were exposed to the war in-utero after their brains were fully formed. This conjecture is also consistent with the result that the probability of entering college is more strongly affected by in-utero exposure to the war than the probability of attending at least primary school (see Chapter 3) because college demands cognitive ability more than middle or high school.

5.2.3. Comparisons between Health Outcomes in 2005 and 2010

The patterns of the differences in disability rates across birth cohorts in the 2010 census (Chapter 4) are similar to the features of the variations in socioeconomic outcomes drawn from the 1990 and 2000 censuses (Chapter 3). When aged 40 to 50, measures of educational attainment, employment, and quality of occupation were significantly lower for the

1951 birth cohort, and the 1951 cohort effect is more strongly revealed for the individuals born in the places that were more seriously devastated by the war.[4] Similarly, the subjects of the 1951 birth cohort emerge as the biggest victims of the Korean War if old-age functional limitations are concerned.

However, the results related to disability obtained from the 2005 and 2010 censuses are considerably different with each other. In 2005, in general, the health consequences of early-life exposure to the Korean War were only weakly presented compared to the impacts on socioeconomic outcomes. Moreover, it was the males born in 1950, not the 1951 birth cohort, whose health was most seriously affected by prenatal exposure to wartime disruptions. No significant health effect of the Korean War is observed for females.

In the 2010 census, by comparison, adverse long-term effects of early-life exposure to the war are more apparently revealed than in 2005. Although the disadvantages of the 1950 birth cohort continue to be observed, the 1951 birth cohort turns out to be more seriously affected by in-utero experiences of the war. As in 2005, the effects of prenatal exposure to the war on health are weaker for females than for males in 2010; however, unlike 2005 census outcomes, the negative long-term impacts of the war on female health became statistically significant for a few health outcomes by 2010.

Although speculative at this point, several possible explanations for the differences in the results drawn from the 2005 and 2010 censuses can be offered. First, in analyzing the 2010 census, the place of birth is considered for identifying the severity of wartime experiences, which is unavailable in the 2005 census. This might help more accurately identify the long-term effects of the war, as in the case of the results on socioeconomic outcomes based on the 1990 and 2000 censuses. Indeed, the 1951 cohort effect is more strongly observed for the natives of the Central Region (Table 4.1).

Second, the long-term effects of in-utero exposure on old-age health

4 The effects of in-utero exposure to the Korean War on educational attainment do not change between 1990 and 2010. Since wage and salary workers retire from their lifetime jobs in the early or mid-50s, it is difficult to investigate the impacts on labor-market outcomes using the census taken in 2010 when the Korean War birth cohorts were aged 57 to 60.

might depend on the age of measuring health outcomes. As apparent from Figure 4.1, the disability rate begins to increase rapidly from the mid-50s (in Figure 4.1, from the 1954 birth cohort who were aged 56 in 2010). The rise in the disability rate after age 55 is particularly sharp for females, whose overall disability rate overtakes the males' at age 60 (Figure 4.1). The persons born in 1951 were aged 54 in 2005, and it is perhaps too early age to observe how early-life experiences eventually affected the risk of suffering from disability, especially for females. This hypothesis might explain why early-life exposure to the Korean War exerts increasingly strong effects on the health over time (e.g. why the 1951 cohort effect estimated from the entire sample is significant in 2010, not in 2005).

Finally, the differences in the features of population selections between the 1950 and 1951 birth cohorts could contribute to the earlier development of health problems among the persons born in 1950 compared to the 1951 birth cohort. The preceding section in this Chapter demonstrates that the parental socioeconomic status is significantly lower for the 1950 birth cohort than the neighboring cohorts. In contrast, the subjects of the 1951 birth cohort were generally privileged compared to other cohorts (except the 1952 birth cohort) in terms of family backgrounds (Tables 5.2 and 5.3). Furthermore, the 1951 birth cohort went through much more pronounced population selection between 1960 and 1990 compared to the 1950 birth cohort.[5] As noted by previous studies (Stanner et al. 1997; Bozzoli, Deaton, and Quintana-Domeque 2009), this stronger population selection should leave more robust persons alive within the 1951 cohort, thus postponing the onset of health conditions at older age. This hypothesis might answer the question of why the 1950 birth cohort began to experience the health consequences of the war-caused shocks earlier (e.g. from 2005) than the 1951 birth cohort.

---

5 For comparing the relative mortality rates of the two cohorts, census survivorship method is applied to the age-specific population from 1960 to 1990. Between 1960 and 1990, the relative size of the male and female cohorts born in 1951 (among the cohorts born from 1945 to 1959) diminished by 0.15% and 0.50% respectively, whereas the relative size of the male and female subjects of the 1950 birth cohort increased by 3.10% and 2.95%.

5.3. Summary

The adverse long-term effects of in-utero exposure to the Korean War found in Chapters 3 and 4 are unlikely driven by bias arising from selections in birth and survival. There is no evidence that the subjects of the 1951 birth cohort were negatively selected in terms of parental characteristics in 1960. Furthermore, it appears that the 1951 birth cohort subjects who were still alive in 2000 were positively selected in terms of health or robustness compared with other cohorts with lower mortality rates since 1960.

The effects of prenatal exposure to the Korean War differed by gender. For instance, the socioeconomic and health outcomes of females were less strongly affected by the war. This gender difference can be explained in part by the influence of the husband's economic and health status on female health in Korea. Women married to the 1950 male subjects were more likely to have disability or limitation in daily activities in 2005 than predicted by smooth cohort trends. In contrast, these married women's own birth years had no significant effect on their health at old age. Stronger population selection among females born in 1951 can be a factor: the mortality rate from 1960 to 2000 was particularly high for the 1951 female cohort, making the female survivors among the 1951 cohort more robust on average than those in neighboring cohorts. Other possible explanations are (a) biological differences in health by gender and (b) gender bias in parental investment on children's health in Korea, a factor that cannot be directly tested.

The type of human capital significantly impaired by war-time in-utero influences differed between the 1950 and 1951 birth cohorts. The 1950 cohort exhibits worse health outcomes while the 1951 cohort shows lower educational attainment and labor market performance. A possible explanation for the difference by year of birth is that the two cohorts were exposed to negative health shocks during different stages of pregnancy. For example, the majority of the 1951 cohort subjects experienced the worst time of the war during the first half of pregnancy, a critical period for the development of the human brain. On the other hand, most of the 1950 birth cohort subjects had already passed the 25th week in pregnancy with complete prenatal brain development when the war broke out. The weaker effect of the war on the health of the 1951 cohort, as noted above, may be attributed to the considerably stronger population selection experienced by this cohort.

The patterns of the variations in the disability rates across birth cohorts considerably differ between 2005 and 2010. First, early-life exposure to the Korean War exerts stronger effects on health outcomes in 2010 than in 2005. It is perhaps attributable to the facts that the rates of functional limitation sharply increase over the late 50s, and that the Korean War birth cohorts were a little too young in 2005 to pay the full prices for the harmful prenatal experiences. Second, the differences in the features of population selections between the 1950 and 1951 birth cohorts might contribute to the earlier development of health problems among the persons born in 1950 compared to the 1951 birth cohort.

CHAPTER 6

Nutrition and Human Capital Development 1: Data and Method

6.1. Background

It is widely believed that the rapid economic growth in South Korea during the second half of the 20th century has immensely improved the standards of living of the country's population. At present, South Koreans enjoy considerably higher levels of material well-being than those with from six or seven decades ago. Current per capita income in dollar value is more than 400 times higher than that in 1953.[1] At present, life expectancy at birth is 30 years longer than that in 1960.[2]

However, the period when the standards of living have begun to flourish is unclear. Available evidence pertaining to several measures of human well-being suggests that improvements have been proceeding since the 1960s. Although vital statistics prior to 1970 are highly unreliable, life expectancy appears to have substantially increased between 1960

1 The per capita GNP in 1953 is estimated at 67 dollars (Song 2003, p. 106); per capita income in 2016 is 28,524 dollars.

2 Life expectancy in 1960 was 52 years (National Statistical Office 1998, p. 54) but increased to 82 years by 2016.

and 1970 (National Statistical Office 1998). Substantial fluctuations were noted in the rates of morbidity and mortality caused by acute infectious disease from 1946 to 1954, although a long-term declining trend has emerged if not for the short-term decrease and increase in 1948 and increase in 1951 (Lee 2016). Age at menarche is often used as an index of the biological standard of living. Several studies determined that menarcheal age declined, particularly after 1946 (Hong et al. 1993; Hwang et al. 2003; Sohn 2016).

Despite this general consensus on the long-term trend in the standards of living, the manner by which the living conditions in South Korea have changed over time and the major factors that produced the changes remain unexplored. For example, substantial knowledge should still be obtained on how the process of improvements differed by socioeconomic characteristics and how the experiences of each birth cohort differed with each other. Moreover, we have yet to completely understand how particular economic or social changes have affected the well-being of the population.

Rigorous research on these issues is often considerably hampered by shortage of the appropriate data, particularly for the periods prior to the 1970s. We can obtain reasonably large and representative micro data on household incomes and consumption expenditures only after the 1970s. Many of the previous studies that utilized the biological measures of standards of living were based on recent survey data, including aging birth cohorts, which are subject to a few shortcomings, such as selective survival of healthy individuals and shrinkage of heights at old age. Other similar studies in the past relied on relatively small samples of particular demographic groups, thereby resulting in difficulty to generalize the results for the entire population. Furthermore, the vast majority of the sources used by these studies restrict us from inferring the socioeconomic backgrounds and ecological environments of individuals in growing ages.

I overcome these limitations of the current data on the standards of living in South Korea prior to the 1970s by analyzing new data on South Korean military records that were collected from the Military Manpower Administration. I also constructed province- and county-level data on local nutritional availability, and matched them with the sample of the conscripts using the information on the place of residence. Using these data, I investigate how nutritional availability in two crucial periods of human growth, namely, early childhood (from conception to age 2) and adolescence (from age 12–16), has affected the heights of South Korean conscripts born from 1946 to 1957. I also explore the extent by which the observed increase in adult heights across birth cohorts can be accounted for by improved nutrition during infancy and adolescence.

I focus on height for the following reasons. First, height is a primary index of cumulative net nutritional status during the growing ages. Adult height is also known as a strong predictor of health and mortality. Therefore, establishing primary determinants of adult height will facilitate the understanding of how and why the standards of living in South Korea have changed over time. Second, the mean adult height slightly declined for the cohorts born prior to1951, presumably due to the adverse effects of early-life exposure to the Korean War (Chapters 3 and 4), and increased rapidly thereafter between the 1951 and 1957 birth cohorts. For these birth cohorts, no clear secular trends in weight were observed. A productive method to understand the causes of long-term changes in standards of living is to focus on heights with changes that reveal secular trends for the cohorts under investigation.

A few studies provided evidence regarding the long-term trends and socioeconomic differences in heights of South Koreans born prior to the 1960s. Several studies compared across different birth cohorts (Hong et al. 1993; Hwang et al. 2003; Schwekendiek and Jun 2010; Pak et al. 2011; Sohn 2016), while others focused on the changes in age-specific anthropometric measures across different years (Lim et al. 1986; National Statistics Office 1998; Pak 2004; Lee and Park 2005; Kim et al. 2006; Kim et al. 2008; Choi and Kim 2012; Korean Agency for Technology and Standards 2011). Compared with the relatively active research on height changes during the Japanese colonial era (Choi and Schwekendiek 2009; Kim and Park 2011), the trends and determinants of heights of individuals born between 1945 and 1960 are less clearly understood.

The studies on cohort-specific stature generally show that the heights of South Koreans increased from the cohorts born after 1945, with substantial differences across birth cohorts and across demographic characteristics observed. Hwang et al. (2003) determined that height increase was slower for the 1940–1959 birth cohorts and the 1960–1969 birth cohorts based on a small sample of females included in the Ansan Health Study. Sohn (2016) also maintained that the trend of male heights was rather flat for the cohorts who experienced the Korean War and its aftermath in childhood. Hong et al. (1993) suggested that the population size of the place of residence was positively related to the heights of girls of menarcheal age.

Differences in height increase by gender and age group have been determined by the studies based on age-and year-specific measures. Between 1965 and 1975, the largest height change was determined at age 7 for boys and girls (Kim et al. 2008; Choi and Kim 2012). The increase in average height of infants and younger children occurred visibly in 1966–1984, which was a period of rapid economic development in South Korea (Kim et al. 2008; Choi and Kim 2012). Kim et al. (2008) reported that the heights in all age group between 12 and 24 stagnated between 1945 and 1950s but rapidly increased thereafter. Lee and Park (2005) determined that the stature of children aged 6 to 11 stagnated or declined between 1953 and 1966.

The research introduced here is distinct from previous studies on South Korean stature in several aspects. First, this is the first attempt to investigate the determinants of adult stature based on a large and representative sample of the birth cohorts born between 1945 and 1960. The birth cohorts born immediately after the Second World War spent their childhood and adolescence during periods of upheavals, including chaotic political and social circumstances that followed the liberation from the Japanese occupation, the Korean War that devastated the entire country, and the long and slow recovery from the destruction caused by the two wars. By contrast, the birth cohorts born toward the end of the 1950s were the first generation to benefit from spending childhood during periods of prolonged peace and rapid economic growth in the 1960s and 1970s. Thus, comparisons of these birth cohorts offer an opportunity to understand how the radical social and economic changes during the three decades after 1945 have affected the standards of living of South Koreans.

Second, the current study is the first to explore how local nutritional availability and other family and environmental characteristics in growth periods have affected the heights of South Korean adults. Similar previous studies were only able to consider the differences in heights across birth cohorts and across regions (Choi and Schwekendiek 2009; Kim and Park 2011). The present study is unique because it analyzes the effects of parental characteristics, which are a key determining factor of living conditions in growth periods. Obtaining data that simultaneously provide information on adult heights of individuals and their parental characteristics is difficult. In addition, I developed and utilized more detailed measures of local nutritional availability than those used in previous studies on nutrition and heights (e.g., Haines et al. 2003). I used four different indices of nutritional availability, namely, total calories and three major nutrients measured in two different crucial periods of human growth (i.e., infancy and adolescence). The improved quality of variables enables me to address several issues that have not been completely understood. For example, I can use the data to analyze which nutrient is considerably important for the growth of South Koreans and how nutritional availability in infancy and adolescence affects adult heights differently.

6.2. Data

6.2.1. Sample of Korean Military Records

After a large-scale recruitment was attempted on a compulsory basis following the outbreak of the Korean War, military service is currently a mandatory duty for all males in South Korea. All males have to take physical examinations for military conscription at age 20. Military record cards are produced for all males, including those who are exempt from service. On the front page of the card, the details on personal and family characteristics and the results of physical examinations are recorded. For veterans, military service records are provided on the back page of the card.

The carded military records (CMR) are kept in the central office of the Military Manpower Administration (MMA). Since 2002 (for the birth cohorts born in 1982 or later), CMRs are available in machine-readable forms. For earlier birth cohorts, either image files or micro films of military records can be obtained. From the total number of records, CMRs may be available for the entire male population at least from the mid-1960s. Figure 6.1 shows a sample of CMR.

By obtaining permission from MMA, I collected a 0.5% sample of CMRs for the birth cohorts born from 1946 to 1957. CMRs for the individuals born between 1948 and 1957 are contained in the forms of image files that can be sorted based on the National Registration Number, the first six digits of which provides the birth dates. I selected men born on the 20th day of each month with IDs ending with 4 or 6, thereby

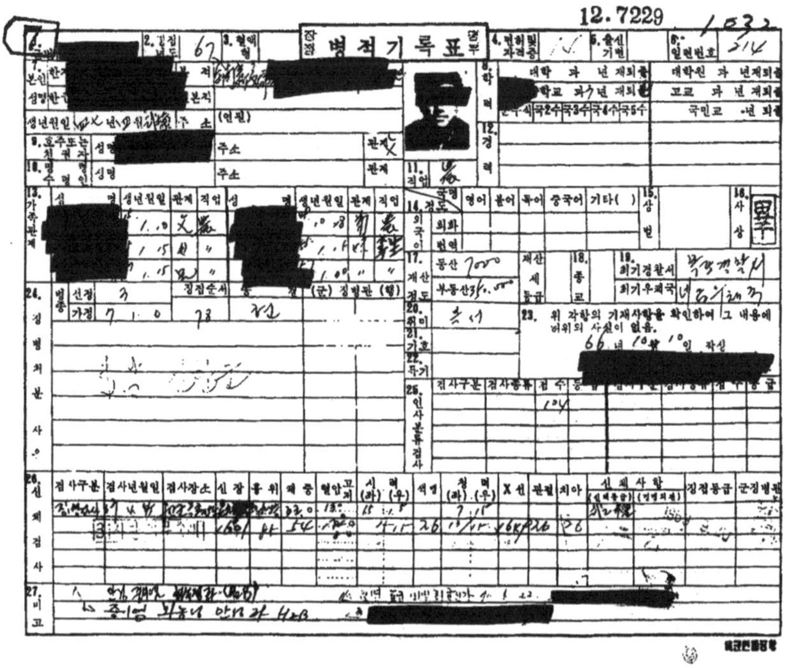

Figure 6.1 | Sample of Carded Military Record

providing a 1-in-150 sample. Further selections of complete and readable records have provided me with approximately 0.5% sample. For the birth cohorts born from 1946 to 1948, CMRs are available in the forms of micro films. I selected the first 15 films from each roll composed of 3,000 films for these cohorts. If the selected film is incomplete or difficult to read, then I replaced it by the next film.

To protect privacy of the individuals included in the sample, I deleted the following information from the selected CMRs: (1) names of the conscript and family members, (2) military ID, (3) last seven digit numbers of the National Registration Number, and (4) address below the county or district level. To obtain the resulting image files, the front and back pages of CMRs with the sensitive personal information deleted were scanned in MMA. After duplicate records were detected and excluded, the information drawn from the image files were inputted into database.

I identified nine different types of CMRs in terms of format and content. Four major types, denoted as Forms 1 to 4, account for the vast

Table 6.1
Number of Military Records by Year of Birth

Year of Birth	(A) Number of Records Collected	(B) Number of Incomplete Records	(C) Number of Duplicated Records	(D) Number of Records Inputted
1946	1,162	0	4	1,158
1947	1,036	0	5	1,031
1948	1,443	1	1	1,441
1949	1,143	0	23	1,120
1950	1,310	1	5	1,304
1951	1,303	0	43	1,260
1952	1,577	0	2	1,575
1953	1,404	11	35	1,358
1954	1,706	4	6	1,696
1955	1,875	0	52	1,823
1956	2,157	1	18	2,138
1957	2,243	3	29	2,211
Total	18,359	21	223	18,115

Source: Sample of Korean Military Records.

majority of the sample. The variables pertaining to the information on conscripts available from all types of CMR include birth dates, place of current residence, place of original residence, education, occupation, specialty, results of physical examinations and aptitude tests, and conscription decision. The data also provide information on the age, occupation, and relationship to the conscript of parents (or guardian) and other family members. The variables on physical examinations include height, weight, chest measurement, blood pressure, eyesight, and particular health problems.

Table 6.1 presents the number of samples by birth year. The total number of CMRs collected and scanned in the MMA is 18,359. Of these CMRs, I found 21 records with a missing page and 233 duplicated records. After excluding these defective records, 18,115 CMRs were inputted into machine readable forms. The sample size for each birth cohort ranges from 1,031 (1947 birth cohort) to 2,211 (1957 birth cohort).

6.2.2. Data on County- and Province-Level Agricultural Productions

Official surveys or statistical reports on agricultural productions in South Korea began publication in the early 1950s (Table 6.2). However,

Table 6.2
Official Surveys or Statistical Reports on Farm Productions

Name	Publication Cycle	Start Year
Farm Household Economy Survey	Annual	1953
Food, Agriculture, Forestry and Fisheries Statistical Yearbook	Annual	1952
Agricultural Production Survey	Annual	1965
Survey of Production Index of Agriculture and Forestry	Annual	1965
Statistical yearbooks of each province or county	Annual	Generally in the middle of 1950s
Agriculture, Forestry and Fisheries Census	5 years	Agriculture survey started in 1960

agricultural statistics compiled at the county level prior to 1960 only include the number of farm households, farm population, cultivated lands, and irrigation associations. Agricultural productions are provided at the province level.3F[3] Previous studies that utilized these data are mainly concerned with estimating country-wide trends of agricultural productions (Hwang et al. 2014; Jeong et al. 2015; Jo 2007; Ko 2007). The only sources that report county-level agricultural outputs annually and in a consistent manner is the statistical yearbooks published by each province (including two autonomous metropolitan cities at the time, namely, Seoul and Busan) and each county. Accordingly, I constructed county-level agricultural production data set generally from provincial or county statistical year books of various years. Moreover, I supplemented such information with province-level data drawn from other sources, including *Korea Statistical Yearbook*, *Food, Agriculture, Forestry and Fisheries Statistical Yearbook*, and recent statistical reports published in a few regions.

Statistical yearbooks employ a bottom–up approach in the process

3 South Korea had 11 provinces (*Do*) and autonomous metropolitan cities (*Gwangyeoksido*) during the periods under study. These largest administrative divisions are referred to as "province" in this book. A province is divided into lower administrative units, including cities (*Si*) and counties (*Gun*), whereas metropolitan city and large cities in provinces have multiple districts (*Gu*). County and district are referred to as "county" throughout this book.

of producing statistics. Each county compiles data reported from lower public administrative centers and publishes its own statistical yearbook annually. Simultaneously, the related sections or bureaus of each province compiles data reported from the counties they control and publish provincial statistical yearbook annually. Lastly, the National Bureau of Statistics collects all of these data and publishes the *Korean Statistical Yearbook* annually. The *Food, Agriculture, Forestry and Fisheries Statistical Yearbook* is also published via bottom-up approach. This yearbook is published annually by the Ministry of Agriculture after receiving data from local public offices under its jurisdiction and independently conducting the related research and analysis. Lastly, regional authorities occasionally collect and compile previous statistical yearbooks and publish new statistical reports.

The records used for the data constructions are available online and in several public libraries. The online sources include the websites of the National Archives of Korea (archives.go.kr), National Assembly Library (nanet.go.kr), Statistics Korea Library (lib1.kostat.go.kr), and several local governments. Many statistical books are deposited in these websites in pdf or e-book files. A few of the records are available only from offline sources. I collected the records that are unavailable online from the Statistics Korea Library, Suwon Library of Seoul National University, National Assembly Library, and National Archives of Korea either through borrowing volumes or reproducing copies with the permission of the library staff members. Table 6.3 presents the list of the sources utilized for constructing our data on local agricultural productions.

These books provide comprehensive information on the following local statistics presented in figures and tables: (1) short history; (2) land area and climate; (3) population; (4) industry and economy, including agriculture; (5) public employees and finance; (6) water works, health, and cleaning; (7) social welfare; (8) education; (9) public peace; (10) price and national account; (11) communication and electric power; (12) foreign trade and exchange; 13) justice of their territories; and (14) international statistics. Recently published statistical yearbooks provide additional detailed information with improved physical design in statistical figures and tables. However, the basic contents and structure remained unchanged over time. Table 6.4 presents common variables contained in the statistical yearbooks of various provinces and years. Figures 6.2, shows a sample page of the *Seoul Statistical Yearbook* on land area, population, and agriculture, including livestock.

Table 6.3
List of Data Sources Used in Construction of Dataset

Data Sources	Publication Year	Form
The *Korea Statistical Yearbook*	1952–1954 1957–1978	Pdf files
The *Food, Agriculture, Forestry and Fisheries Statistical Yearbook*	1955–1978	Pdf files
The *Seoul Statistical Yearbook*	1948–1950 1952–1956 1958–1978	1948, 1950, 1952–1956, 1958–1959: jpg files capturing some pages of books at the National Assembly Library 1949: an e-book from the website of the National Assembly Library. The rest: pdf files
The *Busan Statistical Yearbook*	1962–1978	1964, 1967: e-books from the National Archives of Korea 1973: an e-book from the National Assembly Library The rest: e-books from the Busan Metropolitan City
The *Gyeonggi Statistical Yearbook*	1954–1955 1960–1965 1967–1978	1954–1955, 1960: e-books from the National Assembly Library The rest: pdf files
Statistical yearbooks of counties under the control of Gyeonggi Province	1966	Gapyeong, Suwon, Siheung, Anseong, Incheon, Paju, Pyeongtaek, Hwaseong: pdf files Ganghwa, Goyang, Gwangju, Gimpo, Bucheon, Yangju, Yangpyeong, Yeoju, Yeoncheon, Yongin, Uijeongbu, Icheon, Pocheon: jpg files capturing some pages of books from Statistics Korea Library
The *Gangwon Statistical Yearbook*	1958 1961–1965 1967–1978	1958: a pdf file The rest: e-books from the Gangwon Province
Statistical yearbooks of counties under the control of Gangwon Province	1966	Gangneung: an e-book from the National Assembly Library Goseong, Sokcho, Jeongseon, Cheorwon, Chunseong, Chuncheon: jpg files capturing some pages of books from Statistics Korea Library
The *Chungbuk Statistical Yearbook*	1961–1965 1967–1978	1961, 1963, 1968–1969: jpg files capturing some pages of books from the Statistics Korea Library The rest: e-books from the National Archives of Korea
Statistical yearbooks of Counties under the control of Chungbuk Province	1966	Goesan, Danyang, Boeun, Yeongdong, Okcheon, Eumseong, Jecheon, Jungwon, Jincheon, Cheongwon, Cheongju, Chungju: jpg files capturing some pages of books from Statistics Korea Library
The *Chungnam Statistical Yearbook*	1955–1958 1960–1965 1967–1978	Pdf files
Statistical yearbooks of counties under the control of Chungnam Province	1966	Gongju, Geumsan, Nonsan, Daejeon, Seosan: jpg files capturing pages of books from Statistics Korea Library

Table 6.3 (continued)

Data Sources	Publication Year	Form
The *Jeonbuk Statistical Yearbook*	1957–1958 1960 1962–1965 1967–1978	1957–1958, 1960: e-books from the National Assembly Library 1962–1965, 1967: e-books from the National Archives of Korea The rest: pdf files
Statistical yearbooks of counties under the control of Jeonbuk Province	1966	Gunsan, Gimje, Namwon, Muju, Buan, Okgu, Wanju, Iri, Iksan, Imsil, Jangsu, Jeongeup, Jinan: jpg files capturing some pages of books from the Statistics Korea Library Sunchang, Jeonju: e-books from the National Assembly Library
The *Jeonnam Statistical Yearbook*	1954–1955 1959 1963 1965 1967–1978	1954–1955, 1959: jpg files capturing pages of books from the National Assembly Library 1963: jpg files capturing some pages of books from the Suwon Library of Seoul National University 1965, 1967–1968: jpg files capturing pages of books from the Statistics Korea Library The rest: e-books from the National Archives of Korea
Statistical yearbooks of counties under the control of Jeonnam Province	1961	Mokpo: jpg files capturing pages of books from the Statistics Korea Library
	1964	Muan, Yeocheon, Yeonggwang, Jangheung: jpg files capturing pages of books from the Statistics Korea Library
	1966	Gwangsan, Gwangyang, Damyang, Muan, Suncheon, Yeocheon, Yeonggwang, Wando, Jangheung, Jindo, Hampyeong, Haenam: jpg files capturing pages of books from the Statistics Korea Library
The *Gyeongbuk Statistical Yearbook*	1963–1965 1967–1978	1963, 1964: jpg files capturing pages of books from the Statistics Korea Library 1967: a pdf file. The rest: e-books in homepage of the National Archives of Korea
Statistical yearbooks of counties under the control of Gyeongbuk Province	1960	Pohang: jpg files capturing pages of books from the Statistics Korea Library
	1961	Daegu: jpg files capturing pages of books from the National Assembly Library Pohang: jpg files capturing pages of books from the Statistics Korea Library
	1962	Gyeongsan, Yeongju, Pohang: jpg files capturing pages of books from the Statistics Korea Library
	1966	Gyeongsan, Goryeong, Gunwi, Gimcheon, Dalseong, Bonghwa, Seongju, Andong, Yeongyang, Yeongil, Yeongju, Ulleung, Wolseong, Cheongsong: jpg files capturing pages of books from the Statistics Korea Library

Table 6.3 (continued)

Data Sources	Publication Year	Form
The *Gyeongnam Statistical Yearbook*	1961 1963–1965 1967–1978	1963: jpg files capturing pages of books from the Suwon Library of Seoul National University The rest: e-books from the National Archives of Korea
Statistical yearbooks of counties under the control of Gyeongnam Province	1958	Masan: an e-book from the National Assembly Library
	1966	Geoje, Geochang, Namhae, Sacheon, Sancheong, Ulsan, Changnyeong, Changwon, Chungmu, Hadong, Haman: jpg files capturing pages of books from the Statistics Korea Library
The *Jeju Statistical Yearbook*	1961–1965 1967–1978	1961, 1963: jpg files capturing pages of books from the Statistics Korea Library 1962: jpg files capturing pages of books from the Suwon Library of Seoul National University The rest: e-books from the National Archives of Korea
Statistical yearbooks of counties under the control of Jeju Province	1966	Namjeju, Bukjeju, Jejusi: jpg files capturing pages of books from the Statistics Korea Library
Others		The *Statistical Path of Gangwon* (1993), the *50 Years of Wonju in the Sight of statistics* (2005), the *Statistical Path of Chungbuk* (1996), the *50 Years of Daejeon in the sight of Statistics* (1999): jpg files capturing pages of books from the Statistics Korea Library

I selectively inputted the statistics on land area, population, and agriculture, including livestock, which are highly crucial for our empirical analyses to construct data on agricultural productions and nutritional availability by year, province, and county. Country-wide data by year were created by adding province level data of the same years. The *Korea Statistical Yearbook* and *Food, Agriculture, Forestry and Fisheries Statistical Yearbook* were used as secondary sources to input country-wide and province-specific statistics that are missing from provincial or county statistical yearbooks. Table 6.5 introduces the variables on agricultural productions and nutritional availability that were inputted to our data set.

The land areas and agricultural outputs are originally reported in various units that were traditionally used in South Korea. I converted these into meter-units that are currently used. Thereafter, I converted the physical quantities of agricultural outputs into the magnitudes of calories and particular nutrients. In this process, I used the information on calorie

Table 6.4
Information in Statistical Yearbooks Related to Land, Population, and Agriculture

Category	Contents
Land area	Location Land area by county Land area by land type Land area by land owner (public/ private)
Population	Growth of population House and population by county Population by sex Population by age and sex Population by education level Population by occupation Registered foreigner Movement of population
Agriculture	Number of farm house and farm population Food grain production: rice, barley and wheat, miscellaneous grains, pulse, potatoes, vegetables, fruits, special crops, medicinal plants, tobacco Farm environment: agricultural machines, chemicals, fertilizers Farm disaster Agricultural economy policy: agricultural cooperative federation, farmland improvements, New Community (*Saemaeul*) Movement, government purchase of food grains Livestock things: number of livestock heads by animal type, livestock slaughtered, infectious disease of livestock, veterinarians, improvements of livestock environment

and nutrition ingredient per 100 gram of a variety of foods reported in the Korean Food Composition Table (available on the website of the National Institute of Agricultural Sciences: koreanfood.rea.go.kr). Table 6.6 presents the calories and nutrition ingredients per 100 g of selected foods in the data set. Accordingly, I created county- and province-level variables on the availability of total calories, carbohydrates, protein, fats, calcium, phosphorus, iron, potassium, sodium, and vitamins A, B1, B2, B3, and C.

How accurate are these data on agricultural productions? Given that a few of these sources were produced over six decades ago when South Korea was a poor country recovering from the destruction caused by the war, questions arise about the credibility of the sources we relied upon (e.g., see Ko 2007 and Hwang et al. 2014). Agents conducting public statistical research at the time may lacked the proper skills and knowledge compared with current government employees. A few inconsistencies may arise in the methods of producing statistics across different years

68 농 업

63. 두 류 수 확 고

단위 : 면적…단보, 단수…kg, 수량…M/T

항 목	총계 Grand total			대두 Bay bean			소두 Red bean			녹두 Grean bean		
	면적 Area	단수 Production per dan	수확량 Production	면적 Area	단수 Production per dan	수확량 Production	면적 Area	단수 Production per dan	수확량 Production	면적 Area	단수 Production per dan	수확량 Production
1965	7 291	75	543.2	4 816	83	402.0	826	63	61.8	169	48	8.1
1966	4 658	73	340.2	3 379	77	260.8	443	61	27.1	138	53	7.3
1967	3 610	74	263.7	2 934	79	225.9	374	58	21.8	83	54	4.6
1968	2 883	68	196.3	2 471	70	166.0	292	62	18.2	71	52	3.7
1969	**2 700**	**75**	**202.6**	**2 112**	**80**	**167.9**	**349**	**64**	**22.2**	**101**	**56**	**5.7**
종로	—	—	—	—	—	—	—	—	—	—	—	—
중구	—	—	—	—	—	—	—	—	—	—	—	—
동대문	56	70	3.9	41	69	2.9	14	67	0.9	—	—	—
성동	954	70	67.7	691	74	51.2	179	65	11.7	36	59	2.1
성북	31	72	2.2	25	75	1.8	3	58	0.2	3	54	0.2
서대문	72	48	3.4	9	115	1.0	3	130	0.4	2	130	0.3
마포	—	—	—	—	—	—	—	—	—	—	—	—
용산	—	—	—	—	—	—	—	—	—	—	—	—
영등포	1 587	79	125.4	1 346	82	111.0	150	60	9.0	60	52	3.1

자료 : 산업국 농정과

64. 잡 곡 수 확 고 (정곡)

단위 : 면적…단보, 단수 : kg, 수량…M/T

항 목	총계 Grand total			조 Millet			수수 Sorghuom			옥
	면적	단수 Production per dan	수확량 Production	면적 Area	단수 Production per dan	수확량 Production	면적 Area	단수 Production per dan	수확량 Production	면적 Area
1965	2 273	78	176.9	996	86	86.0	438	84	36.7	206
1966	1 334	69	91.4	502	70	34.9	469	73	34.1	141
1967	699	81	56.6	178	83	41.7	267	92	24.5	117
1968	564	68	38.1	167	64	10.7	176	72	12.7	105
1969	**523**	**69**	**36.1**	**75**	**74**	**5.5**	**242**	**68**	**16.5**	**144**
종로	—	—	—	—	—	—	—	—	—	—
중구	—	—	—	—	—	—	—	—	—	—
동대문	18	85	1.5	1	100	0.1	—	—	—	17
성동	228	72	16.4	43	83	3.5	72	73	5.3	57
성북	21	66	1.4	—	—	—	3	59	0.2	18
서대문	57	85	4.9	10	78	0.8	38	100	3.8	6
마포	—	—	—	—	—	—	—	—	—	—
용산	—	—	—	—	—	—	—	—	—	—
영등포	199	60	11.9	21	53	1.1	129	56	7.2	46

자료 : 산업국 농정과

Figure 6.2 | Sample Table Used for Inputting Data: Part of the *1969 Seoul Statistical Yearbook*

Table 6.5
Variables Inputted into Dataset on Agricultural Output and Nutritional Availability

Category	Contents	Unit
Year	Survey year	
Region	Entire nation, names of provinces and counties	
Land area	Land area by year and locality	m^2
Population	Total, male, female population by year and region Population by age interval and sex for each year and region	
Agriculture: Food grains	Farm population by year and region	
	Farm house by type of management of farm land for each year and region: Paddy field, upland (dry field), fruits, vegetables, special crops, slash-and-burn field, livestock, sericulture, bee-raising, horticulture, wage earner	
	Rice: cultivated area and output by year and region	m^2 and kg, respectively
	Barley and wheat: cultivated area and output by year and region -Barley, naked barley, wheat, rye	〃
	Miscellaneous grains: cultivated area and output by year and region -Foxtail millet (*jo*), barnyard millet (*Pi*), common millet (*Gijang*), sorghum (*susu*), corn, buck wheat (*memil*), oatmeal	〃
	Pulse: cultivated area and output by year and region -Soy bean, red bean, green been, kidney bean, pea, peanut	〃
	Potato and sweet potato: cultivated area and output by year and region	〃
	Vegetables: cultivated area and output by year and region -Radish, Chinese cabbage (*Baechu*), cabbage (*Yangbaechu*), sweet melon (*Chamoe*), cucumber, eggplant (*Gaji*), pumpkin, watermelon, tomato, red pepper (*Gochu*), welsh onion (*Pa*), garlic, spinach, onion, taro (*Toran*), water parsley (*Minari*), burdock (*Ueong*), carrot, ginger, strawberry, asparagus, lettuce (*Sangchu*), head lettuce (*Gyeolgusangchu*), crown daisy (*Ssukgat*), salary, Chinese leek (*Buchu*), cabbage lettuce (*Yangsangchu*), lotus root, pepper (*Pimang*), parsley, greenhouse melon, outdoor melon, seasoned cabbage (*Bomdong*), rakkyo, haruna, Chinese yam (*Ma*), curled mallow (*Auk*), beet greens (*Geundae*), bellflower root (*Doraji*), bourd (*Bak*)	〃
	Fruits: cultivated area and output by year and region -Apple, pear (*Bae*), Persimmon (*Gam*), grape, peach, plum (*Jadu*), apricot (*Salgu*), mandarin, pineapple, Korean cherry (*Aengdu*), cherry, Japanese apricot (*Maesil*), chestnut (*Bam*), jujube (*Daechu*), yuja, Japanese persimmon (*Dangam*), loquat (*Bipa*), quince (*Mogwa*), fig (*Muhwagwa*), pomegranate (*Seokryu*)	〃
Agriculture: livestock	Livestock breeding -Cattle, milk cow, beef cattle, horse, pig, goat, rabbit, chicken, duck, goose, dog, turkey, bee, sheep, deer, pheasant, hawk (*Mae*), donkey, mule	Unit (Bee: box)
	Livestock slaughtering -Cow, pig, chicken, horse, goat, dog, rabbit	Unit, kg

Note: Outputs of rice, barley and wheat, miscellaneous grains, pulse, potato, sweet potato were all weighed as polished grains.

Table 6.6

Calorie and Nutrition Ingredient per 100 g of Each Food in Agricultural Output and Nutritional Availability Dataset

Food	Detailed	Calorie (kcal)	Carbo-hydrate (g)	Protein (g)	Fat (g)	Calcium (mg)	Phosphorus (mg)	Iron (mg)	Kalium (mg)	Natrium (mg)	Vitamin A (RE)	Vitamin B1 (mg)	Vitamin B2 (mg)	Vitamin B3 (Niacin) (mg)	Vitamin C (mg)
Rice	White rice	363	79.5	6.4	0.4	7	87	1.3	170	8	1	0.23	0.02	1.2	0
Barley		352	78	10	1	24	129	1.7	270	18	0	0.27	0.07	1.4	0
Naked barley		347	77.7	9.9	0.6	19	72	1.4	270	5	0	0.41	0.04	0.9	0
Wheat		333	75.8	10.6	1	52	254	4.7	538	17	0	0.43	0.12	2.4	0
Rye	Whole rye	334	70.7	15.9	1.5	10	378	6.4	501	2	0	0.26	0.16	1.8	0
Foxtain millet	Nonglutinous millet	386	76	9.7	4.2	11	184	2.3	368	3	0	0.21	0.09	1.5	0
Barnyard millet		367	72.4	9.7	3.7	7	280	1.6	240	3	0	0.05	0.03	2	0
Common millet		357	74.6	11.2	1.4	14	226	2.8	233	6	0	0.42	0.09	2	0
Sorghum		364	74.1	9.5	2.6	14	290	2.4	410	2	0	0.1	0.03	3	0
Corn	Glutinous corn	142	29.4	4.9	1.2	21	131	2.2	370	1	9	0.25	0.11	2.6	0
Buck wheat		374	74.7	11.5	2.3	18	308	2.6	477	14	17	0.46	0.26	1.2	0
Soy bean		420	30.7	36.2	17.8	245	620	6.5	1340	2	0	0.53	0.28	2.2	0
Red bean		356	68.4	19.3	0.1	82	424	5.6	1180	1	0	0.54	0.14	3.3	0
Green bean		354	62	22.3	1.5	100	335	5.5	1323	2	12	0.4	0.14	2	0
Kidney bean		169	29.2	10	1.2	62	97	3.7	732	5	0	0.48	0.11	1.6	4
Pea		79	13.2	5.8	0.3	25	134	1.6	356	13	1	0.01	0.09	0.8	12
Peanut		568	26	24.5	45.1	68	409	6.7	898	7	5	0.4	0.1	3	6
Potato		63	13.9	2.4	0	14	117	4.2	556	21	1	0.26	0.04	0.4	8
Sweet potato		131	31.2	1.4	0.2	24	54	0.5	429	15	19	0.06	0.05	0.7	25
radish	*Joseon* radish, root	21	4.6	1	0.1	26	38	2.3	257	43	0	0.11	0.03	0.5	15
Chinese cabbage		12	2.7	1.1	0	29	18	0.5	222	15	1	0.2	0.03	0.4	10
Cabbage		20	4.4	1.4	0.1	31	29	0.5	206	16	24	0.07	0.01	0.4	9

Table 6.6 (continued)

Food	Detailed	Calorie (kcal)	Carbo-hydrate (g)	Protein (g)	Fat (g)	Calcium (mg)	Phosphorus (mg)	Iron (mg)	Kalium (mg)	Natrium (mg)	Vitamin A (RE)	Vitamin B1 (mg)	Vitamin B2 (mg)	Vitamin B3 (Niacin) (mg)	Vitamin C (mg)
Sweet melon		38	7.5	2.2	0.4	6	79	0.3	663	10	6	0.07	0.03	0.6	21
Cucumber	Native	11	2.3	0.8	0.1	26	33	0.2	162	5	30	0.03	0.03	0.2	10
Eggplant		17	4	0.8	0.1	18	24	0.2	189	0	63	0.18	0.03	0.4	2
Pumpkin	Green pumpkin	26	5.6	0.9	0.1	30	36	0.4	215	17	34	0.16	0.02	0.4	9
Watermelon		32	8.1	0.8	0	5	14	0.5	169	1	31	0.06	0.01	0.3	0
Tomato		18	4.5	0.8	0	6	12	0.5	196	16	12	0.04	0.01	0.5	12
Red pepper	Dried	300	50.6	11	11	58	230	6.8	2930	56	4623	0.3	1.1	12.5	26
Welsh onion		29	6.7	1.2	0.2	25	26	1	239	17	1	0.02	0.04	0.3	11
Garlic	Green garlic	40	7.6	2.7	0.2	48	79	11	435	30	21	0.3	0.11	0.5	48
Spinach		33	6	3.1	0.5	40	29	2.6	502	54	479	0.12	0.34	0.5	60
Onion		36	8.4	1	0.1	16	30	0.4	144	2	0	0.04	0.01	0.1	8
Carrot		37	8.6	1.1	0.1	40	38	0.7	395	30	1270	0.06	0.05	0.8	8
Apple	*Busa*	49	13.1	0.2	0.1	6	9	0.3	146	16	1	0.05	0.03	0.5	48
Pear	*Singo*	41	10.9	0.3	0.1	2	11	0.2	171	3	0	0.02	0.01	0.1	4
Persimmon	*Daebong*	70	18.9	0.6	0	18	23	3.6	214	2	40	0.06	0.07	0.5	18
Grape	Campbell early	46	12.2	0.5	0.1	5	13	0.2	165	0	2	0.06	0.01	0.2	0
Peach	White peach	36	9.1	0.6	0.1	5	19	0.1	190	2	0	0.03	0.02	0.7	0
Mandarin	Native	39	9.9	0.7	0.1	13	11	0	173	11	1	0.13	0.04	0.4	44
Beef	Native, lean meat, uncooked	190	0.6	19.3	11.3	14	154	3.6	277	259	4	0.06	0.21	4.1	0
Pork	Lean meat, uncooked	241	0.4	17.8	17.5	5	179	2.1	51	17	4	0.78	0.19	4.5	0

Source: The 8th Revision of the Standard Food Composition Table (Published in 2013).

and regions.[4]

Nevertheless, I believe that the quality of the data set on agricultural productions is comparable with that of other historical data. I attempted to determine and correct errors in the sources. For example, I crosschecked among different sources providing similar statistics, discovered typos, and differentiated between 0 and missing values. I also analyzed if the data reveal any discontinuous annual changes that cannot be explained by fluctuations in agricultural productions (e.g., natural disasters or poor crop yields). The results of these analyses suggest the quality and credibility of the data. Although constrained by insufficient resources and manpower, the central and local authorities appear to have exerted effort to produce accurate and consistent statistics that were crucial for planning and implementing national and regional policies. At the very least, the records I utilized are the most reliable sources of local food productions that are currently available. For these reasons, I cautiously claim that the data can provide reasonably reliable estimates of local food availability in South Korea from 1950 to 1980.

6.3. Methods

6.3.1. Measuring Nutritional Status during Growth Periods

Adult stature is associated with the quantity and quality of diet during periods of human growth and other environmental factors, such as exposure to disease. Two growth periods are particularly important for determining adult height: early childhood from conception to 2 years and early adolescence before the onset of puberty. For boys, the second growth spurt occurs between the ages 12 and 16, whereas growth spurt begins early for girls (Abbassi 1998). The crucial period when adult height is determined is the first growth period in early childhood. The

4 For instance, the administrative investigation method that had been used until 1974 was replaced by the sample survey method in 1975, thereby possibly causing discontinuity.

second growth period provides an opportunity for "catch-up growth," which is defined as a more rapid growth than normal for age that follows a period of retardation in early growth. Catch-up growth is generally accepted to be insufficient to completely compensate for deficiencies in early childhood (Perkins et al. 2016). To investigate the association between nutrition and height, I estimated the measures of nutritional intakes separately for two crucial periods of human growth: the first four years in early childhood from conception to age 3 and the five years in early adolescence from age 12 to age 16.

At present, the available data prevent me from connecting the adult height of a person to his or her detailed dietary history during growth. Previous studies inferred the amount of nutritional intakes from the available data on food productions in a particular country or region to establish the relationship between nutritional status and previous health outcomes. Lindert (1994) estimated the per capita food consumption in the UK from 1700 to 1850 by combining the estimates of food productions in England and Wales and statistics on the UK's imports and exports of food items. Floud et al. (2011) estimated the average number of calories for consumption per capita per day in England and Wales from 1700 to 1913 based on crop yields estimated by other scholars. Haines et al. (2003) utilized county-level statistics on farm outputs reported in the US agricultural census and computed the calories and protein productions per adult equivalent per day in each county in the US in the mid-19th century. These studies used the estimates of food consumption as measures of the standard of living and determinants of health outcomes, such as height and mortality.

Following the spirit of previous studies, I inferred nutritional intakes of the conscripts in our sample from the information on food productions in the locality (either county or province) where they lived in early childhood and adolescence. In particular, I estimated the total calories and amounts of major nutrients (including protein, fats, and carbohydrates) for the years covering early childhood (from conception to age 3) and early adolescence (from age 12 to age 16). The county-level statistics on agricultural productions are regularly available only from 1960. Thus, I was unable to obtain county-level measures of nutritional availability in early childhood to match to our conscript sample born from 1946 to 1950. I managed to obtain provincial data on agricultural productions from 1950 on a regular basis. I used these sources to estimate the provincial nutritional availability in early childhood for the individuals born from 1951 to 1957. County-level variables pertaining to nutritional availability in early adolescence are computed for the entire 1946–1957 birth cohorts.

Nutritional requirements differ by gender and age. For example, Fogel (1993) estimated that girls aged 5–9 require two-thirds of the calories needed by males aged 20–39. Given the considerable regional variations in population composition, per capita productions may be misleading measures of true local nutritional availability. Hence, I converted the county or provincial population into adult (prime-age: 20–39) male equivalent population using the estimated average calorie consumption of each age–gender group as a proportion of that of males aged 20–39 (Fogel 1993, p. 9). In the preceding example, a girl aged 5–9 is counted as a 0.6667 adult male. Age- and gender-specific population of each county and province was used for this computation.

Using the aforementioned calories or amounts of nutrients per adult male equivalent population as an index of food availability implicitly assumes that a person's diet is strongly influenced by the size of locally produced nutrients. However, nutrients can be purchased from other regions if insufficiently produced locally. In particular, urban areas are typically net importers of nutrients even in the past when agricultural markets were not considerably integrated. The size of nutritional production per adult equivalent should be extremely low in large cities, such as Seoul and Busan, where only a small fraction of residents are food producers. Arguably, the market for nutrients in mid-20th century South Korea was likely more tightly integrated than the US agricultural market in the mid-19th-century, when the conventional measure of local nutritional availability was applied (Haines et al. 2003).

I circumvented this problem in the following methods. First, I used calories and amounts of major nutrients per farm household male equivalent population (instead of the entire adult male equivalent population) in each county or province as our primary measure of local nutritional availability. Second, I used several alternative subsamples, the diet of whom was likely influenced by local food productions differently. These subsamples include (a) individuals from counties with their nutritional productions per farm household population above a minimum threshold, (b) men from rural counties, and (c) children of farmers in rural counties. These methods are expected to enable me to reduce the problem of understating food availability in large cities. The size of food production per farm household could be regarded as a crude index of agricultural productivity as well as nutritional availability in the locality. If locally produced nutrients were exported to other regions, then rural counties with a high agricultural productivity could still benefit from increased incomes. In summary, my basic assumption is that an increase in food production per standardized farm household population in a locality improves the nutritional status of residents either through increased food availability or increased income.[5]

Table 6.7 explains the measures of nutritional availability. Proxy variables indicating food availability in fetus and infancy include the average productions of calories (calories, infancy), protein (protein, infancy), fat (fat, infancy), and carbohydrates (carbohydrates, infancy) for 4 years (from the year of birth −1 to the year of birth + 2) in the province of residence per farm household adult male equivalent per day. Similarly, the proxy variables for food availability in adolescence include the average productions of calories (calories, adolescence), protein (protein, adolescence), fat (fat, adolescence), and carbohydrates (carbohydrates, adolescence) for 5 years (from age 12 to 16) in the county of residence per farm household adult male equivalent per day. Calories and the three major nutrients per adult male equivalent (where the number of the entire population was applied instead of the number of farm household population) were also employed in our analyses for robustness check.

6.3.2. Other Explanatory Variables

In addition to access to food, environmental factors, such as prevalence of diseases and sanitary conditions, are important determinants of adult height. Previous historical studies suggest that population and urbanization were closely related to considerably short stature and high mortality in the US, the UK, and other advanced countries until the early 20th century (Fogel 1991; Wilson and Pope 2003; Haines et al. 2003; Cain and Hong

5 My data sources do not provide age- and gender-specific farm household population for each county. Thus, a standardized farm household population of a county was estimated by multiplying farm household population in the county by the ratio of the adult male equivalent to the total population in the county. I assumed that the age and gender composition of the farm household population in a county follows that of its entire population.

Table 6.7
Definition of Variable

Variable	Definition
Height	Height at age 20 (in centimeter)
Food availability in fetus & infancy	
Calories, Infancy	Average calorie production for 4 years (from prenatal period to age 2) in the province of residence (1000s of kcals per farm household adult male equivalent per day).
Protein, Infancy	Average protein production for 4 years (from prenatal period to age 2) in the province of residence (100s of grams per farm household adult male equivalent per day).
Fat, Infancy	Average fat production for 4 years (from prenatal period to age 2) in the state of residence (100s of grams per farm household adult male equivalent per day).
Carb, Infancy	Average carbohydrate production for 4 years (from prenatal period to age 2) in the state of residence (100s of grams per farm household adult male equivalent per day).
Food availability in adolescence	
Calories, Adolescence	Average calorie production for 5 years (from age 12 to age 16) in the county of residence (1000s of kcals per farm household adult male equivalent per day).
Protein, Adolescence	Average protein production for 5 years (from age 12 to age 16) in the county of residence (100s of grams per farm household adult male equivalent per day).
Fat, Adolescence	Average fat production for 5 years (from age 12 to age 16) in the county of residence (100s of grams per farm household adult male equivalent per day).
Carb, Adolescence	Average carbohydrate production for 5 years (from age 12 to age 16) in the county of residence (100s of grams per farm household adult male equivalent per day).
Environmental characteristics	
Population density	Population (100s of persons) per 1 square kilometers in the county of residence at age 14.
Nonfarm population share	The share of nonfarm population (percent) in the county of residence at age 14.
Seasonality of birth	
First quarter	Equals 1 if born from January to March.
Second quarter	Equals 1 if born from April to June.
Third quarter	Equals 1 if born from July to September.
Fourth quarter	Equals 1 if born from October to December.
Family size	
Number of family 1–3	Equals 1 if two or less family members are reported.

Table 6.7 (continued)

Variable	Definition
Number of family 4–6	Equals 1 if three to five family members are reported.
Number of family 7 or more	Equals 1 if six family members are reported.
Father's occupation	
Professional	Equals 1 if father had a professional or managerial job.
Clerical	Equals 1 if father had a semi-professional or clerical job.
Service	Equals 1 if father had a service job.
Farming	Equals 1 if father's occupation was farmer.
Manual	Equals 1 if father had a manual job.
No job reported	Equals 1 if father's job is not reported.
Father absent	Equals 1 if father was absent.

2009). For example, in the mid-19th century US, residents in rural areas stood 3.3 cm taller than city dwellers. The advantages of living in the countryside in the past were generally attributed to considerable isolation from other people, thereby reducing the chances of exposure to infectious diseases and improved access to high-quality foods. Moreover, increased pollution caused by industrialization and inflow of city-bound migrants and policy failures in providing proper public health measures and additional housing in the early stage of urbanization are blamed for the highly unhealthy living conditions in urban areas in the past. Whether this is the case in South Korea in the 1950s and 1960s is unclear. Given the potential positive aspects of urbanization, such as high wages and improved access to markets and medical services, it is an empirical question how urbanization and industrialization were associated with the heights of South Koreans born in the mid-20th century. I included the following two variables pertaining to local environmental characteristics: population density (100s of persons per one square kilometer) and percentage of non-farm population in the county where the conscript lived at age 14.

The information on conscripts and their family members kept in military records enables the inclusion of characteristics that affected their early life. First, dummy variables indicating the season of birth were constructed based on each conscript's date of birth. Previous studies have established that the season of birth is significantly related to later outcomes, including adult height, perhaps due to seasonal variations in in-utero conditions, such as nutrition and maternal exposure to disease. In general, individuals born in the winter/spring in the Northern Hemisphere are significantly taller than the average of their birth cohort, whereas those born in the final three months of the year are significantly shorter (McGrath et al. 2006; Tanaka et al. 2007). My analyses classified seasons of birth into four quarters: January to March, April to June, July to September, and October to December.

Second, family size was considered a potential determinant of within-family allocation of nutrients. Previous studies suggest that numerous family members, particularly siblings, tend to reduce parental investments in children (Conley and Glauber 2006; Lee, Jungmin 2008). The format of the Korean Military Records hinders the determination of the precise family size or members or siblings. The table concerning family information has only six lines, thereby allowing up to six other family members to be reported. In selecting family members to be included, the parents and grandparents appear to be prioritized (if alive) followed by the siblings. Thus, a few siblings likely failed to be reported for conscripts from large families. For these reasons, the following categorical variables on family size were included in our analysis: one to three, four to six, and seven or above.

Korean Military Records provide a rare opportunity to connect a person's adult height to parental characteristics. I maximized this unusual feature of our data and included the father's occupation as an index of socioeconomic conditions during childhood and adolescence. Given that my data sources were created when the individuals in our sample were approximately age 20, many of their fathers were presumably dead or retired by the time the former was conscripted. Thus, a considerable proportion of conscripts did not provide information on their fathers. Given the importance of the household head in South Korea at the time, it is likely that the majority of them had lost their fathers. The father's occupation is not reported for approximately one-third of the individuals in the sample, although other paternal characteristics (e.g., relationship or age) are provided. No information is provided whether these fathers were out of the labor force or if their jobs were not reported. In the analyses, the father's occupation was classified into the following categories: professional, clerical, service, farming, manual, no job reported, and father absent.

Military records also provide the personal characteristics of conscripts. The most comprehensively reported characteristic is the conscripts' educational attainment, which is missing in only 0.5% of the sample. Children's education is a useful indicator of parental economic status or their investment in children. However, the causal relationship between education and height is not straightforward. Nutritional status in early childhood is generally accepted to exert influence on cognitive ability, school attendance, and academic performances. Case and Paxson (2008) suggested that height at age 16 is a marker of cognitive ability. Thus, inclusion of one's education in height regression is subject to a reverse causality problem. For this reason, I excluded education in our baseline regressions. Instead, education variable was employed only in robustness tests, where education is classified into five categories: primary school or below, middle school, high school, college or higher, and education missing.

6.3.3. Sample Selection

Table 6.8 compares the measures of food availability and other personal and family characteristics across six selected samples. A total of 17,833 conscripts in the sample were born between 1946 and 1957 and whose date of birth is completely recorded. This sample is defined as the full sample (Col. 1). Of these men, height was successfully identified for 16,838 individuals (Col. 2). Major sample losses also occurred when selecting individuals with information on the county of residence. A total of 13,034 persons survived this selection process. The failure to identify height or county of residence generally resulted from the poor conditions of the original carded military records. The most important predictor of the probability that height or county of residence is unidentified is the year of conscription. Accordingly, the earlier the records produced, the higher the probability of failure.

I selected additional subsamples for regression analyses. Variables on nutritional availability could not be computed in a few counties. I also excluded counties with limited agricultural productions (average calorie production per farm household adult male equivalent per day was below 1,000 kcals in adolescence) and those with extremely high productions (average calorie production per farm household adult male equivalent per day exceeded 20,000 kcals in adolescence). Approximately 2,500 men who lived in those counties between age 12 and 16 were excluded from the sample, thereby leaving me with 11,508 individuals (Col. 3).

Table 6.8
Comparison of Selected Samples

	(1) Full Sample	(2) Information on height	(3) Height + County (nutrition in adolescence)
Measure of net nutritional status			
Height (centimeter)		166.446	166.408
Food availability in fetus & infancy			
Calories (1000s of kcal)			
Protein (100s of grams)			
Fat (100s of grams)			
Carbohydrate (100s of grams)			
Food availability in adolescence			
Calories (1000s of kcal)			4.380
Protein (100s of grams)			1.211
Fat (100s of grams)			0.270
Carbohydrate (100s of grams)			8.987
Environmental characteristics			
Population density (100s/km^2)			20.298
Nonfarm population share (%)			45.661
Seasonality of birth (proportion)			
First quarter	0.286	0.284	0.284
Second quarter	0.230	0.231	0.232
Third quarter	0.242	0.242	0.238
Fourth quarter	0.242	0.242	0.246
Family size (proportion)			
Number of family 1–3	0.096	0.092	0.087
Number of family 4–6	0.609	0.611	0.610
Number of family 7 or more	0.295	0.297	0.303
Father's occupation (proportion)			
Professional	0.007	0.007	0.006
Clerical	0.024	0.024	0.022
Service	0.005	0.005	0.005
Farming	0.391	0.389	0.415
Manual	0.023	0.023	0.022
No job reported	0.341	0.343	0.328
Father absent	0.204	0.204	0.328
Own education (proportion)			
Primary school or less	0.239	0.242	0.254
Middle school	0.282	0.283	0.287
High school	0.363	0.363	0.355
College	0.112	0.108	0.101
Education missing	0.004	0.004	0.003
Number	17833	16838	11508

Table 6.8 (continued)

	(4) Rural counties	(5) Rural counties, 1951–1957 cohorts	(6) Farmer's sons in rural counties, 1951–1957 cohorts
Measure of net nutritional status			
Height (centimeter)	166.338	166.656	166.731
Food availability in fetus & infancy			
Calories (1000s of kcal)		2.811	2.880
Protein (100s of grams)		0.698	0.714
Fat (100s of grams)		0.113	0.115
Carbohydrate (100s of grams)		5.958	6.107
Food availability in adolescence			
Calories (1000s of kcal)	4.662	5.090	5.132
Protein (100s of grams)	1.146	1.257	1.248
Fat (100s of grams)	0.187	0.207	0.195
Carbohydrate (100s of grams)	9.921	10.832	10.960
Environmental characteristics			
Population density (100s/km^2)	4.663	5.155	3.181
Nonfarm population share (%)	25.922	26.240	22.490
Seasonality of birth (proportion)			
First quarter	0.287	0.284	0.290
Second quarter	0.234	0.235	0.229
Third quarter	0.235	0.234	0.238
Fourth quarter	0.244	0.247	0.243
Family size (proportion)			
Number of family 1–3	0.077	0.064	0.023
Number of family 4–6	0.601	0.614	0.600
Number of family 7 or more	0.321	0.322	0.377
Father's occupation (proportion)			
Professional	0.004	0.004	0
Cleric	0.016	0.018	0
Service	0.003	0.003	0
Farming	0.512	0.501	1.000
Manual	0.013	0.015	0
No job reported	0.260	0.279	0
Father absent	0.189	0.177	0
Own education (proportion)			
Primary school or less	0.295	0.281	0.299
Middle school	0.306	0.307	0.323
High school	0.329	0.343	0.329
College	0.067	0.067	0.048
Education unreported	0.003	0.001	0.001
Number	7850	5560	2784

Source. Sample of Korean Military Records matched with province- and county-level data on nutrition.

This sample with information on height and county-level information on nutritional availability in adolescence is not substantially different from the full sample in terms of personal and family characteristics. However, the latter has slightly limited education and likely to include the fathers' sons.

I further restricted the sample to 7,850 individuals from rural counties with information on height and nutritional availability in adolescence (Col. 4). The excluded urban areas are the districts in metropolitan cities, including Seoul, Busan, Incheon, Daejeon, Gwangju, and Daegu. Given that large cities were excluded, this sample unsurprisingly presents a substantially lower population density and higher nonfarm population share compared with the complete sample. In addition, family size is larger, fathers are more likely to be farmers, and schooling is lower in the sample compared with the complete sample. I made an additional selection to have our baseline sample of 5,560 men from rural counties who were born between 1951 and 1957 (Col. 5). The 1946 to 1950 birth cohorts were excluded to include nutritional availability in infancy and adolescence in regressions because the variables on nutritional productions in infancy are available only for the 1951 to 1957 birth cohorts. Lastly, I used a subsample of 2,784 persons from rural counties who were born between 1951 and 1957 and whose fathers were farmers (Col. 6). I used this sample in the analysis to account for the fact that farmers' children were perhaps most strongly influenced by changes in nutritional production per farm household population.

Given the potential sample selection bias, the results from the subsamples may not represent the experiences of the entire conscript population, let alone the young male population at large. By contrast, the first three samples (Cols. 1 to 3) are generally similar with one another in terms of personal and family characteristics. The samples restricted to men from rural counties (Cols. 4 to 6) differ from the considerably large samples. However, except for the evident differences in several characteristics that are fully expected from the nature of the sample selection (e.g., low population density, nonfarm population share, and high percentage of persons whose fathers are farmers), the selected subsamples are reasonably comparable to the full sample in terms of height, nutritional availability, family size, and educational attainment. Figure 6.3 shows that the height changes across birth cohorts observed from three different samples (i.e., full sample, sample with county-level nutritional production is available, and rural county sample) are

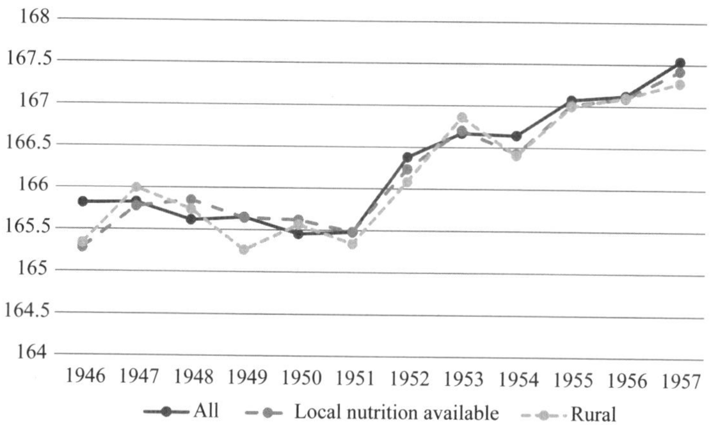

Figure 6.3 | Height at Conscription: Comparison of Different Samples

remarkably similar.

6.4. Summary

This chapter introduced the data and methods used in analyzing how nutritional availability affected physical growth and human capital accumulation in Korea. Rigorous research on these issues is often considerably hampered by limited appropriate data, particularly for the periods prior to the 1970s. To overcome the limitation, I collected new data from archival sources. First, I constructed a sample of military conscripts using South Korean military records collected from the Military Manpower Administration. Second, I constructed province- and county-level data on local nutritional availability from the statistical yearbooks published by each province and each county. By matching these sources, I estimated local nutritional availability in the time and place where each conscript spent his early childhood and adolescence. The amounts of calories and three major nutrients (i.e., protein, fats, and carbohydrates) per farm household adult equivalent in a given province or county were used as the primary measures of local nutritional availability.

CHAPTER 7

Nutrition and Human Capital Development 2: Results

7.1. Nutritional Availability and Height

7.1.1. Results of the Baseline Regressions with a Rural County Sample

My baseline regressions are based on a sample of 5,560 men from rural counties who were born between 1951 and 1957 and who have complete information on local nutritional availability in infancy and adolescence. I use this sample to estimate the following equation:

$$H_{i,j,c} = \beta_0 + \beta_1 N^{I}_{j,c} + \beta_2 N^{A}_{j,c} + \beta_3 Z_{j,c} + \beta_4 X_{i,j,c} + \varepsilon_{i,j,c} \quad \textbf{(7.1)}$$

where $H_{i,j,c}$ is the height of the *i*th person from the *j*th county and who belongs to the *c*th birth cohort; $N^{I}_{j,c}$ and $N^{A}_{j,c}$ represent the vectors of the variables on nutritional availability in infancy and adolescence, respectively; $Z_{j,c}$ is the vector of the variables on environmental conditions in the county of residence at age 14; $X_{i,j,c}$ are the variables on family and personal characteristics; and $\varepsilon_{i,j,c}$ is the error term. Standard errors were clustered at the county level.

Table 7.1 presents the results of the estimation of the four versions of

Table 7.1
Local Nutritional Availability and Height: 1951–1957 Birth Cohort in Rural Counties

Variable	(1) Calories	(2) Protein	(3) Fat	(4) Carbohydrate
Intercept	165.4625***	165.2796***	166.4755***	165.4818***
	(0.3999)	(0.4309)	(0.3309)	(0.3945)
Local Nutritional availability				
Nutrition, Infancy	0.2546**	1.3243***	1.7949	0.1186**
	(0.0995)	(0.4415)	(2.5847)	(0.0458)
Nutrition, Adolescence	0.1303**	0.5698***	1.5865*	0.0585**
	(0.0497)	(0.1941)	(0.9061)	(0.0226)
Local environment				
Population density	0.01689	0.0165	0.0120	0.0169
	(0.0121)	(0.0115)	(0.0113)	(0.0122)
Nonfarm population share	-0.0051	-0.0082	-0.0100	-0.0043
	(0.0084)	(0.0081)	(0.0070)	(0.0085)
Season of Birth				
First quarter	NI	NI	NI	NI
Second quarter	0.2235	0.2253	0.2134	0.2234
	(0.1791)	(0.1795)	(0.1773)	(0.1790)
Third quarter	-0.2126	-0.2019	-0.1925	-0.2141
	(0.1688)	(0.1682)	(0.1688)	(0.1689)
Fourth quarter	-0.3076	-0.3069	-0.3124	-0.3081
	(0.2109)	(0.2103)	(0.2113)	(0.2110)
Family size				
1 to 3	0.3611	0.3733	0.3368	0.3593
	(0.3377)	(0.3389)	(0.3400)	(0.3376)
4 to 6	NI	NI	NI	NI
7 or more	0.0169	0.0082	0.0115	0.0192
	(0.1494)	(0.1501)	(0.1516)	(0.1494)
Father's occupation				
Professional	-0.1198	-0.0932	-0.0897	-0.1262
	(0.9222)	(0.9256)	(0.9325)	(0.9211)
Clerical	1.0196**	1.0070**	1.0074**	1.0212**
	(0.4777)	(0.4787)	(0.4765)	(0.4774)
Service	-0.9528	-0.9629	-0.8128	-0.9545
	(1.6111)	(1.6141)	(1.6371)	(1.6100)
Farming	NI	NI	NI	NI
Manual	-1.2294**	-1.2309**	-1.2340**	-1.2296**
	(0.5973)	(0.5966)	(0.5923)	(0.5973)
No job	-0.2662	-0.2574	-0.2961*	-0.2667
	(0.1735)	(0.1730)	(0.1735)	(0.1736)
Father absent	-0.1025	-0.0935	-0.1079	-0.1044
	(0.2029)	(0.2026)	(0.2035)	(0.2030)
R-square	0.0075	0.0080	0.0051	0.0075
F-value	3.54***	3.75***	2.76***	3.53***
N	5560	5560	5560	5560

Note: Significance level. * 10%, ** 5%, *** 1%.

Equation 7.1, including the different types of nutrients, namely, calories (Col. 1), protein (Col. 2), fats (Col. 3), and carbohydrates (Col. 4). Except for fats, variables on nutritional availability are all positive and statistically significant. The estimated coefficients indicate a person who spent infancy in a province that produced calories per farm household population one standard deviation (i.e., 711 kcal) above the mean becomes 0.18 cm tall at age 20 if other factors are equal. One standard deviation high in protein (15.6 g) and carbohydrates (154.5 g) both during infancy increases adult height by 0.21 cm and 0.18 cm, respectively. The estimated coefficients for food availability in adolescence are smaller than those in infancy. However, the standard deviations for the former are larger than the latter. Consequently, the effects of one standard deviation change in nutritional variables in adolescence and in infancy are similar in magnitude. One standard deviation increase in calories (1.547), protein (0.386), fats (0.107), and carbohydrates (3.421) in the counties where conscripts spent their adolescence is associated with an increase in height at age 20 by 0.20, 0.22, 0.17, and 0.18 cm, respectively.

The population density in the county of residence at age 14 is positively related to adult height, whereas the effect of nonfarm population share on height is negative. The coefficients for these two environment variables are statistically insignificant. The estimated birth season effect is an anticipated one (positive for the second quarter and negative for the fourth quarter), but they are statistically insignificant. Men from families with three or fewer family members are approximately 0.35 cm taller than those with four to six family members. However, the effect of family size is statistically insignificant. Conscripts whose fathers were employed in a clerical job are approximately 1 cm taller than farmers' sons. Having a father engaged in a manual job decreases height by approximately 1.2 cm compared with children of farmers.

Table 7.2 presents the results from additional regressions based on alternative specifications. First, nutritional availability during each of the two stages of growth was included separately in the first two regressions (Panels A and B). Compared with the baseline results (Table 7.1), the effects of nutrition in adolescence (infancy) estimated with and without variables on nutrition in infancy (adolescence) are generally similar, although the magnitudes of the coefficients for nutritional variables increased slightly. This result suggests nutritional status in infancy and in adolescence perhaps independently affected adult height.

The relationship between nutritional availability and height may

Table 7.2
Local Nutritional Availability and Height: Alternative Specifications

Variable	(1) Calories	(2) Protein	(3) Fat	(4) Carbohydrate
(A) Infancy only				
Nutrition, Infancy	0.3280***	1.5530***	3.6797	0.1511***
	(0.0973)	(0.4321)	(2.5611)	(0.0448)
Other controls	Yes	Yes	Yes	Yes
R-square	0.0061	0.0063	0.0068	0.0090
F-value	3.74***	3.82***	6.21***	6.31***
N	5560	5560	5560	5560
(B) Adolescence only				
Nutrition, Adolescence	0.1610***	0.6570***	1.8159**	0.0725***
	(0.0508)	(0.2024)	(0.8880)	(0.0231)
Other controls	Yes	Yes	Yes	Yes
R-square	0.0064	0.0065	0.0050	0.0063
F-value	3.20***	3.34***	2959***	3.19***
N	5560	5560	5560	5560
(C) Categorical variable				
Second quartile, infancy	-0.1361	-0.0085	-0.0793	-0.1420
	(0.1939)	(0.2074)	(0.2553)	(0.1974)
Third quartile, infancy	0.3890*	0.4281**	0.1877	0.4730**
	(0.2182)	(0.1927)	(0.2309)	(0.2233)
Highest quartile, infancy	0.4047*	0.3408	0.5211**	0.3687*
	(0.2112)	(0.2104)	(0.2405)	(0.2127)
Second quartile, Adolescence	0.5211***	0.8108***	0.0375	0.3290*
	(0.1856)	(0.1780)	(0.2207)	(0.1825)
Third quartile, Adolescence	0.5359***	0.7013***	-0.1329	0.4851**
	(0.2010)	(0.1940)	(0.2077)	(0.2032)
Highest quartile, Adolescence	0.6296***	0.6380***	-0.0102	0.5823***
	(0.2015)	(0.1879)	(0.9636)	(0.2073)
Other controls	Yes	Yes	Yes	Yes
R-square	0.0095	0.0102	0.0059	0.0091
F-value	5.17***	3.95***	2.64***	3.07***
N	5560	5560	5560	5560
(D) Infancy / Adolescence				
Low / High	0.5187**	0.5848***	-0.2599	0.5519***
	(0.1986)	(0.2006)	(0.2218)	(0.2009)
High / Low	0.6755***	0.8314***	0.1971	0.7400***
	(0.2125)	(0.2178)	(0.2198)	(0.2088)
High / High	0.8511***	0.7044***	0.3129*	0.8847***
	(0.1990)	(0.1979)	(0.1782)	(0.1992)
Other controls	Yes	Yes	Yes	Yes
R-square	0.0084	0.0083	0.0055	0.0088
F-value	3.22***	3.10***	2.63***	3.27***
N	5560	5560	5560	5560

Note: Significance level. * 10%, ** 5%, *** 1%.

not be linear as implicitly assumed in baseline regressions. To consider such possibility, a dummy variable indicating each quartile of nutritional availability was included in place of nutrition variable measured in calories or grams (Panel C of Table 7.2). Results show discontinuous changes in heights at certain thresholds of nutritional availability: sharp increase in height between the second and third quartiles of nutrition in infancy and between the lowest and second quartiles of nutrition in adolescence. The estimated coefficients for the fourth quartile of nutrition in infancy are slightly smaller than those for the third quartile. This result suggests the positive effects of nutritional availability in early childhood on height largely captured the difference between individuals in the upper and lower halves in terms of nutritional availability. Similarly, the positive relationship between nutrition in adolescence and height could largely be accounted for by the sharp disparity between the lowest quartile and the rest.

Finally, I investigated how nutritional status during the two different growth periods jointly affected adult height. Therefore, I included dummy variables for four combinations of nutritional availability in infancy and adolescence, namely, low-low, low-high, high-low, and high-high in the regressions. The previous regression results (Panel C) suggest that lowering the nutritional availability below a certain threshold was particularly damaging to growth. Based on the regression results, the bottom 50% in terms of nutritional availability in infancy and the lowest quartile of nutrition in adolescence were classified into "low," and those above the thresholds were classified into "high."

Such results are reported in Panel D of Table 7.2. In addition, the estimated coefficients for calories and protein are compared visually across nutrition categories in Figure 7.1. Several features stand out from the results. With the exception of fat, conscripts who belonged to "high" either in infancy or in adolescence are at least 0.5 cm taller than those in the low-low category. Second, high-low individuals are taller than low-high people, confirming that nutrition in infancy is more critical for human growth than nutrition in adolescence. Finally, the marginal effect of changing nutritional status from "low" to "high" is larger in magnitude if nutritional availability in infancy was "low." This result manifests that nutritional intakes in infancy and in adolescence were substitutable. The substitutability between nutritional availability in the two growth periods is revealed more strongly for protein than for calories or carbohydrate. This result indicates remediation in late childhood in the

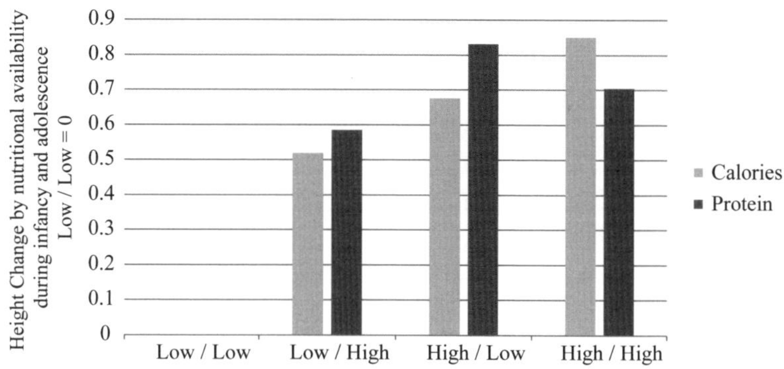

Figure 7.1 | Local Nutritional Availability during Infancy and Adolescence and Height Change (cm)

form of improved nutrition was more effective for individuals who had been poorly nourished in early childhood.

7.1.2. Additional Controls

I analyzed the robustness of the results by including additional controls to Equation 7.1. Table 7.3 summarizes the results. First, I added the Herfindahl indices of concentration of the sources of calories and three nutrients (i.e., rice, barley, and beef) in the county.[1] Doing so examined if the composition of nutritional sources, not just the quantity, had an influence. Panel A shows the Herfindahl indices of calories, fat, and carbohydrates in infancy and adolescence were negatively associated with height, but the results were uniformly insignificant. Only the Herfindahl indices for protein were positively related to height, but the results were statistically insignificant. Adding the concentration indices to the regressions did not change the coefficients of nutrition quantity variables.

Second, a direct measure of local disease environment was added

1 The Herfindahl index is defined as the sum of the squares of the shares of the sources of nutrition. If a given nutrient came entirely from a single source (perfect concentration), then Herfindahl index would equal one. Conversely, if the shares of the sources are equal, the index would equal zero.

Table 7.3
Local Nutritional Availability and Height: Additional Controls

Variable	(1) Calories	(2) Protein	(3) Fat	(4) Carbohydrate
(A) Variety of sources (HI)				
Nutrition, Infancy	0.2983**	1.1501**	2.1780	0.1333**
	(0.1234)	(0.4993)	(2.7865)	(0.0562)
Nutrition, Adolescence	0.1474**	0.8656***	1.6374	0.0621**
	(0.0599)	(0.2983)	(1.0771)	(0.0264)
HI, Infancy	-1.8037	1.2664	-0.5522	-1.2606
	(1.7034)	(1.1713)	(1.3210)	(1.5826)
HI, Adolescence	-0.0551	1.0507	-0.4322	-0.1367
	(0.5452)	(0.6530)	(0.8840)	(0.5622)
Other controls	Yes	Yes	Yes	Yes
R-square	0.0078	0.0089	0.0052	0.0076
F-value	3.29***	3.35***	2.82***	3.32***
N	5560	5560	5560	5560
(B) Sample with information on local disease mortality				
Nutrition, Infancy	0.1055	0.6238	-1.3216	0.0520
	(0.1326)	(0.6238)	(3.5939)	(0.0610)
Nutrition, Adolescence	0.1575**	0.5689**	1.8257	0.0725**
	(0.0736)	(0.2772)	(1.4284)	(0.0338)
Other controls	Yes	Yes	Yes	Yes
R-square	0.0106	0.0105	0.0084	0.0107
F-value	2.11**	2.16**	1.95**	2.10**
N	3025	3025	3025	3025
(C) Local disease mortality				
Nutrition, Infancy	0.1036	0.6290	-1.0079	0.0509
	(0.4357)	(0.5872)	(3.6830)	(0.0609)
Nutrition, Adolescence	0.1612**	0.6135**	1.9076	0.0739**
	(0.0743)	(0.2787)	(1.4357)	(0.0341)
Local disease mortality	0.0025	0.0027	0.0022	0.0023
	(0.0071)	(0.0071)	(0.0075)	(0.0071)
Other controls	Yes	Yes	Yes	Yes
R-square	0.0107	0.0106	0.0085	0.0107
F-value	1.97**	2.02**	1.84**	1.97**
N	3025	3025	3025	3025
(D) Own education				
Nutrition, Infancy	0.2305**	1.1955***	1.7589	0.1070**
	(0.0977)	(0.4375)	(2.6168)	(0.0449)
Nutrition, Adolescence	0.0994**	0.4731**	1.5002*	0.0440*
	(0.0497)	(0.1955)	(0.9050)	(0.0226)
Middle school	0.8319***	0.8309***	0.8698***	0.8314***
	(0.1706)	(0.1707)	(0.1702)	(0.1705)
High school	1.4880***	1.4896***	1.5366***	1.4871***
	(0.1724)	(0.1721)	(0.1714)	(0.1724)
College	1.9143***	1.9163***	1.9549***	1.9147***
	(0.2998)	(0.2994)	(0.2996)	(0.2998)
Education Missing	3.1830*	3.1976*	3.1837	3.1774*
	(1.9007)	(1.8995)	(1.9253)	(1.9007)

Table 7.3 (continued)

Variable	(1) Calories	(2) Protein	(3) Fat	(4) Carbohydrate
Other controls	Yes	Yes	Yes	Yes
R-square	0.0227	0.0232	0.0212	0.0226
F-value	10.49***	10.91***	9.57***	10.44***
N	5560	5560	5560	5560
(E) Education & Province				
Nutrition, Infancy	0.7592***	3.0234***	7.8572*	0.3570***
	(0.1595)	(0.7187)	(2.6168)	(0.0729)
Nutrition, Adolescence	0.1187	0.4278	1.7740	0.0535
	(0.0822)	(0.3591)	(1.4385)	(0.0370)
Education	Yes	Yes	Yes	Yes
Other controls	Yes	Yes	Yes	Yes
Province dummy	Yes	Yes	Yes	Yes
R-square	0.0227	0.0282	0.0240	0.0292
F-value	10.49***	10.04***	8.61***	10.48***
N	5560	5560	5560	5560

Note: Significance level. * 10%, ** 5%, *** 1%.

to the regressions. The degree of exposure to disease in growing ages is regarded as a major determinant of adult height (Wilson and Pope 2003; Haines et al. 2003). Prior to 1970, when the death registration data began to be provided, reliable local mortality statistics were unavailable. However, the number of deaths caused by type-1 infectious diseases (typhoid, diphtheria, dysentery, encephalitis, cholera, paratyphoid fever, and typhus) are reported in statistical yearbooks of selected counties and years. Using these sources, I computed the average disease mortality rate (the number of type-1 infectious disease deaths per 100,000) in the county where the conscripts lived from 12 to 14 years old. I created a variable for about 54% of the baseline sample because of the imperfect coverage.

I first examined the influences of sample selection by estimating the baseline model with the subsample for whom the local disease mortality is available. The coefficients of nutrition variables in infancy diminished in magnitude and lost statistical significance as a consequence of the sample selection (Panel B of Table 7.3). The regression results in which the local disease mortality was included (Panel C of Table 4.3) show the mortality variable is not significantly associated with height. Controlling the local disease mortality did not noticeably change the coefficients for nutritional availability variables.

Third, educational attainment by age 20 was added to the regressions (Panel D of Table 7.3). Including education variables did not substantially change the baseline results on the effects of nutrition. Magnitudes of the coefficients for food availability in infancy and adolescence diminished only slightly. A high educational attainment was positively related to adult height. Conscripts who entered college were nearly 2 cm taller than those with primary school education or below (control group). Males who attended middle school and those who entered high school were taller than the control group by 0.8 cm and 1.5 cm, respectively.

Finally, province fixed effect was controlled along with own education (Panel E of Table 7.3). Including province dummy variables changed the regression results significantly. Effects of nutritional availability in infancy became considerably large in magnitude when controlling for the province fixed effect. By contrast, coefficients of the variables that capture nutrition in adolescence remained slightly changed in magnitude and lost statistical significance. The reason for the inclusion of province dummy variables strengthening the effects of nutritional availability during early childhood is not entirely evident. A possible explanation is that potential underestimation of nutritional availability in considerably urbanized provinces is fixed in part by including the province fixed effect. Nutrition variables in infancy were created from province-level data. The two largest metropolitan cities, namely, Seoul and Busan, were excluded from the rural county sample, but the agricultural statistics from other provinces still included nutritional productions from all counties, including urban areas. Thus, unlike food availability in adolescence (which was constructed from county-level data), early childhood nutrition variables might be subject to potential "urban bias," (local nutritional production is low in urban areas, actual food consumption can be high because of imports of nutrients from other regions). I suspect that including the province fixed effect reduced such bias.

7.1.3. Results from Alternative Samples

A major drawback of the data that served as basis of my analyses is the unknown place of birth. In estimating nutritional availability in infancy, individuals in our sample were assumed implicitly to remain in the same province from birth to conscription. Geographic movements produced

Table 7.4
Local Nutritional Availability and Height: Alternative Samples

Variable	(1) Calories	(2) Protein	(3) Fat	(4) Carbohydrate
(A) Living in province of family place (*Bonjeok*)				
Nutrition, Infancy	0.3010***	1.4468***	0.8730	0.1414***
	(0.1011)	(0.4478)	(2.5709)	(0.0465)
Nutrition, Adolescence	0.1370***	0.5923***	1.7227*	0.0617***
	(0.0515)	(0.1973)	(0.9057)	(0.0234)
Other controls	Yes	Yes	Yes	Yes
R-square	0.0078	0.0081	0.0047	0.0078
F-value	3.13***	3.19***	2.26***	3.15***
N	5044	5044	5044	5044
(B) Farmers' sons in rural counties				
Nutrition, Infancy	0.4594***	2.2225***	5.8666	0.2106***
	(0.1435)	(0.6180)	(3.6528)	(0.0663)
Nutrition, Adolescence	0.0913	0.4459*	0.9934	0.0398
	(0.0677)	(0.2523)	(1.1792)	(0.0311)
Other controls	Yes	Yes	Yes	Yes
R-square	0.0077	0.0083	0.0040	0.0075
F-value	5.29***	5.87***	2.49**	5.19***
N	2784	2784	2784	2784
(C) All persons with local nutritional productions				
Nutrition, Infancy	0.3570***	1.0424***	1.3876*	0.1405***
	(0.0923)	(0.3138)	(0.7584)	(0.0423)
Nutrition, Adolescence	0.0760*	0.1181	-0.0902	0.0427**
	(0.0438)	(0.1057)	(0.1810)	(0.0202)
Other controls	Yes	Yes	Yes	Yes
R-square	0.0074	0.0067	0.0050	0.0069
F-value	4.53***	3.80***	2.93***	4.42***
N	7867	7867	7867	7867
(D) 1946-1950 birth cohorts				
Nutrition, Adolescence	0.2390***	1.0066***	3.2564***	0.1078***
	(0.0455)	(0.1892)	(0.8288)	(0.0206)
Other controls	Yes	Yes	Yes	Yes
R-square	0.0092	0.0095	0.0068	0.0090
F-value	6.31***	6.75***	6.21***	6.31***
N	7850	7850	7850	7850

Note: Significance level. * 10%, ** 5%, *** 1%.

measurement errors in the nutrition variables that could attenuate their effects on height. To alleviate this potential measurement error, I used a subsample of men from rural counties, the province of residence of whom at the time of conscription is the same as the province of "original family place (*Bonjeok*)." For the birth cohorts born in the 1940s and 1950s,

Bonjeok presents their fathers' place of birth or residence in the early Japanese colonial period when the modern household registration system was first introduced. Thus, if a conscript's current address and *Bonjeok* are identical, he was likely born in the current province of residence. Of the 13,999 men in our sample for whom the current address and *Bonjeok* are available, approximately 79% reported identical provinces. The percentage of matches is considerably high for the rural country sample (91%), thereby implying that prior geographic mobility of individuals who lived in rural areas at the time of conscription was probably low.

I estimated Equation 7.1 using a subsample of 5,044 conscripts for whom the current and *Bonjeok* provinces are identical. I expected this additional sample restriction could diminish the magnitude of measurement error resulting from migration. Panel A in Table 7.4 presents similar results to those from the baseline regressions conducted with the full rural county sample. However, the estimated coefficients for nutritional availability, particularly in infancy, are noticeably higher than those obtained from the entire rural county sample (see Table 7.1). If these new estimates are applied, then one standard deviation increase in calories (0.697), protein (0.154), and carbohydrates (1.516) in infancy can increase adult height by 0.21, 0.22, and 0.21 cm, respectively. These effects are slightly higher than the effects drawn from the full rural county sample.

If we select a subsample of conscripts whose nutritional status in the growing ages were most strongly influenced by our measure of local nutritional availability (calories or size of nutrients per farm household adult male equivalent), then such should be men from farm households. We could not determine whether a person lived in a farm household in childhood with available information. Thus, I selected a sample of individuals from rural counties whose fathers were farmers at the time of conscription. This selection process is subject to measurement errors because of possible occupational changes and retirement of the fathers. A certain proportion of the conscripts who lived in farm households in childhood could be excluded from this subsample if their fathers left farming or retired. However, majority of farmers' sons lived in farm households because of the low probability that people in the 1950s and 1960s transferred from nonfarm occupations to farming. This subsample comprises 2,784 men, which is roughly half the size of our baseline sample.

Panel B in Table 7.4 presents the results of using the subsample of farmers' sons. Nutritional availability in infancy exerts considerably stronger effects on adult height compared with the baseline results. Table 7.1 shows the magnitudes of the effects increased by 70% (protein) to three times (fats). By contrast, the effects of nutrition in adolescence modestly diminished in magnitude and became statistically insignificant. These changes are qualitatively similar to the changes that resulted in the addition of the province fixed effect to the baseline regressions (see Panel E of Table 7.3). The sons of non-farmers came from urbanized places. Therefore, excluding these conscripts would reduce the influences of including urban counties in the estimation of food productions, which is similar to the result of including province fixed effect.

I extended the sample to include conscripts from urban areas where nutritional production per farm population exceeded a minimum threshold. Calories per farm household adult male equivalent in the county (district/city) of residence at age 14 were above 1,000 kcal. The extended sample of 7,867 conscripts includes men from urban districts with several farm households specializing in agricultural productions. This sample accounts for approximately 90% of the entire sample of the 1951–1957 birth cohorts for whom height and county of residence are available. That is, a relatively small fraction of the entire sample that represents highly urbanized areas were excluded from our analysis.

Panel C in Table 7.4 reports the results of using the extended sample. The estimated effects of the nutrition variables are similar to the results from the baseline regressions performed based on the rural county sample (see Table 7.1). Major exceptions are the effects of protein and fats in adolescence becoming substantially weak in terms of magnitude and statistical significance. This result suggests the significant positive effects of nutritional availability (particularly during early childhood) on height remained visible for a large proportion of the entire population.

In the baseline regressions, the sample was limited to individuals born from 1951–1957, excluding early birth cohorts. The purpose of the sample restriction was to include the analyses of nutrition variables in infancy that were only available for the 1951–1957 birth cohorts. Whether nutritional availability affected the heights of early birth cohorts as much as it did to those born after 1950 remains unclear. Therefore, I conducted height regressions with two separate samples, the 1946–1950 and 1951–1957 cohorts. I included in the regressions only nutritional availability in adolescence available for the entire birth cohorts.

Panel D in Table 7.4 reports that all nutritional availability variables are positive and significant for the sample of early birth cohorts. Two features stand out from comparisons between the results from the two samples with different birth cohorts (see Panel B of Table 7.2 and Panel D of Table 7.4) and between the results from different specifications (regressions with and without including nutrition variables in infancy: Table 7.1 and Panel D of Table 7.4). First, the heights of the early birth cohorts were affected more strongly by local nutritional availability in adolescence than the heights of the cohorts born after 1950. The coefficients for nutrition variables estimated from the sample of the 1946–1950 cohorts (Panel A in Table 7.4) were 50% to 70% higher than those obtained from the sample of the 1951–1957 cohorts (Panel B of Table 7.2). This result suggests marginal benefits of improved nutrition were probably significant for early birth cohorts who were shorter and more severely undernourished than late birth cohorts.

7.2. Additional Results and Discussion

7.2.1. Nutritional Availability and Education

Educational attainment is another key index to consider in determining the effects of early-life nutrition on human capital development. Nutritional status in early childhood is generally accepted to exert influence on cognitive ability, school attendance, and academic performances. Recent literature has established that negative and positive nutrition-related shocks, including mild ones, can substantially affect adult socioeconomic outcomes, including educational attainment and test scores (Almond et al. 2017).

In South Korea, only primary schooling was compulsory prior to 1985, and the 1946–1957 birth cohorts living in rural areas (the baseline sample) were admitted to middle school, high school, and college based on entrance examination scores.[2] Thus, educational attainment by age

2 Exam-free middle school entrance was first put in force in urban areas, Seoul in 1969 and other metropolitan cities in 1970, and were diffused to the entire

20, available from Korean Military Records, was determined in part by cognitive ability of conscripts, not merely by the economic status of their parents.

Applying a model similar to that used in height regressions, I investigated how the years of schooling at conscription was related to nutritional availability in infancy and in adolescence (Table 7.5). Province fixed effect was included in the regressions, considering possible regional differences in supply of and demand for education. Results show all nutrition variables except for fat availability in adolescence had significantly positive effects on educational attainment. One standard deviation change in calories in adolescence was associated with a change in the years of schooling by 0.28 years. An increase in availability of protein in adolescence and carbohydrate in infancy by one standard deviation lengthened schooling by 0.33 years and 0.29 years, respectively.

Moreover, small family size was significantly associated with high educational attainment. The schooling of conscripts living with three or less family members was 0.31 years longer than those with four to six family members. Father's occupation was a strong determinant of years of schooling. Conscripts whose fathers had professional and clerical jobs were educated more than farmers' sons by 1.7 and 2.4 years, respectively. Conscripts with jobless fathers had more schooling than farmers' sons by 0.5 years, whereas absence of father was associated with a decrease in schooling by about 0.3 years.

Education regressions were conducted by adding height at conscription to the baseline model (Table 7.6). Result shows tall individuals were highly educated. One standard deviation increase in height (5.19 cm) was associated with an increase in schooling by 0.33 years. Controlling height did not change the coefficients for nutritional availability in adolescence estimated from the baseline model, thereby suggesting that nutritional status during puberty affects height and education through different pathways. Conversely, except for fat, the effects of nutritional availability in infancy on height diminished in magnitude and became statistically insignificant. A possible explanation for the result is that nutrition in infancy can affect a common determining factor of stature and cognitive ability.

---

nation by 1971.

Table 7.5
Local Nutritional Availability and Education: 1951–1957 Birth Cohort in Rural Counties

Variable	(1) Calories	(2) Protein	(3) Fat	(4) Carbohydrate
Intercept	9.9545*** (1.0990)	9.8648*** (1.4344)	8.9954*** (1.2912)	9.9364*** (1.0233)
Local Nutritional availability				
Nutrition, Infancy	0.1732* (0.0957)	0.8449* (0.4337)	6.3710** (2.5340)	0.0793* (0.0437)
Nutrition, Adolescence	0.1793*** (0.0451)	0.5418*** (0.2075)	0.3781 (1.0112)	0.0840*** (0.0203)
Local environment				
Population density	-0.0307 (0.0209)	-0.0310 (0.0278)	-0.0052 (0.0288)	-0.0284 (0.0193)
Nonfarm population share	0.0066 (0.0049)	0.0060 (0.0049)	0.0047 (0.0049)	0.0065 (0.0049)
Season of Birth				
First quarter	NI	NI	NI	NI
Second quarter	0.0631 (0.0899)	0.0632 (0.0893)	0.0552 (0.0898)	0.0625 (0.0899)
Third quarter	0.1317 (0.1008)	0.1387 (0.1008)	0.1404 (0.1008)	0.1309 (0.1008)
Fourth quarter	0.0301 (0.0917)	-0.0339 (0.0919)	-0.0404 (0.6620)	-0.0302 (0.0916)
Family size				
1 to 3	0.3152** (0.1541)	0.3149** (0.1542)	0.3011* (0.1545)	0.3148** (0.1541)
4 to 6	NI	NI	NI	NI
7 or more	0.1624* (0.0827)	-0.1704** (0.0819)	-0.1812** (0.0835)	-0.1614* (0.0827)
Father's occupation				
Professional	1.7458*** (0.6031)	1.7758*** (0.6067)	1.7816*** (0.6109)	1.7418*** (0.6027)
Clerical	2.3718*** (0.2058)	2.3674*** (0.2069)	2.3935*** (0.2066)	2.3738*** (0.2055)
Service	0.4717 (0.8630)	0.4653 (0.8665)	0.5444 (0.8708)	0.4747 (0.8619)
Farming	NI	NI	NI	NI
Manual	0.0998 (0.3118)	0.0846 (0.3115)	0.0654 (0.3150)	0.1009 (0.3121)
No job	0.5139*** (0.1019)	0.5201*** (0.1032)	0.5204*** (0.1024)	0.5128*** (0.1017)
Father absent	-0.2827** (0.1105)	-0.2828** (0.1108)	-0.2949*** (0.1101)	-0.2832*** (0.1105)
Province fixed effect	Yes	Yes	Yes	Yes
R-square	0.0447 0.0075	0.0425	0.0391	0.0449
F-value	38.27***	37.12***	34.76***	38.52***
N	5553	5553	5553	5553

Note: Significance level. * 10%, ** 5%, *** 1%.

Table 7.6
Local Nutritional Availability and Education with Controlling for Height: 1951–1957 Birth Cohort in Rural Counties

Variable	(1) Calories	(2) Protein	(3) Fat	(4) Carbohydrate
Intercept	-0.6207 (1.3558)	-0.7651 (1.6017)	-1.8740 (1.5151)	-0.6377 (1.3059)
Local Nutritional availability				
Calories, Infancy	0.1213 (0.0932)	0.6330 (0.4226)	5.7228** (2.4857)	0.0550 (0.0426)
Calories, Adolescence	0.1692*** (0.0445)	0.5067** (0.2068)	0.2528 (1.010)	0.0793*** (0.0201)
Height	0.0636*** (0.0061)	0.0641*** (0.0062)	0.0658*** (0.0062)	0.0636*** (0.0061)
Other Controls	Yes	Yes	Yes	Yes
Province fixed effect	Yes	Yes	Yes	Yes
R-square	0.0593 0.0075	0.0573	0.0549	0.0595
F-value	41.51***	40.49***	38.20***	41.85***
N	5553	5553	5553	5553

Note: Significance level. * 10%, ** 5%, *** 1%.

7.2.2. Remediation: Nutrition in Adolescence and Effect of Exposure to the Korean War

Can increased nutritional availability in late childhood mitigate the negative impact of exposure to negative health shocks sustained in early childhood? The result indicating good substitutability between nutritional intakes in infancy and adolescence (provided in Panel D in Table 7.2) suggests remediation of initial damages in the form of improved nutrition in late childhood would be effective. I attempted to find evidence for remediation by utilizing the experimental episode of the Korean War that majority of the conscripts in our sample experienced in different stages of their childhood.

As explained in Chapters 2 to 4, the Korean War damaged individual maternal and fetal health, especially in the first 9 months of the war following the outbreak of the war in June 1950. I first estimated the following equation to examine if birth cohorts born in 1950 and 1951 (who were exposed to the worst 9 months of the war during pre-natal and/or neo-natal period) deviated from the neighboring birth cohorts in terms of height, weight, and educational attainment:

$$h_i = \alpha + \sum_{t=1950}^{1951} \beta_t I_{it} + \gamma_1 YOB_i + \gamma_2 YOB_i^2 + \gamma_3 YOB_i^3 + \varepsilon_i \quad \textbf{(7.2)}$$

where h_i denotes the anthropometric or educational outcome for individual i; I_t denotes the dummy variable with a value of 1 for individuals born in year t, and 0 otherwise; *YOB* denotes the last two digits of the birth year; and β_t measures the departure of outcomes for the birth cohorts in-utero during the Korean War from the cubic cohort trend. Results in Panel A in Table 7.7 confirm that early-life exposure to the Korean War negatively affected anthropometric and educational outcomes at age 20. Subjects of the 1951 birth cohorts were 0.63 cm shorter, less educated by 0.64 years, and did not enter high school by 11% points compared to the adjacent birth cohorts. Similarly, conscripts born in 1950 were 0.7 kg lighter, had lower schooling by 0.48 years, and did not enter high school by 5.8% points than expected by the cubic cohort trend.

I then estimated Equation 7.3, in which interaction term between dummy variables for 1950 and 1951 birth cohorts and local nutritional availability in adolescence for the corresponding birth cohort (N_{it}) is included.

$$h_i = \alpha + \sum_{t=1950}^{1951} [\beta_t I_{it} + \theta_t (I_{it} \times N_{it})] + \gamma_1 YOB_i + \gamma_2 YOB_i^2 + \gamma_3 YOB_i^3 + \varepsilon_i . \quad \textbf{(7.3)}$$

The estimated equation $\beta_t + (\theta_t \times N_{it})$ shows the magnitude of deviation from smooth cohort trend of the subjects of the birth cohort born in year t (either 1950 or 1951) who spent adolescence in counties with a particular quantity of local nutritional availability.

Panel B of Table 7.7 shows that interaction terms (θ_t) are positive and statistically significant wherever the coefficient for each cohort dummy (β_t) was estimated as significantly negative. This result suggests the negative cohort effects of early exposure to the Korean War were small for those who lived in counties with high nutritional availability during adolescence. Such result also provides suggestive evidence that improved nutrition in late childhood effectively compensated for the

Table 7.7
Early-Life Exposure to the Korean War, Local Nutritional Availability in Adolescence, and Human Capital Outcomes at Conscriptions: Farmers' Sons from Rural Counties

Variable	(1) Height	(2) Weight	(3) Years of schooling	(4) High school entrance
(A)				
1950	-0.2993	-0.7003*	-0.4826**	-0.0580*
	(0.3439)	(0.3919)	(0.1950)	(0.0338)
1951	-0.6252*	-0.5710	-0.6401***	-0.1097***
	(0.3301)	(0.3894)	(0.1877)	(0.0311)
Cubic cohort trend, Birth month	Yes	Yes	Yes	Yes
R-square	0.0244	0.0064	0.0123	0.0080
F-value	5.97***	2.05**	3.30***	2.34***
N	4016	3879	4008	4008
(B)				
1950	-0.2913	-2.7762**	-1.1346**	-0.1014*
	(1.0372)	(1.1667)	(0.5258)	(0.0966)
1950 × Calories, Adolescence	0.0028	0.5083*	0.1597	0.0106
	(0.2339)	(0.2841)	(0.1137)	(0.0211)
1951	-2.5892**	-0.5199	-2.1029***	-0.2811***
	(1.1637)	(1.1425)	(0.6344)	(0.0871)
1951 × Calories, Adolescence	0.4864*	-0.0130	0.3621**	0.0424**
	(0.2642)	(0.2893)	(0.1441)	(0.0189)
Cubic cohort trend, Birth month	Yes	Yes	Yes	Yes
R-square	0.0252	0.0073	0.0144	0.0102
F-value	5.55***	2.16***	3.27***	2.03**
N	4016	3879	4008	4008

Note: Significance level. * 10%, ** 5%, *** 1%.

negative consequences of early exposure to negative shocks caused by the war.

7.2.3. Contribution of Improved Nutrition to Increase in Adult Height across Cohorts

The results provided in section 7.1 of this chapter suggests that local nutritional availability in growth periods is an important determinant of adult height. The average height of South Korean conscripts rapidly increased between the cohort born in 1951 and those born in 1957. For six years, approximately 2 cm was gained. Given that about 6 cm was gained during the next 30 years (0.2 cm per year), the increase in height experienced by males born between 1951 and 1957 (0.33 cm per year)

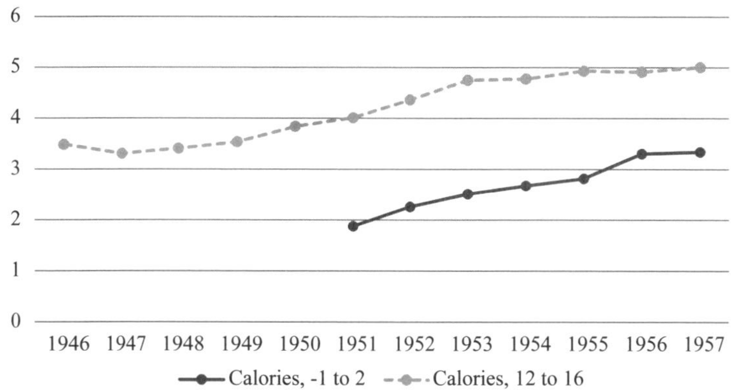

Figure 7.2 | Early-Life Local Calories Availability by Birth Cohort (1,000 kcals per farm household adult male equivalent per day)

was considerably rapid in long-run perspective.[3] As expected from the process of recovery from the aftermath of the Korean War and the increased income and agricultural productivity that followed, the quality and quantity of diet in childhood and adolescence improved across birth cohorts. A question is how much improved nutrition contributed to the rapid increase in height of the birth cohorts under investigation.

Figures 7.2 to 7.5 visually present how nutritional availability in early childhood and adolescence changed across different birth cohorts. Productions of calories and three major nutrients in infancy and adolescence increased substantially between the 1951 and 1957 birth cohorts. Food availability during early childhood, particularly the production of protein and fats, increased more rapidly than nutritional availability did during adolescence. Provisions of protein and fats in early childhood doubled between the 1951 and 1957 cohorts. I was unable to estimate nutritional availability in infancy for men who were born prior to 1951. Productions of calories and major nutrients in adolescence stagnated or increased gradually from the 1946–1951 cohort. Thus, the cohort trends of nutritional availability and of adult height from 1946–

3 The average height at age 20 by year of birth from the late 1950s was obtained from survey reports of the Korea Research Institute of Standards and Science that began to be published from 1979.

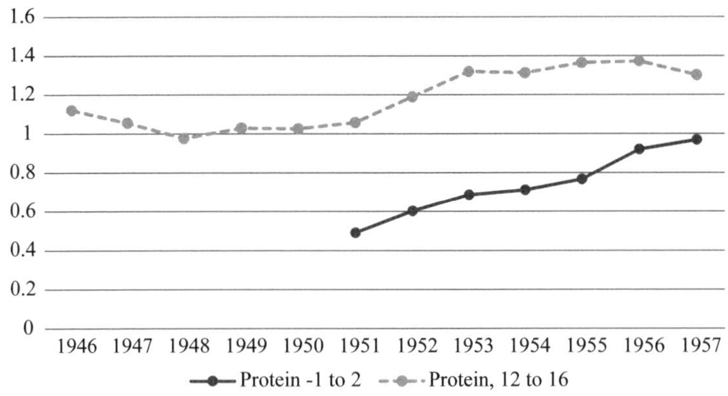

Figure 7.3 | Early-Life Local Protein Availability by Birth Cohort (100 grams per farm household adult male equivalent per day)

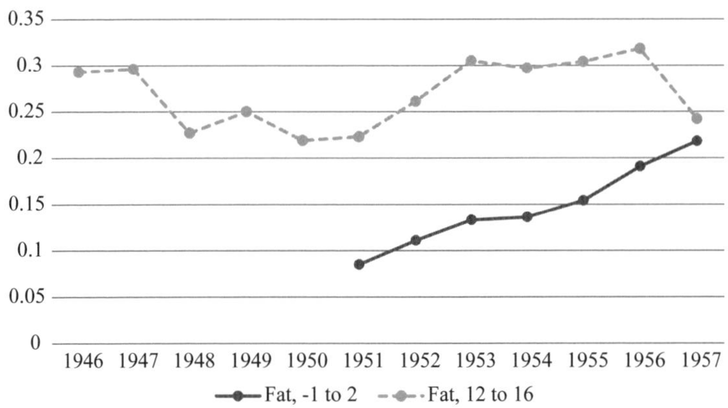

Figure 7.4 | Early-Life Local Fat Availability by Birth Cohort (100 grams per farm household adult male equivalent per day)

1957 match well.

I conducted an exercise to obtain a back-of-envelope estimate on how improved nutrition in growing ages contributed to the increase in heights of conscripts. By using the largest-possible sample for whom nutritional availability in infancy and adolescence is provided (a sample of 7,867 men used in the regressions reported in Panel C of Table 7.4), I first computed the measures of nutritional availability for each cohort from 1951–1957 (see Panels A to G in Table 7.8) and the magnitude

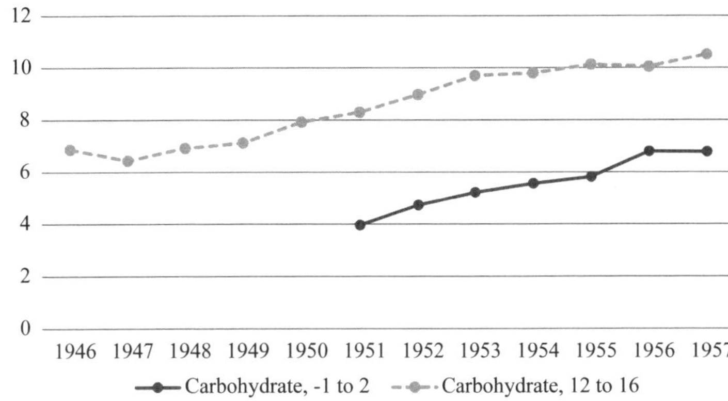

Figure 7.5 | Early-Life Local Carbohydrate Availability by Birth Cohort (100 grams per farm household adult male equivalent per day)

Table 7.8
Height Change Predicted by Increase in Nutritional Production

	(1) Calories (1,000 kcals)		(2) Protein (100 g)		(3) Fat (100 g)		(4) Carbohydrate (100 g)	
	Age -1 to 3	Age 12–16	Age -1 to 3	Age 12–16	Age -1 to 3	Age 12–16	Age -1 to 3	Age 12–16
A. 1951 cohort	1.876	4.011	0.491	1.057	0.085	0.223	3.958	8.296
B. 1952 cohort	2.260	4.361	0.603	1.189	0.111	0.261	4.731	8.973
C. 1953 cohort	2.511	4.747	0.686	1.318	0.133	0.305	5.222	9.698
D. 1954 cohort	2.678	4.773	0.711	1.311	0.136	0.297	5.576	9.792
E. 1955 cohort	2.818	4.929	0.766	1.363	0.154	0.304	5.823	10.121
F. 1956 cohort	3.304	4.910	0.919	1.372	0.191	0.318	6.793	10.042
G. 1957 cohort	3.341	5.002	0.968	1.299	0.218	0.242	6.777	10.521
H. Change (G–A)	1.465	0.991	0.477	0.242	0.133	0.019	2.819	2.225
I. Regression Coefficient	0.357	0.076	1.042	0.118+	1.388	-0.090+	0.141	0.043
J. Predicted height change (H×I)	0.523	0.075	0.497	0	0.185	0	0.397	0.096

Note: The sample includes 11,508 persons born between 1951 and 1957 with information on height and nutritional availability in both infancy (age -1 to 3) and in early adolescence (age 12 to 16). The coefficients for variables regarding local nutritional production are from the regressions conducted based on the same sample (Panel C of Table 4.4). The mean height of this sample is 165.48 cm for 1951 and 167.42 cm for 1957.

of increase in each measure (see Panel H in Table 7.8). For example, calories available in infancy increased by 1,465 kcals between the 1951 and 1957 cohorts. Thereafter, I multiplied the size of the increase by the estimated regression coefficient for the corresponding nutrition variable. I then calculated the magnitude of height change predicted by an increase in the measure of nutrition. The regression results from using the same sample of 7,867 conscripts (see Panel C in Table 7.4) were used.

Result suggests improved nutrition in growth periods, particularly in early childhood, might have contributed substantially to an increase in height from 1951–1957. First, improved calorie availability increased adult height by approximately 0.6 cm. Majority (0.52 cm) of this contribution is attributable to the increased calories in infancy. Moreover, changes in the availability of protein, fats, and carbohydrates resulted in an increase in adult height by 0.5 cm, 0.19 cm, and 0.49 cm, respectively. Given the four measures of nutritional availability are correlated to one another, estimating the combined effect of calories and various nutrients is difficult. If only the effect of calories is concerned, then nutritional improvement accounts for 30% of the increase in average height between the 1951 and 1957 cohorts (i.e., approximately 2 cm). If we assume the three major nutrients (i.e., protein, fat, and carbohydrates) independently contributed to height change, then their joint effect increases in height by 1.1 cm. By applying large estimates of the effect of nutritional availability from using alternative samples (e.g., sample of farmers' sons: Panel B in Table 7.4) or specifications (e.g., adding province fixed effect: Panel E of Table 7.3), the contribution of nutritional improvement becomes more important.

7.3. Summary

This chapter investigated how nutritional availability in two crucial periods for human growth, namely, early childhood (from conception to age 3) and adolescence (from age 12 to age 16), affected the heights of South Korean conscripts born from 1946 to 1957. Results strongly suggest nutrition was an important determining factor of biological standards of living indicated by adult height. Provisions of calories and protein were strongly associated with large stature. Food availability during early childhood was more critical for human growth than nutrition in adolescence. This result is consistent with the consensus that catch-up growth in adolescence is insufficient to compensate completely for deficiencies in early childhood. Nutrition in growing ages also had a strong effect on educational attainment.

The chapter also explored whether increased nutritional availability in late childhood can mitigate the negative impact of exposure to negative health shocks sustained in early childhood. I found that the negative cohort effects of early exposure to the Korean War were small for those who lived in counties with high nutritional availability during adolescence. This result provides suggestive evidence that improved nutrition in late childhood effectively compensated the negative consequences of early exposure to negative shocks caused by the war. I also examined the extent by which improved nutrition contributed to the increase in height between the 1951 and 1957 birth cohorts. Result suggests improved nutrition in early childhood and adolescence accounted for 30% to 50% of the increase in adult height that was gained from the 1951–1957 birth cohorts. Increased nutritional availability during early childhood explains majority of the contribution.

CHAPTER 8

Intergenerational Effect of the Gwangju Uprising: Method

8.1. Intergenerational Transmission of Maternal Stress

Chapters 2 to 5 of this book show strong and persistent effects of in-utero exposure to adverse environment on health and socioeconomic outcomes in older adults. Growing evidence suggests that maternal psychological stress during pregnancy, a more subtle form of negative health shock, negatively affects a wide variety of offspring outcomes. A possible mechanism by which maternal stress affects the health of the next generation is hormonal change. Human studies suggest that maternal stress during pregnancy, associated with raised plasma levels of corticotrophin releasing hormone (CRH) and cortisol, may increase the likelihood of preterm birth, developmental delays, and behavioral abnormalities in the children (Weinstock 2001). Aizer et al. (2009) reports that poor mothers have elevated levels of the stress hormone cortisol. The increased cortisol in pregnancy negatively affects the cognition, health, and educational attainment of their children, even if unobservable differences between mothers are controlled for by making comparisons between siblings.

The influences of a wide range of stressors have been reported. For example, Os and Selten (1998) found that prenatal exposure to maternal stress caused by the invasion of the German army in the May

1940 increased the risk of lifetime diagnosis of schizophrenia. Maternal stress caused by the loss of a husband among the Finnish population between 1925 and 1957 increased the incidence of psychiatric disorders (Huttunen and Niskanen 1978). Israeli male cohorts exposed to maternal stress caused by the Six-Day War in 1967 were more likely to experience developmental delays and behavioral disorders (Meijer 2007). Epidemiological studies based on human experiences and animal experiments have shown that exposure to excessive noise in pregnancy can cause stillbirth, birth defects, and decreased birth weight (Geber 1970; Jones and Tauscher 1978; Knipschild et al. 1981).

An emerging research by economists and other social scientists provides evidence pertaining to the effects of maternal stress on offspring health and economic outcomes based on semi-experimental episodes. Lauderdale (2006) finds that Arabic-named women in California, who went through a period of increased harassment, violence, and workplace discrimination immediately after September 11, 2001, had increased risk of preterm birth and low birth weight. Eccleston (2011) reports that individuals exposed to the stress of the September 11, 2001 terrorist attacks in-utero weighed less, had a shorter duration of gestation, and had lower initial educational attainment. According to Currie and Rossin-Slater (2012), exposure to a hurricane during pregnancy increased the probability of complications of labor and delivery. Torche (2011) reports maternal exposure to stress caused by the 2005 Tarapaca earthquake in Chile resulted in a significant decline in birth weight and an increase in the proportion of low birth weight. Chapters 4 to 5 of this book show strong negative effects of in-utero exposure to the Korean War on economic and health outcomes in older adults, and suggest that increased maternal stress from exposure to combat activities and war-related atrocities is probably a major mechanism of the effects.

Animal studies suggest that the negative influences of maternal stress during pregnancy persist across multiple generations. For example, a study of a mammal (snowshoe hare) reports that a predator-induced increase in maternal stress hormone levels resulted in a decline in reproduction, and that the effect persisted across several generations even after the predators have disappeared (Sheriff et al. 2010). The negative effect of poor maternal diet on birth weight among black-and-white hooded rats persisted for approximately three generations despite the resumption of normal nutrition (Stewart et al. 1975; Stewart et al. 1980). Maternal exercise during pregnancy resulted in the low birth weight of the second-generation pups although the growth-retarded first generation remained sedentary during pregnancy (Pinto and Shetty 1995).

The presence of the multi-generational effect of maternal stress in human populations is less clear, although some circumstantial evidence from research on historical famine exists.[1] Epidemiological studies reported that parental and offspring birth weights are positively related, and that matrilineal intergenerational effect on birth weight is stronger than relationship between paternal and offspring birth weight (Emanuel et al. 1992). Currie and Moretti (2007) found that if a mother was born with low birth weight, her child is significantly more likely to have low birth weight, even if the comparison is between mothers who are sisters. Guven, Hoang, Rahman, and Ulubaşoğlu (2021) found that early exposure to the 1944–1945 Great Vietnam Famine lowered the school attendance rate of the second generation. If these findings are combined with the result demonstrating that maternal stress in pregnancy reduces offspring birth weights, we might expect to find the multi-generational effects of maternal stress.

A possible mechanism behind the intergenerational transmission of birth weight is maternal growth, especially the uterine and ovarian size. Exposure of the fetus to a negative shock in-utero may permanently alter physiology in adulthood. Such physiological changes may result in an adverse intrauterine environment for the offspring of the mother, leading to physiological changes in the next generation. Evidence shows that maternal size is associated with the size of the offspring (Hackman et al. 1983; Emanuel 1997). Another possible explanation is that a stimulus or insult received during critical periods of growth and development may permanently alter the programming of physiology by epigenetic modification (Rakyan et al. 2001).

---

1 Recent research suggests that early-life exposure to famine has negative effects on the health and socioeconomic status of the next generation (Fung and Ha 2010; Kim and Fleisher 2010). Although a different type of shock is examined, and prenatal exposure is not clearly identified in these studies, this evidence highlights the possibility of the multi-generational transmission of the consequences of maternal stress.

8.2. The Gwangju Uprising in May 1980

The Gwangju uprising occurred in May 1980 in the course of the political turmoil that followed the assassination of President Park Chung Hee on the night of October 26, 1979. As Park's 18-year authoritarian regime ended abruptly, the country entered a period of political instability. The prime minister who immediately succeeded Park as the new president had little power to lead the nation through the political crisis. On December 12, the new military regime headed by Generals Chun Doo Hwan and Roh Tae Woo took control of the government through a military coup.

Many Koreans, especially college students, were frustrated and angered by the rise of another military dictatorship that filled the power vacuum created by Park's downfall. Through protests and demonstrations, they demanded that Chun resign from key positions and called for immediate democratic reform, including an end to martial law (declared after Park's assassination), direct presidential election, and freedom of the press. These pro-democracy activities culminated in the demonstration at Seoul station on May 15, 1980 where an estimated 150,000 students and citizens gathered to protest the new military regime.

General Chun and his collaborators responded by taking several oppressive measures. On May 17, they extended martial law to the entire nation, which was not applied previously to the island of Jeju. The new martial law suspended the cabinet and closed the National Assembly. The military regime also closed down all university campuses and arrested many political leaders. Among those who were arrested was Kim Dae Jung, a highly popular political leader from the southwest (*Honam*) region where Gwangju is located. To enforce the new martial law, troops were deployed to various parts of the country. In Gwangju, too, the provincial office and other key official buildings as well as universities were under the occupation of riot police and soldiers.

The first clash between civilian demonstrators and soldiers occurred on the morning of May 18 when about 200 college students who gathered at the gate of Jeonnam National University were brutally attacked by a squad of paratroopers. In the afternoon that same day, a larger number of students and citizens who demonstrated in downtown Gwangju were mercilessly suppressed by paratroopers (special troops trained for guerrilla warfare). Testimonial and photographic evidence shows that martial law soldiers assaulted both demonstrators and onlookers using batons and bayonets. The first known fatality was a 29-year-old deaf man who was clubbed to death on May 18 while passing by the scene. According to a martial law document, 68 people were injured and 405 were arrested that day.

The eyewitness news of excessive repression by the military spread around the city, which prompted more students and citizens to come out onto the street and to become anxious to know what had happened the previous day. On May 19, the number of students and citizens who participated in demonstrations grew to several thousands. The martial law troops once again attempted to suppress the protests with brutality. Soldiers in small teams searched buildings and houses and indiscriminately assaulted any young man they found and took him into custody. Soldiers forced the captured young men to strip down to their underwear and beat them on the street with their hands tied. This scene became one of the most symbolic images of the Gwangju uprising.

As ordinary citizens were infuriated by the ruthless acts of violence conducted by martial law troops, the number of protestors on the street rapidly increased and exceeded tens of thousands by May 20. Angered protesters burned down television station buildings for false broadcasting, and rammed cars into soldiers and policemen. As the conflict escalated, the army opened fire on citizens, killing or seriously injuring at least 20 people. The violence climaxed on May 21. The martial law troops fired at protestors gathered in front of the Provincial Office, killing at least 54 people and injuring about 500. In response, civilian protestors armed themselves with rifles by raiding armories and police stations. Later that afternoon, the "Citizen's Army" and the government troops began to engage in bloody gunfights. Concerned with the growing number of casualties, the government troops finally retreated to suburban areas to wait for reinforcement. Gwangju citizens took full control of the city for five days (May 22 to 26).

During this period, Gwangju was completely isolated from the rest of the country as the army blocked all routes and communications leading in and out of the city. On May 23, soldiers fired at a bus that attempted to break out of the city, killing 17 out of the 18 passengers. The following day, soldiers mistook boys swimming in a reservoir as attempting to cross, and shot and killed one of them. Meanwhile, a remarkable degree of order in the self-governed city under siege was established. Markets reopened and basic necessities such as food, water, and electricity were supplied to the residents without interruption. On May 22, the Citizens

Settlement Committee was formed and negotiated with the army to demand the release of arrested citizens, compensation for victims, and prohibition of retaliation in exchange for the disarmament of militias. However, the negotiations came to a deadlock, as the army insisted that the militias should unconditionally disarm themselves. Before dawn of May 27, government troops moved into the city with the aid of tanks and guns. By late morning, the military had retaken the city, defeating the Citizen Army garrisoned at the Provincial Office. The 10-day Gwangju uprising was finally crushed.

Even today, the exact number of people who were killed or injured during the Gwangju uprising is uncertain. Shortly after the tragedy, the Martial Law Command announced that 170 people died (144 civilians, 22 soldiers, and 4 policemen) and 380 were wounded. These official figures have been criticized by some as being too low. In particular, these estimates fail to account for the number of people who are still missing and presumed dead. A recent scholarly work on the Gwangju uprising argues that the best estimate available today is about 500 civilians killed and over 3,000 wounded (Shin and Hwang 2003, p. xvii).

The estimated number of individuals directly victimized by the Gwangju uprising (dead, missing, injured, or detained) is over 4,000. Although quantitative documentations are rare, the Gwangju uprising left lasting scars on the surviving victims and their families. Testimonials frequently refer to ongoing medical problems (including nervous anxiety and depression, as well as lingering illnesses and death), financial difficulties (including unemployment), and general hardship (Byun and Lewis 2000). A more systematic study by a medical anthropologist/nurse found that 92% of Gwangju victims developed post-traumatic stress disorders; they were much more likely to suffer from physical ailments, anxiety, and depression than nonvictims in Gwangju (Byun 1996).

Determining how the traumatic experiences during the Gwangju uprising affected the lives of the vast majority of the citizens who were not visibly influenced by the violence during the event is less clear. Even for the more fortunate residents of Gwangju who avoided any direct damage, the incident must be extremely stressful in several respects. Many citizens, including those who did not actively participate in demonstrations, encountered brutal acts of violence that are unthinkable in a peace-time city. War-like conflicts on the street, media coverage depicting Gwangju protestors as North Korean communists' espionage, and blocked communications with the outside of community perhaps generated great fear and anxiety among ordinary citizens.

The time was difficult for mothers and young wives, including pregnant women, whose sons and husbands were the major targets of oppression. Based on the findings from previous literature on the effects of maternal stress in pregnancy, fetal and maternal health could be negatively affected by the exposure to the disruptions caused by the Gwangju uprising. No attempts have been made to understand the impact of the tragic event on the offspring outcomes. Micro files of birth records are unavailable for the period prior to 1991; thus, studying the birth outcomes of the children who were exposed to the Gwangju uprising while in-utero is impossible.

The Gwangju uprising provides a unique opportunity for identifying the impact of maternal psychological stress on pregnancy. First, the tragic incident of May 1980 was a completely unanticipated shock that was unavoidably sustained by all citizens of Gwangju. The aggressive move of the new military regime to suppress the democratization movement was largely unknown to the public until it actually happened. Once the crackdown started, the citizens could not keep away from the terror by moving out of the city because all routes leading into and out of Gwangju were blocked by government troops.

Second, the major type of negative shocks to fetal health caused by the Gwangju uprising is likely to be maternal psychological stress. Although the incident was highly violent, the vast majority of the citizens and almost all pregnant women were physically unaffected. The primary targets of the brutal assault of martial law troops were young males. A number of public buildings (including a broadcasting company, the provincial office, and police stations) were burnt or destroyed, but the majority of residential and commercial buildings were untouched. Provisions of foods and public utilities (including water and electricity) were uninterrupted.

Finally, the duration of potential exposure to maternal stress was brief: only 10 days between May 18 and May 27 in 1980. Shortly after the Citizen Army rebellion was crushed by the government troops at the provincial office on May 27, the uprising ended abruptly. On the surface, the city resumed its ordinary life only in a few days.[2] A few politicians,

---

2 A testimony of a factory worker, Jung Hee Lee, shows her company (Honam

activists, and students were arrested and jailed on the accusation of instigating the uprising. The agony and anger of the Gwangju citizens continued as they were often treated as "mobsters" or "communist spies." Nevertheless, the direct exposure to intense violence lasted about 10 days.

8.3. Data and Methods

I hypothesize that maternal stress negatively affected the fetal health of the children, and that the impact of the adverse early-life shock even transmitted to the health of the next generation. More specifically, I suspect that maternal stress during pregnancy from the Gwangju uprising adversely affected the birth outcomes of the mother's grandchildren.

The first step of the research is to select the female birth cohorts who were exposed to maternal stress caused by the Gwangju uprising. I assume that individuals whose mother resided in Gwangju in May 1980 and who were born between June 1980 and February 1981 were exposed to the violence in-utero. I do not regard persons born during and shortly after the incident (May 18 to 31) as "treated," because their births could be negatively influenced by the chaotic conditions of hospitals in Gwangju during the uprising as well as maternal stress.[3]

To study the intergenerational transmission of maternal stress caused by the violence during the Gwangju uprising, the following difference-in-difference model is employed in the regression analyses:

$$\textbf{(8.1)} \quad y_i = \alpha + \beta_1 I_i + \beta_2 (I_i \times S_i) + \beta_3 S_i + \gamma_1 YOB_i + \gamma_2 YOB_i^2 + \gamma_3 YOB^3 + \delta X_i + \varepsilon_i$$

Electric Co. located in Gwangju) resumed normal operation from the beginning of June (Lee 2012, p. 130).

3 Medical facilities in the city of Gwangju and its vicinity were similar to wartime field hospitals. Emergency rooms, regular wards, and even hospital corridors were full of wounded citizens and soldiers. Some physicians and nurses were mobilized by martial law troops to inspect dead bodies (Lee 2012, pp. 231–238).

where y denotes birth outcomes, I is the dummy variable that identifies a mother as in-utero between June 1980 and February 1981, S is the dummy variable that indicates whether the child was born in the city of Gwangju, YOB stands for the mother's year of birth, and X represents other characteristics of the child and parents that potentially influence birth outcomes, including year of birth, sex, multiple births, and parents' education and occupation.

The data used in this research are micro files of the 2000 and 2002 Vital Statistics for birth in Korea. These data contain the universe of the digitalized birth registration records for all children born in the given years, which provide information on the characteristics of the parents and the newborn babies. The variables offered by the data include the child's sex, place of birth, date of birth, length of gestation (in week), birth weight, and age, education, and occupation of the parents. The micro files of the data are available from 1991 (although birth weight was only reported beginning in 1993), but the exact birth dates of the parents are reported only in the 2000 and 2002 micro data. The data for the other years only provide the ages of the parents at the time of registration. For the years except 2000 and 2002, thus, accurately identifying the year and month of birth is difficult. Only the birth records of children born in 2000 or 2002 are utilized in this study due to this data feature.

Variables on birth outcomes available from the Korean Vital Statistics are birth weight and the length of gestation. In addition to these measures, I also consider if the birth weight is lower than 2.5 kg (referred to as low birth weight, or LBW) and if the length of gestation is less than 37 weeks (referred to as preterm birth). A voluminous literature has established that low birth weight has persistent adverse effects on health and socioeconomic outcomes over the life cycle (Currie and Hyson 1999; Behrman and Rosenzweig 2004; Black, Devereux, and Salvanes 2007; Currie and Moretti 2007). For example, Black, Devereux, and Salvanes (2007) analyzed Norwegian twins and found that LBW has long-run adverse effects on adult height, IQ, earnings, and education. Currie and Moretti (2007) stated that LBW among individuals born in California has modest but statistically significant negative effects on educational attainment and the probability of living in a wealthy neighborhood.

Several drawbacks of the data used in this study limit the scope and quality of the study. First, neither the place of residence of the grandmother in May 1980 nor the birthplace of the mother is reported in the Vital Statistics. Thus, the actual birthplace of the mother cannot be identified from the data, and I cannot but use the birthplace of the child as a proxy for the place of residence of the grandmother or the birthplace of the mother 20 years earlier.

If geographic migrations are considered, some of the young women who gave birth in Gwangju in the early 2000s were born elsewhere. This type of measurement error results in downward bias in the estimated effect of exposure to the Gwangju uprising, which confirms the negative effects of in-utero exposure to the incident. If either of the following two assumptions is satisfied, the measurement error in the birthplace of the mother is not a serious problem in the context of this study: (a) Selections in migrations out of and into Gwangju from 1980 to the early 2000s are not correlated to in-utero exposure to the Gwangju uprising, or (b) female out-migrants born in Gwangju between June 1980 and February 1981 are not more positively selected than those born in Gwangju just before or after the period. This potential bias problem arising from geographic mobility is discussed in detail in Chapter 9.

Second, the cohorts who were in-utero during the 1980 Gwangju uprising and who were included in the 2000 and 2002 birth records were aged 20 to 22 years at the time of delivery. Given that the average age of marriage and first birth in the early 2000s was the late 20s, available data allow us to examine the birth outcomes of children born to a selected group of mothers who gave birth at a relatively young age. I make comparisons among children whose mothers gave birth to them at almost the same age. However, I cannot preclude the possibility that the results are peculiar to women who gave birth at a relatively young age. Possible bias issues related to this drawback are addressed in Chapter 9.

Before conducting regression analyses, I simply compare some measures of birth outcomes, namely, average birth weight, probability of LBW, length of gestation, and probability of preterm birth, between children born in Gwangju to women born between June 1980 and February 1981 (hereafter referred to as Gwangju grandchildren) and the rest of the children (non-Gwangju grandchildren). If the impact of maternal stress caused by the Gwangju incident transmitted across two generations, the children of women who were prenatally exposed to the Gwangju uprising might reveal worse birth outcomes than babies whose grandmothers were not influenced by the incident.

Figure 8.1 provides the average birth weight (in grams) of children grouped according to the year and month of birth of the mother (classified into five nine-month intervals) for the entire nation and for

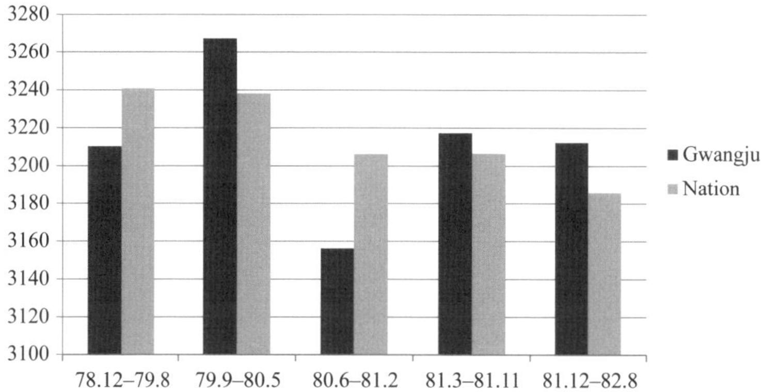

Figure 8.1 | Birthweight (grams) by Mother's Year and Month of Birth

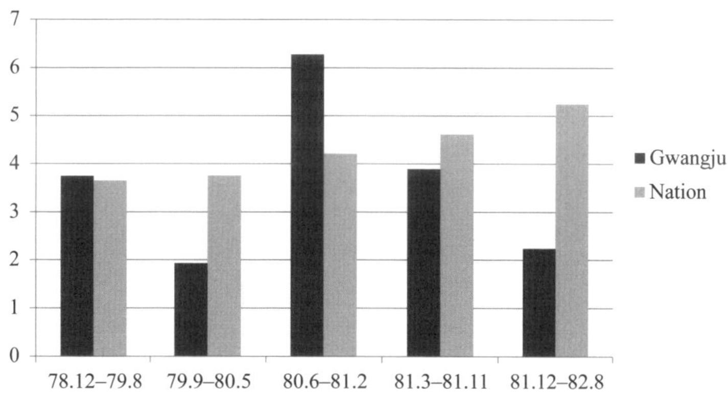

Figure 8.2 | % Low Birth Weight (< 2.5 kg) by Mother's Year and Month of Birth

Gwangju. Gwangju grandchildren weigh notably less at birth than the other grandchildren of women who born between the end of 1978 and early 1982. The disadvantage of having a mother who spent a part of the prenatal period during the Gwangju uprising is observed only among those born in Gwangju. Gwangju grandchildren faced a higher risk of LBW than babies whose grandmother did not experience the violent incident (Figure 8.2). Babies born in Gwangju between December 1978 and August 1982 had a slightly shorter length of gestation than the national average, but the disadvantage of birth in Gwangju is particularly greater among babies whose mothers experienced the Gwangju incidence while

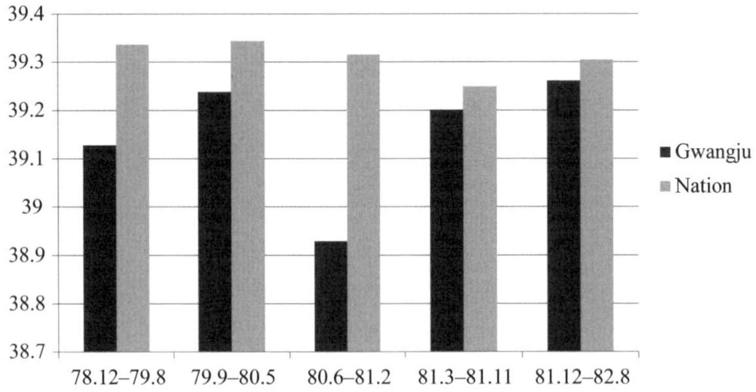

Figure 8.3 | Length of Gestation (weeks) by Mother's Year and Month of Birth

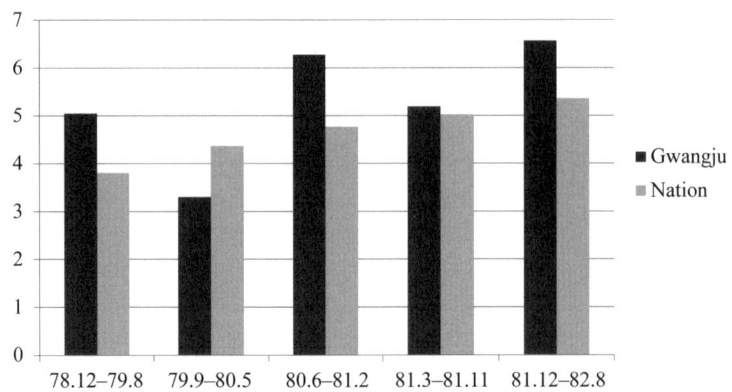

Figure 8.4 | % Preterm Births (< 37 weeks) by Mother's Year and Month of Birth

in-utero (Figure 8.3). For the risk of preterm birth, the disadvantage of the Gwangju grandchildren is less clearly revealed (Figure 8.4).

8.4. Summary

Growing evidence demonstrates that maternal psychological stress during pregnancy, a more subtle form of health shock, negatively affects a variety of offspring outcomes. Animal studies suggest that negative influences of maternal stress during pregnancy persist across multiple generations, but limited direct evidence confirms that the negative influences are present among human populations. The Gwangju uprising provides a unique opportunity for identifying the impact of maternal psychological stress on pregnancy. First, the tragic incident of May 1980 was a completely unanticipated shock that was unavoidably sustained by all citizens of Gwangju. Second, the major type of negative shocks to fetal health caused by the Gwangju uprising is likely to be maternal psychological stress. Finally, the duration of potential exposure to maternal stress was brief: only 10 days between May 18 and May 27 in 1980, which allows me to identify the exact timing of prenatal exposure.

CHAPTER 9

Intergenerational Effects of Exposure to Maternal Stress

9.1. Major Results

9.1.1. Result of Baseline Model Estimation

Ordinary least squares regressions for birth weight and gestation period are conducted according to the difference-in-difference model of Equation 8.1 introduced in Chapter 8. In all statistical tests, standard errors are adjusted for clustering at the levels of child's province of birth and mother's year of birth. If the exposure of a pregnant woman to the Gwangju uprising negatively affected the birth outcomes of their grandchildren, then the coefficient of the interaction between the dummy variable for birth in Gwangju (B_Gwangju) and that for having a mother born between June 1980 and February 1981 (B_Jun80-Feb81) should be negative.

In the baseline model (Column 1), polynomial terms of the year of birth of the mother (YOB, YOB^2, and YOB^3) are included to consider long-term changes in birth weight across birth cohorts. The variables of key determinants of birth weight, such as year of birth (year 2002, omitted category is year 2000), sex of the child (male), multiple birth (twins or triplets), and parity order (second, third or higher), are also included. In

Table 9.1
Mother's In-Utero Exposure to the Gwangju Uprising and Offspring Birth Weight (in grams)

	Mean	(1)		(2)		(3)	
		∂y/∂x	P-value	∂y/∂x	P-value	∂y/∂x	P-value
Intercept		4704.42	<.0001	4479.98	<.0001	4526.38	<.0001
Mother's place & timing of birth							
B_GWANGJU	0.03259	5.20	0.0059	3.63	0.0475	2.68	0.1440
B_GWANGJU*B_Jun80-Feb81	0.00021	-55.82	<.0001	-57.56	<.0001	-57.27	<.0001
B_Jun80-Feb81	0.00607	-15.17	0.0075	-16.19	0.0045	-15.89	0.0053
Mother YOB	71.6	-105.28	0.0125	-88.38	0.0300	-87.68	0.0279
Mother YOB^2	5144.7	2.06	0.0007	1.71	0.0034	1.66	0.0036
Mother YOB^3	370645.7	-0.01	<.0001	-0.01	0.0003	-0.01	0.0004
Characteristics of Birth							
Year 2002	0.43653	14.63	<.0001	13.22	<.0001	13.43	<.0001
Male	0.52389	101.26	<.0001	101.21	<.0001	101.19	<.0001
Twins	0.01793	-834.89	<.0001	-835.36	<.0001	-835.87	<.0001
Triplets	0.00017	-1232.68	<.0001	-1230.06	<.0001	-1229.99	<.0001
Birth parity: second	0.41977	14.87	<.0001	16.80	<.0001	16.52	<.0001
Birth parity: third or higher	0.09843	72.86	<.0001	78.24	<.0001	78.60	<.0001
Mother's SES							
Mother Middle school or less	0.03731			-42.68	<.0001	-28.02	<.0001
Mother High school	0.55457			NI		NI	
Mother college or higher	0.40549			10.12	<.0001	1.93	0.0835
Mother's education unknown	0.00263			-196.21	<.0001	-169.67	<.0001
Mother Professional job	0.04831			-3.92	0.0374	-5.65	0.0025
Mother Clerical job	0.06670			11.86	<.0001	9.43	<.0001
Mother Service/Sales	0.01336			7.67	0.0330	6.94	0.0514
Mother Farming	0.00594			-10.93	0.0971	1.79	0.7849
Mother Skilled job	0.00265			7.18	0.3489	10.23	0.1872
Mother Unskilled job	0.00188			-14.82	0.1377	-9.81	0.3285
Mother Not working	0.84368			NI		NI	
Mother Occupation unknown	0.00628			-32.36	<.0001	-28.07	<.0001
Father's SES							
Father Middle school or less	0.04728					-20.44	<.0001
Father High school	0.44835					NI	
Father college or higher	0.49977					12.21	<.0001
Father's education unknown	0.00460					-97.55	<.0001

Table 9.1 (continued)

	Mean	(1)		(2)		(3)	
		∂y/∂x	P-value	∂y/∂x	P-value	∂y/∂x	P-value
Father Professional job	0.17894					-0.45	0.6666
Father Clerical job	0.34924					NI	
Father Service/Sales	0.13535					2.55	0.0778
Father Farming	0.03093					-12.36	<.0001
Father Skilled job	0.08688					-5.72	0.0016
Father Unskilled job	0.06344					-7.79	<.0001
Father Not working	0.06096					-7.04	0.0009
Father Occupation unknown	0.00823					-7.19	0.2912
R-square		0.0764		0.0772		0.0777	
F-value		5659.43		3343.32		2478.93	
P-value		<.0001		<.0001		<.0001	

Source: Micro data on the Korean Vital Statistics (Birth) for 2000 and 2002.

Note: The number of observation is 1,124,848. The dependent mean is 3262.142 grams. NI denotes the omitted category (control group). Standard errors are adjusted for clustering at the levels of child's province of birth and mother's year of birth.

the second model (Column 2), the variables of the educational attainment and occupation of the mother are added. Schooling is classified into four categories: (a) middle school or lower, (b) high school, (c) college or higher, and (d) education unknown. Occupation is classified into eight categories: (a) professional (b) clerical job, (c) service and sales, (d) farming, (e) skilled, (f) unskilled, (g) not working, and (h) occupation unknown. In the final model (Column 3), the variables of the socioeconomic status of the father and mother are included.

The regression results for birth weight are reported in Table 9.1. The prenatal exposure of the mother to the Gwangju uprising reduced the offspring birth weight. The coefficient for the interaction term (B_Gwangju*B_Jun80-Feb81) is negative and significant (p-value < 0.0001). The magnitude of the coefficient suggests that the average birth weight of Gwangju grandchildren is lower than that of non-Gwangju grandchildren by about 56 grams, controlling for the year of birth of the mother and some key birth characteristics. Adding parental socioeconomic characteristics does not significantly change the result. The coefficient for the interaction term is marginally changed in terms of magnitude (about 57 grams).

The year of birth of the mother is negatively related to birth weight.

Table 9.2
Mother's In-Utero Exposure to the Gwangju Uprising and the Length of Gestation (in weeks)

	Mean	(1)		(2)		(3)	
		∂y/∂x	P-value	∂y/∂x	P-value	∂y/∂x	P-value
Intercept		72.248	<.0001	72.153	<.0001	72.456	<.0001
Mother's place & timing of birth							
B_GWANGJU	0.03259	-0.078	<.0001	-0.080	<.0001	-0.081	<.0001
B_GWANGJU*B_Jun80-Feb81	0.00021	-0.328	0.0095	-0.329	0.0089	-0.328	0.0097
B_Jun80-Feb81	0.00607	0.023	0.2934	0.022	0.2975	0.022	0.2983
Mother YOB	71.6	-1.561	<.0001	-1.551	<.0001	-1.562	<.0001
Mother YOB^2	5144.7	0.024	<.0001	0.024	<.0001	0.024	<.0001
Mother YOB^3	370645.7	0.000	<.0001	0.000	<.0001	0.000	<.0001
Characteristics of Birth							
Year 2002	0.43653	-0.150	<.0001	-0.153	<.0001	-0.153	<.0001
Male	0.52389	-0.106	<.0001	-0.106	<.0001	-0.106	<.0001
Twins	0.01793	-2.635	<.0001	-2.636	<.0001	-2.636	<.0001
Triplets	0.00017	-5.073	<.0001	-5.072	<.0001	-5.069	<.0001
Birth parity: second	0.41977	-0.308	<.0001	-0.304	<.0001	-0.304	<.0001
Birth parity: third or higher	0.09843	-0.150	<.0001	-0.142	<.0001	-0.141	<.0001
Mother's SES							
Mother Middle school or less	0.03731			-0.020	0.0205	-0.010	0.2706
Mother High school	0.55457			NI		NI	
Mother college or higher	0.40549			0.026	<.0001	0.009	0.0276
Mother's education unknown	0.00263			0.058	0.2263	0.070	0.1503
Mother Professional job	0.04831			-0.023	0.0039	-0.025	0.0016
Mother Clerical job	0.06670			0.024	0.0012	0.018	0.0092
Mother Service/Sales	0.01336			-0.010	0.4087	-0.015	0.2415
Mother Farming	0.00594			0.068	0.0025	0.061	0.0058
Mother Skilled job	0.00265			0.009	0.7024	0.023	0.3621
Mother Unskilled job	0.00188			-0.068	0.0673	-0.055	0.1327
Mother Not working	0.84368			NI		NI	
Mother Occupation unknown	0.00628			0.037	0.0940	0.041	0.0664
Father's SES							
Father Middle school or less	0.04728					0.001	0.8501
Father High school	0.44835					NI	
Father college or higher	0.49977					0.026	<.0001
Father's education unknown	0.00460					-0.094	0.0197
Father Professional job	0.17894					-0.006	0.1237

Table 9.2 (continued)

	Mean	(1)		(2)		(3)	
		∂y/∂x	P-value	∂y/∂x	P-value	∂y/∂x	P-value
Father Clerical job	0.34924					NI	
Father Service/Sales	0.13535					0.008	0.1278
Father Farming	0.03093					0.004	0.7270
Father Skilled job	0.08688					-0.032	<.0001
Father Unskilled job	0.06344					-0.029	<.0001
Father Not working	0.06096					0.002	0.8239
Father Occupation unknown	0.00823					-0.027	0.2677
R-square		0.0754		0.0755		0.0757	
F-value		1609.16		973.71		702.38	
P-value		<.0001		<.0001		<.0001	

Source: Micro data on the Korean Vital Statistics (Birth) for 2000 and 2002.

Note: The number of observation is 1,124,848. The dependent mean is 39.175 weeks. NI denotes the omitted category (control group). Standard errors are adjusted for clustering at the levels of child's province of birth and mother's year of birth.

Given that the analysis is based on the 2000 and 2002 birth records, it perhaps captures the effect of early-age delivery. The effects of birth characteristics and parental socioeconomic status (SES) show largely anticipated signs. Boys are heavier at birth than girls. Multiple births reduce birth weight, and higher-parity children are heavier at birth. Parental education is positively related to birth weight. The quality of parental occupation is not perfectly matched with offspring birth weight. For example, children of professional mothers are significantly lighter than those of non-working mothers and mothers with clerical, service/sales, or skilled jobs. Similarly, children of fathers with service/sales jobs are slightly heavier at birth than those of fathers with professional jobs.

Table 9.2 reports the regression results for the length of gestation. The in-utero exposure of the mother to the Gwangju uprising had a significantly negative effect on the gestation period of the child, although the magnitude was rather small: the length of gestation of Gwangju grandchildren was about 2.3 days shorter than that of non-Gwangju grandchildren, with the year of birth of the mother and some key birth characteristics held constant. As with birth weight, adding parental SES does not change the magnitude and statistical significance of the coefficient for the interaction term.

The year of birth of the mother is negatively associated with

Table 9.3
Mother's In-Utero Exposure to the Gwangju Uprising and Probability of Offspring Low Birth Weight (< 2.5 kg)

	Mean	(1)		(2)		(3)	
		$\partial y/\partial x$	P-value	$\partial y/\partial x$	P-value	$\partial y/\partial x$	P-value
Intercept		-1.5804	<.0001	-1.5352	<.0001	-1.5483	<.0001
B_GWANGJU	0.032591	-0.0008	0.2831	-0.0001	0.9042	0.0002	0.8075
B_GWANGJU*B_Jun80-Feb81	0.000067	0.0232	<.0001	0.0238	<.0001	0.0236	<.0001
B_Jun80-Feb81	0.001949	-0.0020	0.4700	-0.0017	0.5449	-0.0017	0.5252
Mother YOB, YOB^2, YOB^3		Yes		Yes		Yes	
Characteristics of Birth		Yes		Yes		Yes	
Mother's SES		No		Yes		Yes	
Father's SES		No		No		Yes	
R-square		0.1063		0.1070		0.1073	
F-value		1260.32		757.79		542.44	
P-value		<.0001		<.0001		<.0001	

Source: Micro data on the Korean Vital Statistics (Birth) for 2000 and 2002.

Note: The number of observation is 1,124,848. The dependent mean is 0.0388. The same independent variables used in the regressions presented in Table 9.1 are included. Standard errors are adjusted for clustering at the levels of child's province of birth and mother's year of birth.

the length of gestation, which perhaps reflects the effect of early-age pregnancy, as in the case of birth weight. Length of gestation for multiple births is much shorter than that for singleton babies. Differences in the length of gestation according to parental SES are small in magnitude.

Table 9.3 and Table 9.4 present the results of linear probability model estimations of how the in-utero exposure of the mother to the Gwangju uprising influenced the risks of low birth weight (i.e., under 2.5 kg) and pre-term birth (i.e., gestation period shorter than 37 weeks). Maternal exposure to stress in pregnancy not only reduces the average birth weight of the grandchildren, but also increases the probability that they are born with LBW. With parental SES controlled for, Gwangju grandchildren were about 2.4% more likely to have LBW than non-Gwangju grandchildren, and the difference is statistically significant (p-value < 0.0001). Similarly, the grandchildren of women who experienced the Gwangju massacre during pregnancy were at a higher risk of preterm birth, although the effect is statistically less significant (p-value = 0.0146). Again, three different specifications (Columns 1 to 3 in Tables 9.3 and 9.4) yield virtually the same results.

Table 9.4
Mother's In-Utero Exposure to the Gwangju Uprising and Probability of Offspring Preterm Birth (< 37 weeks)

	Mean	(1)		(2)		(3)	
		∂y/∂x	P-value	∂y/∂x	P-value	∂y/∂x	P-value
Intercept		-2.4381	<.0001	-2.2697	<.0001	-2.2503	<.0001
B_GWANGJU	0.032591	0.0026	0.0042	0.0030	0.0009	0.0031	0.0006
B_GWANGJU*B_Jun80-Feb81	0.000067	0.0146	0.0161	0.0161	0.0074	0.0152	0.0218
B_Jun80-Feb81	0.001949	-0.0002	0.9395	0.0005	0.8480	0.0003	0.8890
Mother YOB, YOB^2, YOB^3		Yes		Yes		Yes	
Characteristics of Birth		Yes		Yes		Yes	
Mother's SES		No		Yes		Yes	
Father's SES		No		No		Yes	
R-square		0.0585		0.0772		0.0787	
F-value		596.11		500.36		463.21	
P-value		<.0001		<.0001		<.0001	

Source: Micro data on the Korean Vital Statistics (Birth) for 2000 and 2002.

Note: The number of observation is 1,124,848. The dependent mean is 0.0406. The same independent variables used in the regressions presented in Table 9.2 are included. Standard errors are adjusted for clustering at the levels of child's province of birth and mother's year of birth.

9.1.2. Differences by Trimester

The impact of exposure to maternal stress could differ by stage of pregnancy when the shock is received. To verify this possibility, children born to mothers exposed to the Gwangju uprising in-utero are classified into three groups, depending on which trimester of pregnancy their mothers experienced the event. For example, mothers born between December 1980 and February 1981 were in the first trimester when the Gwangju uprising occurred. Similarly, those born between September 1980 and November 1980 and between June 1980 and August 1980 were exposed to the Gwangju incident when they were in the second and third trimesters, respectively.

In the new regression equations, three dummy variables of the month or year of birth of the mothers corresponding to the three groups (B_Dec80-Feb81, B_Sep80-Nov80, and B_Jun80-Aug80) and their interactions with the dummy variable for birth in Gwangju (B_Gwangju)

Table 9.5
Mother's In-Utero Exposure to the Gwangju Uprising and Offspring Birth Weight by Stage of Pregnancy

	Mean	(1)		(2)		(3)	
		∂y/∂x	P-value	∂y/∂x	P-value	∂y/∂x	P-value
Intercept		4676.97	<.0001	4448.58	<.0001	4493.39	<.0001
B_GWANGJU	0.032591	5.20	0.0058	3.62	0.0475	2.68	0.1440
B_GWANGJU*B_Dec80-Feb81	0.000067	-39.29	0.0095	-41.22	0.0055	-36.80	0.0227
B_GWANGJU*B_Sep80-Nov80	0.000075	-102.62	<.0001	-103.55	<.0001	-104.65	<.0001
B_GWANGJU*B_Jun80-Aug80	0.000070	-22.52	0.0407	-24.92	0.0235	-27.11	0.0141
B_Dec80-Feb81	0.001949	-26.38	0.0103	-28.88	0.0040	-29.37	0.0037
B_Sep80-Nov80	0.002019	-5.32	0.5835	-5.86	0.5528	-5.48	0.5798
B_Jun80-Aug80	0.002105	-14.56	0.1855	-14.69	0.1817	-13.79	0.2110
Mother YOB, YOB^2, YOB^3		Yes		Yes		Yes	
Characteristics of Birth		Yes		Yes		Yes	
Mother's SES		No		Yes		Yes	
Father's SES		No		No		Yes	
R-square		0.0764		0.0772		0.0777	
F-value		6227.85		3.28E+09		3556.46	
P-value		<.0001		<.0001		<.0001	

Source: Micro data on the Korean Vital Statistics (Birth) for 2000 and 2002.

Note: The number of observation is 1,124,848. The dependent mean is 3262.142 grams. The same independent variables used in the regressions presented in Table 9.1 are included. Standard errors are adjusted for clustering at the levels of child's province of birth and mother's year of birth.

are included, replacing B_Jun80-Feb81 and B_Gwangju*B_Jun80-Feb81. Other control variables of the year of birth of the mother, birth characteristics, and parental SES are also included.

Table 9.5 shows how the in-utero exposure of the mother to the Gwangju incident in each trimester affects offspring birth weight. In-utero exposure to stress during the second trimester exerted the strongest negative effect on offspring birth weight, diminishing birth weight by 103 grams (p-value < 0.0001). Maternal exposure to stress during the first and final trimesters also reduces the birth weight of the grandchildren, but the effects are less significant and smaller in magnitude (39 and 23 grams, respectively). The results remain unchanged if parental SES is controlled for.

Table 9.6 presents the estimated effect of the in-utero exposure of

Table 9.6
Mother's In-Utero Exposure to the Gwangju Uprising and Offspring Length of Gestation by Stage of Pregnancy

	Mean	(1)		(2)		(3)	
		∂y/∂x	P-value	∂y/∂x	P-value	∂y/∂x	P-value
Intercept		72.206	<.0001	72.107	<.0001	72.408	<.0001
B_GWANGJU	0.032591	-0.078	<.0001	-0.080	<.0001	-0.081	<.0001
B_GWANGJU*B_Dec80-Feb81	0.000067	0.085	0.1196	0.083	0.1260	0.090	0.1084
B_GWANGJU*B_Sep80-Nov80	0.000075	-0.537	<.0001	-0.539	<.0001	-0.539	<.0001
B_GWANGJU*B_Jun80-Aug80	0.000070	-0.507	<.0001	-0.508	<.0001	-0.510	<.0001
B_Dec80-Feb81	0.001949	-0.010	0.7690	-0.011	0.7315	-0.013	0.7028
B_Sep80-Nov80	0.002019	0.066	0.0239	0.066	0.0229	0.066	0.0216
B_Jun80-Aug80	0.002105	0.011	0.7824	0.011	0.7736	0.012	0.7622
Mother YOB, YOB^2, YOB^3		Yes		Yes		Yes	
Characteristics of Birth		Yes		Yes		Yes	
Mother's SES		No		Yes		Yes	
Father's SES		No		No		Yes	
R-square		0.0754		0.0756		0.0757	
F-value		1.93E+08		7.57E+08		1031.86	
P-value		<.0001		<.0001		<.0001	

Source: Micro data on the Korean Vital Statistics (Birth) for 2000 and 2002.

Note: The number of observation is 1,123,814. The dependent mean is 39.175 weeks. The same independent variables used in the regressions presented in Table 9.2 are included. Standard errors are adjusted for clustering at the levels of child's province of birth and mother's year of birth.

the mother to the Gwangju incident in each trimester on the offspring length of gestation. In contrast to birth weight, prenatal exposure of the mother to stress during the second and third trimesters has equally strong negative effects on the offspring length of gestation, reducing the length of gestation by slightly more than half a week (p-values < 0.0001). Again, adding parental SES does not change the results.

Similar regression analyses are conducted for the probabilities of low birth weight and preterm birth, in linear probability models (Table 9.7 and Table 9.8). Maternal exposure to stress during the second trimester of pregnancy is particularly harmful for offspring birth outcomes. Consistent with the results for average birth weight (Table 9.5), maternal exposure to the Gwangju uprising during the second trimester of pregnancy (birth of the mother between September and November 1980)

Table 9.7
Mother's In-Utero Exposure to the Gwangju Uprising and Probability of Offspring Low Birth Weight by Stage of Pregnancy

	Mean	(1)		(2)		(3)	
		∂y/∂x	P-value	∂y/∂x	P-value	∂y/∂x	P-value
Intercept		-1.5888	<.0001	-1.5421	<.0001	-1.5547	<.0001
B_GWANGJU	0.032591	-0.0008	0.2831	-0.0001	0.9040	0.0002	0.8077
B_GWANGJU*B_Dec80-Feb81	0.000067	0.0180	0.0075	0.0187	0.0056	0.0171	0.0075
B_GWANGJU*B_Sep80-Nov80	0.000075	0.0397	<.0001	0.0400	<.0001	0.0403	<.0001
B_GWANGJU*B_Jun80-Aug80	0.000070	0.0111	0.0011	0.0118	0.0005	0.0125	0.0002
B_Dec80-Feb81	0.001949	-0.0050	0.3417	-0.0041	0.4356	-0.0039	0.4583
B_Sep80-Nov80	0.002019	-0.0050	0.0685	-0.0048	0.0828	-0.0049	0.0814
B_Jun80-Aug80	0.002105	0.0036	0.3050	0.0035	0.3094	0.0032	0.3443
Mother YOB, YOB^2, YOB^3		Yes		Yes		Yes	
Characteristics of Birth		Yes		Yes		Yes	
Mother's SES		No		Yes		Yes	
Father's SES		No		No		Yes	
R-square		0.1063		0.1070		0.1073	
F-value		4335.80		3272.27		2591.73	
P-value		<.0001		<.0001		<.0001	

Source: Micro data on the Korean Vital Statistics (Birth) for 2000 and 2002.

Note: The number of observation is 1,124,848. The dependent mean is 0.0388. The same independent variables used in the regressions presented in Table 9.1 are included. Standard errors are adjusted for clustering at the levels of child's province of birth and mother's year of birth.

strongly increases the probability that the child weighs less than 2.5 kg at birth. The magnitude of the coefficient for the interaction term (0.0403 in Column 3 of Table 9.7) is much larger than the result for the entire period of pregnancy (0.0236 in Column 3 of Table 9.3). Prenatal exposure of the mother to stress during the first and third trimesters also increases the risk of LBW, but the effects are much smaller in magnitude (0.0171 and 0.0125, respectively, in Column 3 of Table 9.7).

For offspring preterm birth, the second trimester also stands out as the most critical period. The probability of preterm birth is most strongly increased by maternal exposure to the Gwangju uprising during the second trimester of pregnancy (Table 9.8). Compared with the results of regressions of the influences of exposure through the entire pregnancy (Column 3 of Table 9.4), the coefficient for the interaction term (Column 3) has much a larger magnitude (0.0462 versus 0.152) and

Table 9.8
Mother's In-Utero Exposure to the Gwangju Uprising and Probability of Offspring Preterm Birth by Stage of Pregnancy

	Mean	(1)		(2)		(3)	
		∂y/∂x	P-value	∂y/∂x	P-value	∂y/∂x	P-value
Intercept		-2.4224	<.0001	-2.2581	<.0001	-2.2387	<.0001
B_GWANGJU	0.032591	0.0026	0.0042	0.0030	0.0009	0.0031	0.0006
B_GWANGJU*B_Dec80-Feb81	0.000067	-0.0169	0.1466	-0.0133	0.2146	-0.0188	0.1637
B_GWANGJU*B_Sep80-Nov80	0.000075	0.0464	<.0001	0.0452	<.0001	0.0462	<.0001
B_GWANGJU*B_Jun80-Aug80	0.000070	0.0117	0.0003	0.0139	<.0001	0.0153	<.0001
B_Dec80-Feb81	0.001949	0.0070	0.1953	0.0060	0.1924	0.0061	0.1875
B_Sep80-Nov80	0.002019	-0.0069	0.0468	-0.0050	0.1429	-0.0049	0.1598
B_Jun80-Aug80	0.002105	-0.0004	0.9028	0.0006	0.8342	0.0001	0.9749
Mother YOB, YOB^2, YOB^3		Yes		Yes		Yes	
Characteristics of Birth		Yes		Yes		Yes	
Mother's SES		No		Yes		Yes	
Father's SES		No		No		Yes	
R-square		0.0585		0.0772		0.0787	
F-value		3697.43		2946.67		2398.11	
P-value		<.0001		<.0001		<.0001	

Source: Micro data on the Korean Vital Statistics (Birth) for 2000 and 2002.

Note: The number of observation is 1,123,814. The dependent mean is 0.0429. The same independent variables used in the regressions presented in Table 9.2 are included. Standard errors are adjusted for clustering at the levels of child's province of birth and mother's year of birth.

statistically more significant (p-value of <0.0001 versus 0.0218). This contrast is partly explained by the fact that maternal exposure during the first trimester of pregnancy actually decreases the risk of preterm birth, although the estimated coefficient is statistically insignificant.

Whether the intergenerational consequences of the in-utero exposure of the mother to the Gwangju uprising differs by offspring gender is also examined by separate regression analyses for boys and girls. Table 9.9 provides the results of how the prenatal exposure of the mother to stress during the entire pregnancy (Panel A) and during a particular trimester of pregnancy (Panel B) affected the four birth outcomes of her child. Results in Panel A suggest that the overall effects of the in-utero exposure of the mother to the Gwangju uprising are stronger for boys than for girls. The estimated coefficients of interaction terms for girls are mostly smaller in magnitude than those for boys.

Table 9.9

Mother's In-Utero Exposure to the Gwangju Uprising and Offspring Birth Outcomes by Gender

	(1) Birth Weight		(2) LBW		(3) Gestation		(4) Preterm Birth	
	∂y/∂x	P-value	∂y/∂x	P-value	∂y/∂x	P-value	∂y/∂x	P-value
(A) Boys								
(1) B_GWANGJU*B_Jun80-Feb81	-65.459	0.0681	0.0406	0.0561	-0.4218	0.2158	0.0309	0.2231
(2) B_GWANGJU*B_Dec80-Feb81	50.632	0.1627	-0.0069	0.4075	0.3439	<.0001	-0.0405	0.0012
B_GWANGJU*B_Sep80-Nov80	-142.049	<.0001	0.0556	<.0001	-0.8727	<.0001	0.0628	<.0001
B_GWANGJU*B_Jun80-Aug80	-126.229	<.0001	0.0877	<.0001	-0.9027	<.0001	0.0854	<.0001
(B) Girls								
(1) B_GWANGJU*B_Jun80-Feb81	-50.487	0.1334	0.0091	0.3217	-0.2458	<.0001	0.0009	0.9221
(2) B_GWANGJU*B_Dec80-Feb81	-150.166	<.0001	0.0497	<.0001	-0.2424	0.1566	0.0098	0.6416
B_GWANGJU*B_Sep80-Nov80	-71.790	<.0001	0.0268	<.0001	-0.2566	<.0001	0.0312	<.0001
B_GWANGJU*B_Jun80-Aug80	38.754	0.0224	-0.0375	<.0001	-0.2459	<.0001	-0.0342	<.0001

Source: Micro data on the Korean Vital Statistics (Birth) for 2000 and 2002.

Note: The number of observation is 589,247 for boys and 535,601 for girls. The dependent means for boys and girls are respectively 3311.68 and 3207.64 for (1); 0.0346 and 0.0434 for (2); 39.12 and 39.23 for (3); and 0.0454 and 0.0400 for (4). The same independent variables used in the regressions presented in the Column 3 of Table 9.1 are included. Standard errors are adjusted for clustering at the levels of child's province of birth and mother's year of birth.

The results in Panel B further suggest that the mechanism by which maternal stress in pregnancy transmitted across generations might be different between sons and daughters. For boys, the in-utero exposure of the mother to the Gwangju uprising during the second trimester had a particularly strong negative effect on all birth outcomes, especially on the length of gestation and probability of preterm birth. In sharp contrast, maternal stress received in the first trimester had a particularly strong adverse effect on birth weight and risk of LBW for girls. This effect is not mediated by the reduced length of gestation. Length of gestation and probability of preterm birth for girls are not significantly influenced by the exposure of their mothers to prenatal stress.

9.2. Discussion: Robustness and Potential Bias

9.2.1. Robustness

Several robustness checks are performed. First, to compare mothers with similar year of birth, the children of women born between 1975 and 1985 are included in regressions, excluding the children of mothers who are much older or younger than the cohort who experienced the Gwangju uprising in-utero (Panel A of Table 9.10). The results for birth weight, LBW, and preterm birth are practically the same as the baseline regression based on the full sample of babies in terms of the magnitude and statistical significance of each of the estimated coefficients (Columns 1, 2, and 3). For length of gestation, the result also does not change significantly, although the absolute magnitudes of the coefficients for the interaction terms are slightly smaller than those obtained from the baseline regressions.

Second, only babies born in the six metropolitan cities (i.e., Seoul, Busan, Incheon, Daejeon, Daegu, and Gwangju) are included in regression analyses to make comparisons across mothers living under similar conditions (e.g., similar medical facilities and ecological environment) (Panel B of Table 9.10). For all four measures of birth outcomes, regression results based on the urban sample are remarkably similar to the results from the whole sample.

Third, children born in counties adjacent to Gwangju are included in the treated group along with those born in Gwangju to consider the potential spillover effects of the uprising (Panel C of Table 9.10). Although major clashes between martial law troops and citizens occurred in Gwangju, neighboring areas could have been affected by the uprising to some extent. After retreating from the city on May 21, 1980, the government army stationed and regrouped in the outskirts of the city while attempting to prevent the democratic movement from spreading to wider areas by blockading the major routes connecting Gwangju and

Table 9.10
Mother's In-Utero Exposure to the Gwangju Uprising and Offspring Birth Outcomes: Robustness Tests

	(1) Birth Weight		(2) LBW		(3) Gestation		(4) Preterm Birth	
	∂y/∂x	P-value	∂y/∂x	P-value	∂y/∂x	P-value	∂y/∂x	P-value
(A) Sample: 1975-85 Cohorts								
(1)								
B_GWANGJU*B_Jun80-Feb81	-53.530	<.0001	0.0261	<.0001	-0.2755	0.0272	0.0148	0.0397
(2)								
B_GWANGJU*B_Dec80-Feb81	-36.722	0.0125	0.0210	0.0037	0.1393	0.0172	-0.0206	0.1620
B_GWANGJU*B_Sep80-Nov80	-100.644	<.0001	0.0428	<.0001	-0.4865	<.0001	0.0468	<.0001
B_GWANGJU*B_Jun80-Aug80	-20.178	0.0805	0.0136	0.0004	-0.4553	<.0001	0.0153	<.0001
(B) Sample: Six Large Cities								
(1)								
B_GWANGJU*B_Jun80-Feb81	-60.273	<.0001	0.0233	0.0002	-0.3168	0.0159	0.0177	0.0206
(2)								
B_GWANGJU*B_Dec80-Feb81	-38.802	0.0660	0.0201	0.0371	0.0805	0.1859	-0.0144	0.3347
B_GWANGJU*B_Sep80-Nov80	-124.765	<.0001	0.0428	<.0001	-0.5507	<.0001	0.0457	<.0001
B_GWANGJU*B_Jun80-Aug80	-14.220	0.5694	0.0059	0.2016	-0.4561	<.0001	0.0192	0.0001
(C) Treated: Adjacent Counties								
(1)								
B_GWANGJU*B_Jun80-Feb81	-26.702	0.3254	0.0086	0.5576	-0.2373	0.0800	0.0034	0.7510
(2)								
B_GWANGJU*B_Dec80-Feb81	-11.154	0.7087	0.0133	0.0540	0.1244	0.0575	-0.0281	0.0462
B_GWANGJU*B_Sep80-Nov80	-85.984	0.0001	0.0220	0.2476	-0.4393	0.0002	0.0342	0.0039
B_GWANGJU*B_Jun80-Aug80	12.618	0.7315	-0.0076	0.6735	-0.3574	0.0192	0.0021	0.8526
(D) Treated: Jeonnam Province								
(1)								
B_GWANGJU*B_Jun80-Feb81	2.5947	0.6885	-0.0090	0.0623	0.0182	0.5020	-0.0139	<.0001

Table 9.10 (continued)

	(1) Birth Weight		(2) LBW		(3) Gestation		(4) Preterm Birth	
	∂y/∂x	P-value	∂y/∂x	P-value	∂y/∂x	P-value	∂y/∂x	P-value
(2)								
B_GWANGJU*B_Dec80-Feb81	20.3973	0.1452	-0.0253	0.0001	-0.0637	0.6095	-0.0065	0.7485
B_GWANGJU*B_Sep80-Nov80	-7.3406	0.5137	-0.0072	0.0277	0.0905	0.0167	-0.0216	<.0001
B_GWANGJU*B_Jun80-Aug80	-3.9495	0.7344	0.0025	0.4825	0.0150	0.7455	-0.0123	0.0002

Source: Micro data on the Korean Vital Statistics (Birth) for 2000 and 2002.

Note: The number of observation is 239,786 for (A); 490,001 for (B); and 1,123,814 for (C) and (D). The same independent variables used in the regressions presented in Col. 3 of Table 9.1 are included. Standard errors are adjusted for clustering at the levels of child's province of birth and mother's year of birth.

nearby towns. Violent incidents took place outside Gwangju, such as the shooting and killing of children who were misidentified as escaping demonstrators. Regression results show that the prenatal exposure of the mother to the Gwangju uprising during the second trimester of pregnancy had significantly negative effects on birth outcomes. However, the overall effects are weaker than those of the baseline results, in which only the children born in Gwangju are regarded as treated.

Finally, children born anywhere in Jeonnam Province are regarded as treated by the Gwangju incident. Gwangju and Jeonnam residents probably share similar political, social, and cultural backgrounds, although they differ in terms of the extent of urbanization. In particular, the entire region supported Former President Kim Dae Jung and most actively protested against the military regime that emerged in 1980. The purpose of the final robustness check is to determine if the negative effect of having a mother born between June 1980 and February 1981 captures the influences of exposure to the violence during the Gwangju uprising or the effects of the political oppression of the military regime during the period that were felt by a larger population in the region. Regression results do not support this conjecture (Panel D). The coefficients for the interaction terms are much smaller than those of baseline regressions and statistically insignificant for birth weight. The negative effect of maternal exposure to the Gwangju uprising is likely to reflect the negative intergenerational effects of stress caused by the first-hand experience of the violent event.[1]

9.2.2. Potential Bias Problems

A critical weakness of the data used in this study is that the birthplace of the parent is not reported. The place of residence of women in the sample at the time of giving birth must be an inaccurate proxy for their birthplace because of geographic mobility. The direction and magnitude of potential bias arising from the problem depend on the extent and pattern of migrations from and to Gwangju.

Table 9.11 presents two types of statistics computed from the 2% sample of the 2000 census providing the magnitude and pattern of geographic mobility of female birth cohorts born around 1980 (those aged 18 to 22 years in 2000) from their birth to 2000. The first column shows where Gwangju natives were located in 2000. The second column gives the birthplaces of the same female cohorts residing in Gwangju in 2000. Both columns suggest considerably high geographic mobility. Nearly half of the women born in Gwangju had remained in Gwangju

Table 9.11
Geographic Mobility of the Female Cohorts aged 18 to 22 in 2000 (percent)

	Place of residence in 2000 of women born in Gwangju		Place of birth of women residing in Gwangju in 2000	
	All N=424	Married in 2000 N=15	All N=887	Married in 2000 N=54
Gwangju	43.6	46.7	20.9	13.0
Neighboring Counties	3.3	6.8	19.8	22.2
Other Jeonnam Counties	6.8	13.3	41.3	44.4
Other Provinces	46.2	33.3	18.0	20.4

Source: The 2% micro sample of the 2000 census.

1 This finding is confirmed by the results of additional regressions not reported here, where only the birth records of those born in Gwangju or Jeonnam Province, which surrounds Gwangju, are considered. Overall, the results based on the Gwangju and Jeonnam samples are similar to those of baseline regressions, although the effect on birth weight is somewhat less significant, implying that the experiences of Gwangju citizens should be different from those of Jeonnam residents.

or adjacent counties by 2000, and about an equal proportion had moved out of the Jeonnam Province (Column 1 of Table 9.11). Of the Gwangju female citizens aged 18 to 22 years in 2000, 20% were Gwangju natives, another 20% came from adjacent counties, 40% from other Jeonnam areas, and the remaining 20% from other provinces (Column 2 of Table 9.11).

The considerably high geographic mobility must lead to a misidentification of treated persons. That is, the newly born regarded as the treated group in this study include both the children of women actually exposed to the Gwangju uprising while in-utero and the children of those who were born elsewhere and migrated to Gwangju. As noted above, any negative effects of the Gwangju uprising were likely limited to those who were directly exposed to the incident. This conjecture is consistent with the result that the adverse intergenerational effects of the Gwangju uprising become weaker or disappear if children born in counties adjacent to Gwangju or in other places within Jeonnam Province are added to the treated group. If this type of bias is considered, I suspect that the actual negative effects of in-utero exposure to the Gwangju uprising on offspring birth outcomes might be even more serious than suggested by the results of this study.

Another possible concern related to geographic mobility is that the results of this chapter (i.e., worse birth outcomes of children born in Gwangju to mothers who were in-utero during the Gwangju uprising) might be attributed to the consequences of selective migration. As difference-in-difference estimation is employed and the socioeconomic characteristics of parents (i.e., education and occupation) are controlled for, the so-called "selective migration story" is plausible if the following condition holds: the selection of Gwangju residents around 2000 out of all women born in Gwangju was discontinuously negative for the cohort born between June 1980 and February 1981 in terms of unobservable personal characteristics.

Although the validity of the selective migration story is difficult to examine directly, some circumstantial evidence can be offered based on the micro-sample of the 2000 census. Using a sample of women born in Gwangju aged 18 to 22 years in 2000, the following difference-in-difference regressions were conducted to determine if educational attainment as of 2000 was significantly lower for Gwangju citizens born in 1980.

Table 9.12

Logistic Regression: Migration, Birth in 1980, and Schooling of Gwangju Natives Aged 18 to 22 in 2000

	Mean	(1) No High School Diploma		(2) College	
		∂y/∂x	P-value	∂y/∂x	P-value
Age	19.969	-2.630	<.0001	2.743	<.0001
Age^2	400.649	0.064	<.0001	-0.066	<.0001
Gwangju in 2000	0.436	-0.035	0.1520	0.197	0.0002
Gwangju in 2000*Born in 1980	0.099	0.044	0.6025	-0.115	0.2848
Born in 1980	0.214	0.112	0.1567	-0.025	0.7529
-2 Log L w/o Covariates		330.986		568.539	
-2 Log L w/ Covariates		161.023		503.117	
Chi-Square		169.962		65.422	
P-value		<.0001		<.0001	

Source: The 2% micro sample of the 2000 census.

Note: The number of observation is 424. The dependent mean is 0.132 for (1) and 0.489 for (2).

$$\textbf{(9.1)} \quad E_i = \alpha + \beta_1 I_i + \beta_2 (I_i \times K_i) + \beta_3 K_i + \gamma_1 AGE_i + \gamma_2 AGE_i^2 + \varepsilon_i$$

where E denotes educational attainment (dummy variables for no high school diploma and for entering college), I denotes the dummy variable for women born in 1980 (Born in 1980: a proxy variable for being in-utero during the Gwangju uprising), K is the dummy variable for whether the woman lived in Gwangju in 2000 (Gwangju in 2000), and AGE stands for the age of the woman in 2000. The results of logistic regressions (Table 9.12) suggest out-migrants from Gwangju were positively selected (as shown by the estimated coefficient β_3), but migrant selections were not significantly different between the 1980 birth cohort and neighboring cohorts (as indicated by the estimated coefficient β_2).

Selective marriage is another possible source of bias. As only the 2000 and 2002 Vital Statistics on birth provide information on the dates of birth of parents, the empirical analyses above were restricted to babies born to relatively young mothers. Mothers exposed to the Gwangju uprising while in-utero were in their early 20s at the time of giving birth. If only selected women married early and selections in marriage among young women were discontinuously negative for those who were in-utero during the Gwangju uprising, the results of this chapter regarding the intergenerational impact of prenatal exposure to stress could be

Table 9.13
Logistic Regression: Marriage, Birth in 1980, and Schooling of Gwangju Natives Aged 18 to 22 in 2000

	Mean	(1) No High School Diploma		(2) College	
		∂y/∂x	P-value	∂y/∂x	P-value
Age	20.086	-2.032	<.0001	2.268	<.0001
Age^2	405.306	0.049	<.0001	-0.055	<.0001
Married	0.061	0.201	<.0001	-0.451	0.0001
Married*Born in 1980	0.003	-0.007	0.9490	-33.340	0.9825
Born in 1980	0.202	0.144	0.0007	-0.084	0.1021
-2 Log L w/o Covariates		536.583		1005.351	
-2 Log L w/ Covariates		320.882		910.942	
Chi-Square		215.701		94.409	
P-value		<.0001		<.0001	

Source: The 2% micro sample of the 2000 census.
Note: The number of observation is 743. The dependent mean is 0.117 for (1) and 0.591 for (2).

explained by selective marriage.

To examine if this selective marriage hypothesis is plausible, difference-in-difference regressions were performed employing similar methods used for those conducted regarding selective migration. Based on the sample of women in the 2000 census who were born in either Gwangju or neighboring counties and who were aged 18 to 22 years in 2000, the following equation is estimated to verify if educational attainment was significantly lower for married women born in 1980.

$$\textbf{(9.2)} \quad E_i = \alpha + \beta_1 I_i + \beta_2 (I_i \times M_i) + \beta_3 M_i + \gamma_1 AGE_i + \gamma_2 AGE_i^2 + \varepsilon_i$$

where E denotes educational attainment (dummy variables for no high school diploma and for entering college), I denotes the dummy variable for women born in 1980 (Born in 1980: a proxy variable for being in-utero during the Gwangju uprising), M is the dummy variable for the marital status of the woman (Married), and AGE stands for the age of the woman in 2000. The results of logistic regressions (Table 9.13) show that married women are less educated (as suggested by the estimated coefficient β_3), but selections in marriage are not significantly different between the 1980 birth cohort and neighboring cohorts (as indicated by the estimated coefficient β_2). Overall, circumstantial evidence suggests that the negative intergenerational effects of maternal stress in pregnancy are not attributable to bias problems related to selective migration or marriage.

Finally, potential bias problem resulting from selections in early-life deaths is a matter of possible concern in interpreting the results of this study. If individuals who were in-utero during the Gwangju uprising were positively selected in terms of characteristics correlated with offspring birth outcomes, the effect of exposure to maternal stress in pregnancy estimated in this study is subject to a downward bias. Furthermore, if the risk of stress-caused miscarriage is particularly high in the early stage of pregnancy, the effect of exposure to the uprising during the first trimester of pregnancy could be more seriously underestimated.

It is difficult to obtain direct evidence regarding selections in live birth such as incidence of miscarriage. Micro data on birth registrations this study is based upon are not available for the period prior to 1991, either. Thus, I had to rely on a highly indirect measure of early-life mortality, namely, the sex ratio (the male-to-female ratio) by year and place of birth that can be drawn from micro samples of censuses. The basis for using this method is the finding that increased prenatal mortality caused unfavorable in-utero circumstance result in a lower sex ratio at birth because boys are more fragile than girls in early stages of life (Andersson and Bergström 1998; Almond et al. 2010). It is examined if the sex ratio is particularly low for children who were born in Gwangju in 1980 or 1981 by estimating the following difference-in-difference model, based on the 2% micro sample of the 1990 census:

$$S_i = \alpha + \beta_1 I_i + \beta_2 (I_i \times B_i) + \beta_3 B_i + \gamma_1 YOB_i + \gamma_2 YOB_i^2 + \varepsilon_i \tag{9.3}$$

where S denotes the dummy variable for males (= 1 if male, and = 0 otherwise), I denotes the dummy variable for individuals born in 1980 (or in 1981), B is the dummy variable for birth in the city of Gwangju (Gwangju), and YOB stands for the year of birth of the person.

The results of regressions (Table 9.14) show that the individuals who were exposed to the Gwangju uprising in-utero were no different from the rest of the population in terms the sex ratio (as suggested by the estimated coefficient for Born in Gwangju*Born in 1980 in Table 9.14). Because the micro sample of the census does not provide information on the month of birth, it is difficult to determine whether the persons who were prenatally exposed to the Gwangju uprising during the first

Table 9.14
Logistic Regression: Exposure to the Gwangju Uprising and Sex Ratio of Individuals Aged 5 to 14 in 1990

	Mean	(1)		(2)	
		$\partial y/\partial x$	P-value	$\partial y/\partial x$	P-value
YOB	80.305	-0.087	0.0757	-0.228	0.3237
YOB^2	6456.600	0.001	0.0772	0.001	0.3283
Born in Gwangju	0.018	-0.004	0.8168	-0.009	0.8854
Born in Gwangju*Born in 1980	0.002	-0.012	0.8183		
Born in 1980	0.111	0.015	0.0383		
Born in Gwangju*Born in 1981	0.002			-0.015	0.9371
Born in 1981	0.111			0.014	0.6361
-2 Log L w/o Covariates		84022.054		84022.054	
-2 Log L w/ Covariates		84015.926		84020.216	
Chi-Square		6.123		1.836	
P-value		0.295		0.871	

Source: The 2% micro sample of the 1990 census.
Note: The number of observation is 60,683. The dependent mean is 0.521.

trimester of pregnancy were at particularly higher risk of miscarriage. To provide a rough test, we exploit the fact that the individuals born in the first two months of 1981 were in the first stage of gestation when the Gwangju incidence took place. The negligibly small and statistically insignificant coefficient for the interaction term of birth in Gwangju and 1981 birth cohort (Born in Gwangju*Born in 1981 in Table 9.14) is not consistent with the hypothesis that strong selections in prenatal mortality produced the relatively mild effect of in-utero exposure to maternal stress in the first trimester of pregnancy found in this study.

9.3. Summary

This chapter investigated how the stress experienced by women during the 1980 Gwangju uprising in South Korea affected the birth outcomes of their grandchildren. The prenatal exposure of the mother to the violent incident is estimated to reduce offspring birth weight and length of gestation by 57 grams and 2.3 days, respectively, and increase the probability of LBW by 2.4%. Similarly, the probabilities of LBW and preterm birth of treated children were higher by, respectively, 2.4% and 1.5%. The in-utero exposure of the mother to stress during the second trimester exerted the strongest adverse effect on offspring birth outcomes, reducing birth weight and length of gestation by 103 grams and 3.8 days, respectively, and increasing the probability of LBW and preterm birth by 4.0% and 4.6%, respectively. The offspring length of gestation was also significantly diminished by the prenatal exposure of the mother to stress during the third trimester. The intergenerational effects of exposure to stress in pregnancy were stronger for boys than for girls. It is unlikely that the negative intergenerational effects of maternal stress in pregnancy were caused by bias problems related to selective migration or marriage.

The results of this chapter suggests that a traumatic experience can have a lasting impact on the life of a person even if he or she is physically unaffected. These invisible scars are often ignored when assessing the severity of a disastrous event. In the case of the Gwangju uprising, only about 4,000 dead, missing, injured, and detained people are regarded as its victims, and eligible to receive compensation for their losses. In reality, however, a much larger fraction of Gwangju citizens of the time must have been victimized by the violence.

CHAPTER 10

Conclusion

It has been established by research across various disciplines that in-utero exposure to negative health shocks has strong and persistent effects on health and socioeconomic outcomes at older ages. The so-called fetal origins hypothesis is supported by growing evidence drawn from experimental events. In spite of the remarkable growth in the scholarly attention to the area, how the long-term effects of early-life conditions differ across countries and times is not fully understood, partly because existing evidence is drawn largely from North America and from Europe. The effect of an adverse shock to health in-utero depends on the patterns of postnatal investments in health and other types of human capital. Thus, the relationship between early-life conditions and later health outcomes is likely to differ across periods and countries. The differences depend on income, quality of medical care, and educational system, political and social structures, as well as cultural and social norms.

This book provides new evidence as to the long-term consequences of early-life experiences based on Korean cases that have not been thoroughly studied. The modern Korean history offers experimental episodes that generated dramatic changes in early-life circumstances across birth cohorts and across regions. As a consequence of the rapid economic development and dramatic social changes associated with it, early-life experiences of the cohorts born shortly after 1945 substantially differed according to the year of birth. For instance, the birth cohorts born after the recovery from the Korean War likely spent their childhood in better conditions than those born before or during the Korean War. Potential adverse shocks to fetal and childhood health caused by violence and malnutrition differed across regions of residence. This book utilizes semi-experimental features of several events in Korean history, namely, the Korean War, differential changes in food availability across regions, and the Gwangju uprising.

The Korean War (June 1950–July 1953) likely damaged individual maternal and fetal health, especially in the first nine months of the war following the surprise invasion of North Korea. The frontline dramatically moved back and forth across the region, forcing civilians to suffer from severe war-related disruptions. The extent of war-related disruptions experienced by a particular locality was strongly influenced by the distance to the border (the 38th parallel). That is, the closer to the 38th parallel a person was located, the more arduous his or her wartime experiences would be. Utilizing these experimental features of the Korean War, Chapters 2 to 5 investigated how in-utero exposure to such arduous wartime experiences (refugee experience, occupation, hunger, and combat) affected socioeconomic and health outcomes at older ages.

The results suggest that prenatal exposure to the disruptions caused by the Korean War negatively affected the individual socioeconomic and health outcomes at older ages. The educational attainment, labor market performance, and other socioeconomic outcomes of the subjects of the 1951 birth cohort, who were in-utero during the worst time of the war, were significantly lower in 1990 and in 2000. Similarly, the probabilities of suffering from a particular type of functional limitation as well as having any disability were significantly higher in 2010 among the individuals born in 1951. The results of difference-in-difference estimations suggest that the magnitude of the negative cohort effect is significantly larger for individuals who were more seriously traumatized by the war. The long-term effects of in-utero circumstances differed by gender. This difference may be partly attributed to the strong population selection for the 1951 female cohort and the potent influence of the husband's health status over the woman's own health. Different aspects of human capital (e.g., health and cognitive skills) were impaired by in-utero exposure to the war, depending on the stage of pregnancy when the negative shocks were experienced. The adverse long-term effects of in-utero exposure to the Korean War found in this study are unlikely driven by selection bias: the subjects of the 1951 birth cohort were not negatively selected in conception, birth, and survival.

It is widely accepted that net nutritional status in early life course is critical in determining physical growth, health formation, and development of cognitive and non-cognitive abilities. Despite the general consensus that provision of nutrition improved as a result of rapid economic growth in Korea, it is not fully understood how nutritional availability changed and how improved provision of nutrition in early ages affected human capital development over the life course. Rigorous research on these issues is often considerably hampered by shortage of the appropriate data, particularly for the periods prior to the 1970s. Chapter 6 introduced the newly-collected data that can overcome the limitations of the current data on the standards of living in South Korea prior to the 1970s. These data include South Korean military records that were collected from the Military Manpower Administration and province- and county-level data on local nutritional availability matched with the sample of the conscripts.

Using these data, Chapter 7 investigated how nutritional availability in two crucial periods for human growth, namely, early childhood (from conception to age 3) and adolescence (from age 12 to 16), affected the heights and other measures of human capital development of South Korean conscripts born from 1946–1957. Results strongly suggest nutrition was an important determining factor of biological standards of living as indicated by adult height. Provisions of calories and protein were associated strongly with larger stature. Food availability during early childhood was more critical for human growth than nutrition in adolescence. This result is consistent with the consensus that catch-up growth in adolescence is insufficient to compensate completely for deficiencies in early childhood. Nutrition in growing ages also had a strong effect on educational attainment. I also found that increased nutritional supply in adolescence mitigated the negative consequences of early-life exposure to the Korean War. This result provides suggestive evidence that improved nutrition in late childhood effectively compensated the negative consequences of early exposure to negative shocks. Improved nutrition in early childhood and adolescence accounted for 30% to 50% of the increase in adult height (about 2 cm) that was gained between the 1951 and 1957 birth cohorts, respectively. Increased nutritional availability during early childhood explains the majority of the contribution.

The Gwangju uprising is arguably the bloodiest incident that occurred in South Korea since the end of the Korean War. The tragic event took place on May 18, 1980 in the course of political crisis that followed the assassination of President Park in October 1979. In several aspects, it provides a unique opportunity for identifying the impact of maternal psychological stress on pregnancy. First, the tragic incident of May 1980 was a completely unanticipated shock that was unavoidably sustained by all citizens of Gwangju. Second, the major type of negative shocks to fetal health caused by the Gwangju uprising is likely to be maternal psychological stress, because the vast majority of the citizens and almost all pregnant women were physically unaffected. Finally, the duration of potential exposure to maternal stress was brief so that the exact timing of exposure can be identified.

Chapters 8 and 9 investigated how the stress experienced by women during the 1980 Gwangju uprising affected the birth outcomes of their grandchildren. The prenatal exposure of the mother to the violent incident is estimated to reduce offspring birth weight and length of gestation by 57 grams and 2.3 days, respectively, and increase the probability of low birth weight (LBW) by 2.4%. Similarly, the probabilities of LBW and preterm birth of treated children were higher by, respectively, 2.4% and 1.5%. The impact of exposure to maternal stress varied with the stage of pregnancy when stress was received. The in-utero exposure of the mother to stress during the second trimester exerted the strongest adverse effect on offspring birth outcomes, reducing birth weight and length of gestation by 103 grams and 3.8 days, respectively, and increasing the probability of LBW and preterm birth by 4.0% and 4.6%, respectively. The offspring length of gestation is also significantly diminished by the prenatal exposure of the mother to stress during the third trimester. The intergenerational effects of exposure to stress in pregnancy were stronger for boys than for girls. If the treated group is extended to children born in counties adjacent to Gwangju or to those born in the Jeonnam Province, the intergenerational effects of the prenatal exposure of the mother to the Gwangju uprising weaken or disappear, which suggests that the negative effect of maternal exposure to the Gwangju uprising reflects the effects of the stress caused by the first-hand experience of the violent event. It is unlikely that the negative intergenerational effects of maternal stress in pregnancy are caused by bias problems related to selective migration or marriage.

The findings of this book obtained from South Korea in the mid and late twentieth century are generally consistent with the predictions of previous studies suggesting that early-life conditions are critical to the formation and development of health and human capital of individuals. The results of Chapters 2 to 5 confirm the fetal origins hypothesis that prenatal exposure to negative shocks have persistent negative effects on old-age health and socioeconomic outcomes in older ages. Chapters 6 and 7 suggest that early-life nutritional availability is a strong determinant of growth and cognitive development. Chapters 8 and 9 provide rate evidence that the adverse effect of maternal stress in pregnancy can be transmitted even to the next generation.

Several findings of this book shed some new lights into the mechanisms of and heterogeneity in the long-term consequences of early-life experiences. For example, the evidence from the Korean War suggests that the type of human capital significantly impaired by war-time in-utero influences may depend on the timing of exposure. Chapter 4 shows that whereas the health outcomes of both the 1950 and 1951 cohorts were negatively influenced by the war, only the 1951 cohort shows lower educational attainment and labor market performance. A possible explanation for the difference by year of birth is that the two cohorts were exposed to negative health shocks during different stages of pregnancy. That is, the majority of the 1951 cohort subjects experienced the worst time of the war during the first half of pregnancy, a critical period for the development of the human brain. On the other hand, most of the 1950 birth cohort subjects had already passed the 25th week in pregnancy with complete prenatal brain development when the war broke out.

This book also suggests that the long-term effects of prenatal exposure to a negative health shock could differ by gender. Chapters 3 and 4 show that socioeconomic and health outcomes of females were less strongly affected by prenatal exposure to the Korean War than were males. Such gender differences found in this book could be explained by socioeconomic and cultural characteristics peculiar to the Korean society. As Chapter 5 shows, the gender difference can be explained in part by the particularly strong influence of the husband's economic and health status on female health in Korea. Since only a small fraction of females born during the Korean War participated in the labor market and virtually all of them eventually married, the husband's characteristics possibly played a more important role in determining the health and socioeconomic outcomes of older women. Another possible account of the differences in the effects of the Korean War between men and women is the presence of gender bias in parental investments in children.

In addition, this book provides new evidence as to the relationship between investments in human capital in different stages of human growth and the effectiveness of compensatory investment. The evidence given in Chapter 7 suggests that nutritional intakes in infancy and in adolescence are substitutable. That is, the marginal effect of improving nutrition in late childhood was larger in magnitude if nutritional availability in infancy was low. This indicates that compensatory investment in late childhood in the form of improved nutrition would be more effective for individuals who were poorly nourished in early childhood. The chapter also suggests the negative cohort effects of early exposure to the Korean War were small for those who lived in counties with high nutritional availability during adolescence. Such result offers rare evidence that improved nutrition in late childhood effectively compensated for the negative consequences of early exposure to negative shocks.

The findings of this book and other studies on the subject suggests that traumatic events such as military conflicts and natural disasters can lead to long-term negative health and economic consequences by adversely affecting maternal and fetal health. The adverse effects of early exposure tend to persist during the entire life course of an individual, and even transmit to the next generation. If the long-term and intergenerational consequences are considered, the economic cost of a traumatic event or stressful circumstance could be larger than suggested by an estimate obtained through short-term consideration. This leads to a policy implication that the long-run potential benefits of efforts to prevent children or pregnant women from being exposed to stressful events or environments are greater than conventionally believed.

Acknowledgements

This book is based on my research over the last decade on early-life determinants of later health and socioeconomic status in Korea. Some of the contents in these chapters appeared in papers published in *Journal of Health Economics*, *Social Science & Medicine*, and *Asian Population Studies*, and several unpublished manuscripts presented in seminars and conferences. I would like to thank everyone who commented on various drafts of these papers, including Douglas Almond, Tommy Bengtsson, Young Jun Cho, Dora Costa, Joe Ferrie, Alain Gagnon, Sok Chul Hong, Daeil Kim, Dohyung Kim, Taejong Kim, Tae Woo Kim, Adriana Lleras-Muney, Eun Kyung Lee, Seung Kyu Shim, and Hyunju Yang. I also thank Min Young Do, Hyeong Suk Kim, Ki-Sung Kim, Young Long Kim, and Eunmi Ko for their excellent research assistance. I benefited from criticisms of the participants of seminars at UCLA, University of Chicago, Institut National d'Études Démographiques, KDI School, Korea University, Sogang University, Seoul National University, Stanford University, and University of Tokyo. I would also like to thank the staffs of the Seoul National University Press for an excellent editorial work. I gratefully acknowledge that this work was supported by the Ministry of Education of the Republic of Korea and the National Research Foundation of Korea (NRF-2015S1A5B1009529).

References

Abbassi, Val (1998): "Growth and Normal Puberty," *Pediatrics* 102. S(3), 507–511.

Aizer, Anna, Laura Stroud, and Stephen Buka (2009): "Maternal Stress and Child Well-Being: Evidence from Siblings," Brown University Working Paper.

Aizer, A., L. Stroud, and S. Buka (2016): "Maternal Stress and Child Outcomes: Evidence from Siblings," *Journal of Human Resources* 51(3), 523–555.

Akbulut-Yuksel, M. (2017): "War during Childhood: The Long Run Effects of Warfare on Health," *Journal of Health Economics* 53, 117–130.

Akbulut-Yuksel, M. and M. Yuksel (2017): "Heterogeneity in the Long Term Health Effects of Warfare," *Economics & Human Biology* 27, 126–136.

Akresh, R., S. Bhalotra, M. Leone, and U. O. Osili (2012): "War and Stature: Growing up during the Nigerian Civil War," *American Economic Review: Papers and Proceedings* 102(3), 273–277.

Akresh, R., L. Lucchetti, and H. Thirumurthy (2012): "Wars and Child Health: Evidence from the Eritrean–Ethiopian Conflict," *Journal of Development Economics* 99(2), 330–340.

Akresh, R., S. Bhalotra, M. Leone, and U. O. Osili (2017): "First and Second Generation Impacts of the Biafran War (No. w23721)," National Bureau of Economic Research.

Almond, Douglas (2006): "Is the 1918 Influenza Pandemic Over? Long-Term Effects of In Utero Influenza Exposure in the Post-1940 Population," *Journal of Political Economy* 114(4), 672–712.

Almond, Douglas, Kenneth Y. Chay, and David S. Lee (2005): "The Cost of Low Birth Weight," *Quarterly Journal of Economics* 120(3), 1031–1084.

Almond, Douglas and Bhashkar Mazumder (2005): "The 1918 Influenza Pandemic and Subsequent Health Outcomes: An Analysis of SIPP Data," *American Economic Review Papers and Proceedings* 95(2), 258–262.

Almond, Douglas, Lena Edlund, and Marten Palme (2009): "Chernobyl's Subclinical Legacy: Prenatal Exposure to Radio Active Fallout and School Outcomes in Sweden," *Quarterly Journal of Economics* 124(4), 1729–1772.

Almond, Douglas and Janet Currie (2010): "Human Capital Development before Age Five," NBER Working Paper No. 15827.

Almond, Douglas, Lena Edlund, Hongbin Li, and Junsen Zhang (2010): "Long-Term Effects of Early-Life Development: Evidence from the 1959 to 1961 Chinese Famine," in Takatoshi Ito and Andrew Rose eds., *The Economic Consequences of Demographic Change in East Asia*, Chicago: University of Chicago Press, 321–350.

Almond, Douglas and Janet Currie (2011): "Killing Me Softly: The Fetal Origins Hypothesis," *Journal of Economic Perspectives* 25(3), 153–172.

Almond, D., J. Currie, and V. Duque (2017): "Childhood Circumstance and Adult Outcomes: Act II," NBER Working Paper No. 23017.

Andersson, Roland and Staffan Bergström (1998): "Is Maternal Malnutrition Associated with a Low Sex Ratio at Birth?" *Human Biology* 70(6), 1101–1106.

Barker, David J. P. (1992): "Fetal and Infant Origins of Adult Disease, London," British Medical Journal of Publishing Group.

Barker, David J. P. (1994): "Mothers, Babies, and Disease in Later Life, London," British Medical Journal of Publishing Group.

Beebe, Gilbert W. (1975): "Follow-up Studies of World War II and Korean War Prisoners, II: Morbidity, Disability, and Maladjustments," *American Journal of Epidemiology* 101, 400–422.

Behrman, Jere R. and Mark R. Rosenzweig (2004): "Returns to Birth Weight," *Review of Economics and Statistics* 86(2), 586–601.

Black, Sandra E., Paul J. Devereux, and Kjell G. Salvanes (2007): "From the Cradle to the Labor Market? The Effect of Birth Weight on Adult Outcomes," *Quarterly Journal of Economics* 122(1), 409–439.

Black, S. E., P. J. Devereux, and K. G. Salvanes (2016): "Does Grief Transfer Across Generations? Bereavements during Pregnancy and Child Outcomes," *American Economic Journal: Applied Economics* 8(1), 193–223.

Bleker, O. P., T. J. Roseboom, A. C. J. Ravelli, G. A. van Montfans, C. Osmond, and D. J. P. Barker (2005): "Cardiovascular Disease in Survivors of the Dutch Famine," in G. Hornstra, R. Uauy, and X. Yang eds., *The Impact of Maternal Malnutrition on the Offspring: Nestle Nutrition Workshop Series Pediatric Program* 55, 183–195. Basel, Switzerland: Karger.

Bozzoli, Carlos, Angus Deaton, and Climent Quintana-Domeque (2009): "Adult Height and Childhood Disease," *Demography* 46(4), 647–669.

Brakman, Steven, Harry Garretsen, and Marc Schramm (2004): "The Strategic Bombing of Cities in Germany in World War II and Its Impact on City Growth," *Journal of Economic Geography* 4(1), 1–18.

Brown, Ryan (2011): "The 1918 U.S. Influenza Pandemic as a Natural Experiment, Revisited," Duke University Working Paper.

Bundervoet, T. and S. Fransen (2018): "The Educational Impact of Shocks in Utero: Evidence from Rwanda," *Economics & Human Biology* 29, 88–101.

Byun, Ju-na (1996): "15-Year Aftermath-victim-syndrome of the 5-18 Kwangju Civil Uprising," *Korean Cultural Anthropology* 29(2), 221–259 (in Korean).

Byun, Ju-na and Linda S. Lewis eds. (2000): *The Kwangju Uprising after 20 Years; The Unhealed Wounds of the Victims*, Seoul: Dahaes.

Cain, Louis and Sok Chul Hong (2009): "Survival in the 19th Century Cities: The Larger the City, the Smaller Your Chances," *Explorations in Economic History* 46, 450–463.

Camacho, Adriana (2008): "Stress and Birth Weight: Evidence from Terrorist Attack," *American Economic Review Papers and Proceedings* 98(2), 511–515.

Case, Anne and Christina Paxson (2008): "Stature and Status: Height, Ability, and Labor Market Outcomes," *Journal of Political Economy* 116 (3), 499–532.

Cecchi, F. and J. Duchoslav (2018): "The Effect of Prenatal Stress on Cooperation: Evidence from Violent Conflict in Uganda," *European Economic Review* 101, 35–56.

Cha, Myung-Soo (2014): *The Origins of a Growth Miracle: An Economic History of Korea, 1700–2010*, Seoul: Haenam (in Korean).

Chay, Kenneth Y. and Michael Greenstone (2003): "The Impact of Air Pollution on Infant Mortality: Evidence from the Geographic Variation in Pollution Shocks Induced by Recession," *Quarterly Journal of Economics* 118(3), 1121–1167.

Chen, Y. and L. A. Zhou (2007): "The Long-Term Health and Economic Consequences of 1959–1961 Famine in China," *Journal of Health Economics* 26(4), 659–681.

Choi, Joong-Myung and Ji-Yeong Kim (2012): "Secular Changes in Anthropometric Indices of Children and Adolescents: Studies from Korea," in Victor R. Preedy ed., *Handbook of Anthropometry: Physical Measures of Human Form in Health and Disease*, New York: Springer-Verlag, 2615–2627.

Choi, Seong-Jin and Daniel Schwekendiek (2009): "The Biological Standard of Living in Colonial Korea, 1910–1944," *Economics and Human Biology* 7, 259–264.

Chun, S. K. (2006): "The Korean War that I Experienced," D. Park ed., *The One Hundred Scenes of the Korean War*, Seoul: Nunbit, 153–160 (in Korean).

Chun, W. Y. (2011): *The Birth of Modern Men*, Seoul: Isoon (in Korean).

Chung, B. J. (2010): "The Types and Characteristics of the Civilian Casualties in South Korea during the Korean War," in The Group for Korean Historical Studies ed., *The Korean War in Historical Perspectives*, Seoul: Humanist, 471–504 (in Korean).

Conley, Dalton and Rebecca Glauber (2006): "Parental Educational Investment and Children's Academic Risk: Estimates of the Impact of Sibship Size and Birth Order from Exogenous Variation in Fertility," *Journal of Human Resources* 41(4), 722–737.

Conti, Gabriella, James Heckman, Junjian Yi, and Junsen Zhang (2011): "Early Health Shocks, Prenatal Responses, and Child Outcomes," Paper presented at the 2011 NBER Cohort Studies Meeting (April, 2011).

Costa, Dora L. and Matthew E. Kahn (2008): *Heroes and Cowards*, Princeton: Princeton University Press.

Cumings, Bruce (1981): *The Origins of the Korean War, I: Liberation and the Emergence of Separate Regimes, 1945–1947*, Princeton: Princeton University Press.

Cumings, Bruce (1990): *The Origins of the Korean War, II: The Roaring of the Cataract, 1947–1950*, Princeton: Princeton University Press.

Cumings, Bruce (2010): *The Korean War: A History*, New York: Modern Library.

Currie, Janet and Rosemary Hyson (1999): "Is the Impact of Shock Cushioned by Socioeconomic Status? The Case of Low Birth Weight," *American Economic Review* 89(2), 245–250.

Currie, Janet and Enrico Moretti (2007): "Biology as Destiny? Short- and Long-Run Determinants of Intergenerational Transmission of Birth Weight," *Journal of Labor Economics* 25(2), 231–264.

Currie, Janet and Maya Rossin-Slater (2012): "Weathering the Storm: Hurricanes and Birth Outcomes," NBER Working Paper No. 18070.

Dahl, Gordon and Enrico Meretti (2008): "The Demand for Sons," *Review of Economic Studies* 75, 1085–1120.

Davis, Donald and David Weinstein (2002): "Bones, Bombs, and Break Points: The Geography of Economic Activity," *American Economic Review* 92(5), 1269–1289.

Drake, A. J. and B. R. Walker (2004): "The Intergenerational Effects of Fetal Programming: Non-genomic Mechanisms for the Inheritance of Low Birth Weight and Cardiovascular Risk," *Journal of Endocrinology* 180, 1–16.

Duque, V. (2017): "Early-life Conditions and Child Development: Evidence from a Violent Conflict," *SSM-population Health* 3, 121–131.

Eccleston, Melissa (2011): "In Utero Exposure to Maternal Stress: Effects of 9/11 on Birth and Early Schooling Outcomes in New York City," Harvard University Working Paper.

Edwards, Ryan D. (2010): "U.S. War Costs: Two Parts Temporary, One Part Permanent," NBER Working Paper No. 16108.

Emanuel, I. (1997): "Invited Commentary: An Assessment of Maternal Intergenerational Factors in Pregnancy Outcomes," *American Journal of Epidemiology* 146, 820–825.

Emanuel, I., H. Filakti, E. Alberman, and S. J. Evans (1992): "Intergenerational Studies of Human Birth Weight from the 1958 Birth Cohort: Evidence for a Multigenerational Effect," *British Journal of Obstetrics and Gynecology* 99, 67–74.

Fenoll, Aparicio A. and L. González (2021): "Political Instability and Birth Outcomes: Evidence from the 1981 Military Coup in Spain," *Health Economics* 30(2), 328–341.

Floud, R., R. W. Fogel, B. Harris, and S. Hong (2011): *The Changing Body: Health, Nutrition, and Human Development in the Western World since 1700*, Cambridge: Cambridge University Press.

Fogel, Robert William (1991): "The Conquest of High Mortality and Hunger in Europe and America: Timing and Mechanisms," in P. Hilgonnet, D. Landes, and H. Rosovsky eds., *Favorites of Fortune: Technology, Growth, and Economic Development since the Industrial Revolution*, Cambridge: Harvard University Press, 33–71.

Fogel, Robert William (1993): "New Sources and New Techniques for the Study of Secular Trends in Nutritional Status, Health, Mortality, and the Process of Aging," *Historical Methods* 26(1), 5–43.

Fogel, Robert William (2004): *The Escape from Hunger and Premature Death, 1700–2100*, Cambridge: Cambridge University Press.

Fung, Winnie and Wei Ha (2010): "Intergenerational Effects of the 1959–61 China Famine," Working Paper.

Geber, W. F. (1970): "Cardiovascular and Teratogenic Effects of Chronic Intermittent Noise Stress," in B. L. Welch and A. S. Welch eds., *Physiological Effects of Noise*, New York: Plenum Press, 85–90.

Goldin, Claudia D. and Frank D. Lewis (1975): "The Economic Cost of the American Civil War: Estimates and Implications," *Journal of Economic History* 35(2), 299–326.

Grossman, D., U. Khalil, and A. Ray (2019): "Terrorism and Early Childhood Health Outcomes: Evidence from Pakistan," *Social Science & Medicine* 237, 112–453.

Guven, C., T. Hoang, M. H. Rahman, and M. A. Ulubaşoğlu (2021): "Long-term Effects of Malnutrition on Early-Life Famine Survivors and Their Offspring: New Evidence from the Great Vietnam Famine 1944–45," *Health Economics* 30(7), 1600–1627.

Hackman, E., I. Emanuel, G. van Belle, and J. Daling (1983): "Maternal Birth Weight and Subsequent Pregnancy Outcome," *Journal of the American Medical Association* 250, 2016–2019.

Haines, Michael R., A. Craig Lee, and Thomas Weiss (2003): "The Short and the Dead: Nutrition, Mortality, and the "Antebellum Puzzle" in the United States," *Journal of Economic History* 63(2), 382–413.

Halberstam, David (2007): "The Coldest Winter: American and the Korean War," New York: Hyperion.

Higonnet, P., D. S. Landes, and H. Rosovksy eds. (1998): *Favorites of Fortune: Technology, Growth, and Economic Development since the Industrial Revolution*, Cambridge: Harvard University Press.

Hong, Chang-Ho, Hyung-Rae Cho, and Kye-Suk Park (1993): "The Secular Trend of Menarcheal Age in Korea," *Korean Journal of Pediatrics* 36(2), 239–243 (in Korean).

Huttunen, M. O. and P. Niskanen (1978): "Prenatal Loss of Father and Psychiatric Disorders," *Archives of General Psychiatry* 35(4), 429–431.

Hwang, Ji-Yun, Chol Shin, Edward A. Frongillo, Kyung-Rim Shin, and In-ho Jo (2003): "Secular Trend in Age at Menarche for South Korea Women Born between 1920 and 1986: the Ansan Study," *Annals of Human Biology* 30(4), 434–442.

Hwang, Su-Chul., Li-Na Yu, and Young-Bong Yu (2014): "An Estimation and Analysis of Agricultural Output in Korea (1955–2012)," *Korean Journal of Food Marketing Economics* 31(4), 21–43 (in Korean).

Ichino, Andrea and Rudolf Winter-Ebmer (2004): "The Long-Run Educational Cost of World War II," *Journal of Labor Economics* 22(1), 57–87.

Islam, A., C. Ouch, R. Smyth, and L. C. Wang (2017): "The Intergenerational Effect of Cambodia's Genocide on Children's Education and Health," *Population and Development Review*, 43(2), 331–353. doi:10.1111/padr.12047.

Islam, A., P. Raschky, and R. Smyth (2017): "The Long-Term Health Effects of Mass Political Violence: Evidence from China's Cultural Revolution," *Social Indicators Research* 132(1), 257–272.

Jeong, Hyeok, Young-Bong Yu, Su-Chul Hwang, Myung-Hun Lee, Hong-Sang Kim, and Seok-Gon Jo (2015): "Understanding Korean Economic Development from the Perspectives of Agricultural Development and Structural Transformation," Sejong: Korea Development Institute (in Korean).

Jo, Seok-Gon (2007): "The Effects of Land Survey (1912–1918) and Land Reform (1950–1969) on Land Productivity in Korea," *Trends and Perspectives* 71, 304–335 (in Korean).

Jones, F. N. and J. T. Tauscher (1978): "Residence under an Airport Landing Pattern as a Factor in Teratism," *Archives of Environmental Health* 33(1), 10–12.

Karbownik, K. and A. Wray (2019): "Long-run Consequences of Exposure to Natural Disasters," *Journal of Labor Economics* 37(3), 949–1007.

Kelly, Elaine (2009): "The Scourge of Asian Flu: In Utero Exposure to Pandemic Influenza and the Development of a Cohort of British Children," Institute for Fiscal Studies Working Paper 09/17, University College London.

Kesternich, Iris, Bettina Siflinger, James P. Smith, and Joachim K. Winter (2011): "The Effects of World War II on Economic and Health Outcomes across Europe," Working Paper.

Kim, Dong Choon (2009): *War and Society*, Paju: Dolbege (in Korean).

Kim, Doo-Sub, S. Park, and K. Eun (2002): "Population of Korea 1," Korea National Statistical Office.

Kim, Duol, and Heejin Park (2011): "Measuring Living Standards from the Lowest: Height of the Male Hangryu Deceased in Colonial Korea," *Explorations in Economic History* 48, 590–599.

Kim, Ji-Yeong, In-Hwan Oh, Eun-Young Lee, Kyung-Sik Choi, Bong-Keun Choi, Tai-Young Yoon, Chong-Guk Lee, Jin-Soo Moon, Sung-Hee Shin, and Joong-Myung Choi (2008): "Anthropometric Changes in Children and Adolescents from 1965 to 2005 in Korea," *American Journal of Physical Anthropology* 136(2), 230–236.

Kim, Nak Nyeon ed. (2012): *National Accounts of Korea 1911–2010*, Seoul: Seoul National University Press (in Korean).

Kim, Nak-Nyeon (2012): "Long Term Statistics of National Accounts 1911–2010," in Nak-Nyeon Kim ed., *National Accounts of Korea 1911–2010*, Seoul: Seoul National University Press, 295–331 (in Korean).

Kim, Seonghoon and Belton M. Fleisher (2010): "The China Leap Forward Famine: The Lasting Impact of Mother's Fetal Malnutrition on Their Offspring," Ohio State University Working Paper.

Kim, Tae Woo (2008): "A Study of the Aerial Bombing by the United States Air Force during the Korean War," Ph.D. Dissertation, Department of History, Seoul National University (in Korean).

Kim, Won Il (2006): "Three Months in Seoul Under the North Korean Occupation," D. Park ed., *The One Hundred Scenes of the Korean War*, Seoul: Nunbit, 33–43 (in Korean).

Kim, Yeon-Sung, Bong-Kun Choi, Tai-Young Yoon, Jung-Myung Choi, and Soon-Young Park (2006): "A Study on the Literatures of the Korean Youth's Physique Change from 1940 to 1995," *Journal of the Korean Society of Maternal and Child Health* 10(1), 96–109 (in Korean).

Knipschild, Paul, Hans Meijer, and Herman Sallé (1981): "Aircraft Noise and Birth Weight," *International Archives of Occupational and Environmental Health* 48, 131–136.

Ko, Jeong-Soon (2007): "An Estimation and Analysis of the Agricultural Production Statistics in Korea: 1955–2005," Unpublished doctoral dissertation, Jeju National University (in Korean).

Korean Agency for Technology and Standards (2011): "7th Size Korea: Final Report" (in Korean).

Korean Office Military Manpower (1985): "History of Military Manpower Administration," 1, Office of Military Manpower

Lauderdale, Diane S. (2006): "Birth Outcomes for Arabic-Named Women in California before and after September 11," *Demography* 43(1), 185–201.

Lawlor, Debbie A., Shah Ebrahim, and George Davey Smith (2002): "Is There a Sex Difference in the Association between Birth Weight and Systolic Blood Pressure in Later Life? Findings from a Mega-Regression Analysis," *American Journal of Epidemiology* 156(12), 1100–1104.

Lee, Chulhee (2005): "Wealth Accumulation and the Health of Union Army Veterans, 1860–1870," *Journal of Economic History* 65(2), 352–385.

Lee, Chulhee (2008): "Health, Information, and Migration: Post-Service Geographic Mobility of Union Army Veterans, 1860–1880," *Journal of Economic History* 65, 352–385.

Lee, Chulhee (2014a): "In Utero Exposure to the Korean War and Its Long-Term Effects on Socioeconomic and Health Outcomes," *Journal of Health Economics* 33, 76–93.

Lee, Chulhee (2014b): "Intergenerational Health Consequences of In Utero Exposure to Maternal Stress: Evidence from the 1980 Kwangju Uprising," *Social Science & Medicine* 119, 284–291.

Lee, Chulhee (2016): "Changes in Anthropometric Measures of Wellbeing in Korea from 1945 to 1977: Evidence from Korean Military Records," Research Working Paper Series: 2015 Cliometric Study Program to Focus on Korea's Development Experiences, KDI School of Public Policy and Management.

Lee, Chulhee (2017a): "Long-Term Health Consequences of In-Utero Exposure to the Korean War," *Asian Population Studies* 13(1), 101–117.

Lee, Chulhee (2017b): "Local Nutritional Availability and Adult Height: Evidence from South Korea, 1946 to 1977," Research Working Paper Series: 2016 Cliometric Study Program to Focus on Korea's Development Experiences, KDI School of Public Policy and Management.

Lee, Hwan-Ho and Soon-Young Park (2005): "The Secular Trend 2020 of Body Height and Weight of Korean Youth According to Chronological Change with Reference to 2000," *Korean Public Health Research* 31(2), 192–209 (in Korean).

Lee, Jong Won (2001): "The Impact of the Korean War on the Korean Economy," *International Journal of Korean Studies* 5(1), 97–118.

Lee, Jung Woo ed. (2012): *Kwangju, Women*, Seoul: Humanitas (in Korean).

Lee, Jungmin (2008): "Sibling Size and Investment in Children's Education: Asian Instrument," *Journal of Population Economics* 21(4), 855–875.

Lhila, Aparna and Kosali I. Simon (2008): "Prenatal Health Investment Decisions: Does the Child Sex Matter?" *Demography* 45(4), 885–905.

Lim, Song-Son, Soon-Young Park, Do-Sue Koo, and Yang-Won Park (1986): "Studies on the Secular Trend of Body Height and Weight of Korea Youth According to Chronological Change," *Journal of Kyung Hee University* 2(2), 183–214 (in Korean).

Lindeboom, M. and R. Van Ewijk (2015): "Babies of the War: The Effect of War Exposure Early in Life on Mortality Throughout Life," *Biodemography and Social Biology*, 61(2), 167–186.

Lindert, Peter (1994): "Unequal Living Standards," in Roderick Floud, and Deidre N. McCloskey eds., *The Economic History of Britain since 1700*, 1: 1900–1860, Cambridge: Cambridge University Press.

Luo, Z., R. Mu, and X. Zhang (2006): "Famine and Overweight in China," R*eview of Agricultural Economics* 28(3), 296–304.

McGrath, John, S. Saha, D. E. Lieberman, and S. Buka (2006): "Season of Birth is Associated with Anthropometric and Neurocognitive Outcomes during Infancy and Childhood in a General Population Birth Cohort," *Schizophrenia Research* 81(1), 91–100.

Meijer, A. (2007): "Child Psychiatric Sequelae of Maternal War Stress," *Acta Psychiatrica Scandinavica* 72(6), 505–511.

Menclova, A. K. and S. Stillman (2020): "Maternal Stress and Birth Outcomes: Evidence from an Unexpected Earthquake Swarm," *Health Economics* 29(12), 1705–1720.

Meng, X. and N. Qian (2009): "The Long-Term Consequences of Famine on Survivors: Evidence from a Unique Natural Experiment Using China's Great Famine," NBER Working Paper No. 14917.

Miguel, Edward and Gérald Roland (2008): "The Long-Run Impact of Bombing Vietnam," *Journal of Development Economics* 96(1), 1–15.

Minoiu, C. and O. Shemyakina (2012): "Child Health and Conflict in Côte d'Ivoire," *American Economic Review: Papers and Proceedings* 102(3), 294–299.

Minoiu, C. and O. N. Shemyakina (2014): "Armed Conflict, Household Victimization, and Child Health in Côte d'Ivoire," *Journal of Development Economics* 108, 237–255.

Mu, Ren and Xiaobo Zhang (2008): "Gender Difference in the Long-Term Impact of Famine," International Food Policy Research Institute Discussion Paper 00760.

National Statistical Office (1998): "Socioeconomic Changes in Korea in the Past 50 Years" (in Korean).

Neelsen, Sven and Thomas Stratman (2011): "Effects of Prenatal and Early Life Malnutrition: Evidence from the Greek Famine," *Journal of Health Economics* 30, 479–488.

Nefzger, M. Dean (1970): "Follow-up Studies of World War II and Korean War Prisoners, I. Study Plan and Mortality Findings," *American Journal of Epidemiology* 91, 123–138.

Neugebauer, R., H. Wijbrand Hoek, and E. Susser (1999): "Prenatal Exposure to Wartime Famine and Development of Antisocial Personality Disorder in Adulthood," *Journal of the American Medical Association* 281(5), 455–462.

Os, Jim Van and Jean-Paul Selten (1998): "Prenatal Exposure to Maternal Stress and Subsequent Schizophrenia. The May 1940 Invasion of The Netherlands," *British Journal of Psychology* 172, 324–326.

Oskorouchi, H. R. (2019): "Learning to Fight: Afghan Child Health and In-utero Exposure to

Conflict," *Population and Development Review* 45(2), 275–300.
Ouili, I. (2017): "Armed Conflicts, Children's Education and Mortality: New Evidence from Ivory Coast," *Journal of Family and Economic Issues* 38(2), 163–183.
Pak, Sun-Young (2004): "The Biological Standard of Living in the Two Koreas," *Economics and Human Biology* 2(3), 511–521.
Pak, Sun-Young, Daniel Schwekendiek, and Hee-Kyoung Kim (2011): "Height and Living Standards in North Korea, 1930–1980s," *Economic History Review* 64(S1), 142–158.
Perkins, J. M., S. V. Subramanian, G. D. Smith, and E. Ozaltin (2016): "Adult Height, Nutrition, and Population Health," *Nutrition Review* 74(3), 149–165.
Persson, P. and M. Rossin-Slater (2018): "Family Ruptures, Stress, and the Mental Health of the Next Generation," *American Economic Review* 108(4–5), 1214–1252.
Phadera, L. (2019): "Unfortunate Moms and Unfortunate Children: Impact of the Nepali Civil War on Women's Stature and Intergenerational Health," The World Bank.
Pinto, M. and P. Shetty (1995): "Influence of Exercise-Induced Maternal Stress on Fetal Outcomes in Wistar Rats: Intergenerational Effects," *British Journal of Nutrition* 73, 645–653.
Pyo, Hak K. (2001): "Economic Growth in Korea (1911–1999): A Long-Term Trend and Perspective," *Seoul Journal of Economics* 14(1), 59–125.
Pyo, I. et al. (2003): *War and People*, Paju: Han-ul (in Korean).
Rakyan, V. K., J. Preis, H. D. Morgan, and E. Whitelaw (2001): "The Marks, Mechanisms and Memory of Epigenetic States in Mammals," *Biochemical Journal* 356 (1), 1–10.
Robson, D., E. Welch, N. J. Beeching, and G. V. Gill (2009): "Consequences of Captivity: Health Effects of Far East Imprisonment in World War II," *Quarterly Journal of Medicine* 102(2), 87–96.
Rofe, Yacov and Joel Goldberg (2011): "Prolonged Exposure to a War Environment and Its Effects on the Blood Pressure of Pregnant Women," *British Journal of Medical Psychology* 56(4), 305–311.
Roseboom, T. J., J. H. P. Meulen, C. Osmond, D. J. P. Barker, A. C. J. Ravelli, and O. P. Bleker (2001): "Effects of Prenatal Exposure to the Dutch Famine on Adult Disease in Later Life: An Overview," *Twins Research* 4(5), 293–298.
Saing, C. H. and H. Kazianga (2019): "The Long-Term Impacts of Violent Conflicts on Human Capital: US Bombing and Education, Earnings, Health, Fertility and Marriage in Cambodia," *The Journal of Development Studies*, 1–16.
Sardoschau, S. (2019): "Children of War: In-Utero Stress and Child Health in Iraq," Available at SSRN 3383653.
Schiman, J. C., R. Kaestner, and A. T. L. Sasso (2019): "Infant Mortality and Adult Wellbeing: Evidence from Wartime Britain," *Labour Economics* 60, 12–29.
Schwekendiek, Daniel and Seong-Ho Jun (2010): "From the Poorest to the Tallest in East Asia: The Secular Trend in Height of South Koreans," *Korea Journal* 50(3), 151–175.
Scott-Strokes, Henry and Jai Eui Lee (2000): *The Kwangju Uprising: Eyewitness Press Accounts of Korea's Tiananmen*, Armonk: M. E. Sharp.
Selten, J., E. Cantor-Graae, D. Nahon, I. Levav, A. Aleman, and R. Kahn (2003): "No Relationship between Risk of Schizophrenia and Prenatal Exposure to Stress during the Six-Day War or Yom Kippur War in Israel," *Schizophrenia Research* 63, 131–135.
Sheriff, Michael J., Charles. J. Krebs, and Rudy Boonstra (2010): "The Ghosts of Predators Past: Population Cycles and the Roles of Maternal Programming under Fluctuating Predation Risk," *Ecology* 91(10), 2983–2994.

Shih, H. H. and M. J. Lin (2018): "Long-term Impacts of Early-life Exposure to Malaria: Evidence from Taiwan's Eradication Campaign in the 1950s," *Health Economics*, 27(10), 1484–1512.

Shin, Gi-Wook and Kyung Moon Hwang (2003): *Contentious Kwangju: The May 18 Uprising in Korea's Past and Present*, Lanham: Rowman & Littlefield Publishers.

Singhal, S. (2019): "Early Life Shocks and Mental Health: The Long-term Effect of War in Vietnam," *Journal of Development Economics* 141, 102244.

Sohn, Ki-Tae (2016): "Improvement in the Biological Standard of Living in 20th Century Korea: Evidence from Age at Menarche," *American Journal of Human Biology* 28(4), 1–7.

Song, Byung-Nak (2003): *The Rise of the Korean Economy, 3rd Edition*, New York: Oxford University Press.

St. Clair, D., M. Xu, P. Wang, Y. Yu, Y. Fang, F. Zhang, X. Zheng, N. Gu, G. Feng, P. Sham, and L. He (2005): "Rates of Adult Schizophrenia Following Prenatal Exposure to the Chinese Famines of 1959–1961," *Journal of the American Medical Association* 294(5), 557–562.

Stanner, S. A., K. Bulmer, C. Andrès, O. E. Lantseva, V. Borodina, V. Poteen, and J. S. Yudkin (1997): "Does Malnutrition in Utero Determine Diabetes and Coronary Heart Disease in Adulthood?" *British Medical Journal* 315(7119), 1342–1348.

Stewart, R., R. Preece, and H. G. Sheppard (1975): "Twelve Generations of Marginal Protein Deficiency," *British Journal of Nutrition* 33, 233–253.

Stewart, R. J., H. Sheppard, R. Preece, and J. Waterlow (1980): "The Effect of Rehabilitation at Different Stages of Development of Rats Marginally Malnourished for Ten to Twelve Generations," *British Journal of Nutrition* 43, 403–412.

Sutker, P., D. Winstead, Z. Galina, and A. Allan (1991): "Cognitive Deficits and Psychopathology among Former Prisoners of War and Combat Veterans of the Korean Conflicts," *American Journal of Psychiatry* 148, 67–72.

Tanaka, H., M. Sei, T. Q. Bihn, H. Munakata, K. Yuasa, and Y. Nakahori (2007): "Correlation of Month and Season of Birth with Height, Weight, and Degree of Obesity of Rural Japanese Children," *Journal of Medical Investigation* 54, 133–139.

Torche, Florencia (2011): "The Effect of Maternal Stress on Birth Outcomes: Exploiting a Natural Experiment," *Demography* 48, 1473–1491.

Tsujimoto, T. and Y. Kijima (2020): "Effects of Conflict on Child Health: Evidence from the 1990–1994 Northern Mali Conflict," *Health Economics* 29(11), 1456–1474.

Tucker, Spencer C. ed. (2002): *Encyclopedia of The Korean War: A Political, Social, and Military History*, New York: Checkmark Book.

Van Ewijk, R. and M. Lindeboom (2017): "Why People Born during World War II Are Healthier," Available at SSRN 3054480.

Weinstock, M. (2001): "Alterations Induced by Gestational Stress in Brain Morphology and Behaviour of the Offspring," *Progress in Neurobiology* 65, 427–451.

Wilson, Sven E. and Clayne L. Pope (2003): "The Height of Union Army Recruits: Family and Community Influences," in Dora L. Costa ed., *Health and Labor Force Participation over the Life Cycle: Evidence from the Past*, Chicago: University of Chicago Press.

Yang, Y. C. (2010): "The Conditions of Refugees and Aid Activities in Daegu Area during the Korean War," in The Group for Korean Historical Studies ed., *The Korean War in Historical Perspectives*, Seoul: Humanist, 569–594 (in Korean).

Index

G

H

I

K

L

M